Donald J. Trump :
Accused & Guilty

DONALD J. TRUMP :
ACCUSED & GUILTY

JPL. Mimo

Archway Publishing books may be ordered through booksellers or by contacting:

Archway Publishing
1663 Liberty Drive
Bloomington, IN 47403
www.archwaypublishing.com
844-669-3957

ISBN: 978-1-6657-6242-7 (sc)
ISBN: 978-1-6657-6244-1 (hc)
ISBN: 978-1-6657-6243-4 (e)

Library of Congress Control Number: 2024918653

Print information available on the last page.

Archway Publishing rev. date: 10/10/2024

CONTENTS

FOREWORD

In this book I was first of all focused, on Trump's and his followers, at every stage. This book is neither a romance, nor a biography. And, no longer science fiction. This book is more a collection of short stories, and finally, I added a little of my own.

Trump uses carefully calibrated language to impress his supporters. He is aware of the magnitude of the impact on his enablers, and also on 40% of the population, who believe in him.

Trump possesses a cult-like power over his supporters. Some of them, demonstrably unhinged, are willing to do anything to please him.

Trump is like Mister America to his supporters. To them, he represents the new ideal. He's their god of fate in the Western civilization.

Trump said of his enablers that they knew what he could do for them. To them, Trump represents something fundamentally different in politics.

You will see for yourself what sort of President Donald Trump was during his time in the White House. History will teach you all the right and wrong paths this man traveled for half a century.

We now know that 40 % of the population shares these opinions; but what about the rest of the population. We will see, later on in this book, a completely different story of this man.

Please believe me, I do not denigrate the fact that this person was and is a very good communicator. How many times did Trump say, we are going to make America great again -- and strong again. Or bring back the American Dream. Everybody remembers, on inauguration day, Trump saying that he was going to "drain the swamp" and everyone cheered.

He lives for their applause. Without it, he is lost. He doesn't know why he seeks their plaudits. He reassured the public in a rally by saying that he was "a very stable genius", and again, everyone clapped.

President Donald Trump long exulted in superlatives. The first. The best. The most. The greatest. "No president has ever done what I've done," he boasts. "No president has ever even come close," he says.

One of his supporters, a cowboy wearing a black felt hat, said that "he believed Trump was GOD".

In his own mind, he is more like a persona than a person, more like a primal force or superhero, rather than a fully realized human being.

When you start reading this book, you will have a hard time putting it down, thanks to the depth of the topics covered all the way to the last page.

My research is mainly focused on newspaper articles, stories told in various media around the world for over a decade, as well as facts and stories from books and magazines.

Chapter 1 through the end is a Goldmine of information on Trump.

This book will give you hours of pleasure; I wish you a good read.

INTRODUCTION

IGNORANCE AND TRAITORS

When I hear elected officials of this party, who are Republicans, say that they could never have imagined foreseeing what happened on January 6th in the Temple of American Democracy, I almost want to laugh. How can they not understand the consequences of a phenomenon of which they are the main cause? This attempt at sedition, that they find surprising, is only the culmination of their four years of tacit or ostensible complicity with Donald J. Trump's salvos on American democratic institutions.

What hypocrisy! How many times have we heard that the president just crossed the line? And this, with the blessing of elected Republican officials, who were in collusion, no doubt, with this demagogue, for four years!

Trump has come to understand that no line, however sacred it may be, is insurmountable. When you know how to handle bullying as a tool of control, nothing is easier. Also, as soon as we wander away from his will, he stalls. In my book, all of these Republicans are traitors.

Mike Pence, his staunch servant who, until recently, acted to make Trump believe he had actually won the election, is one of these men who are part of that brotherhood of hypocritical people and «Yes-Men» and, the fact that there were a lot of friends without any experience, one could say that these people were surely puppets; what a circus.

Finally, Pence comes to realize the hard way that loyalty is not part of the vocabulary of the Grand Bully when one is not ready to break the law to fulfill, on command, his autocratic wishes.

The elected Republicans, for the most part, fell into the clutches of the monster whose ego they generously fattened; which they did not know to be an endless abyss. Despite all these dictatorial drifts, some did not hesitate to solicit him, up until this day of certification of the results, thinking of what he could bring them in 2024.

So, even if they pretend not to understand, they know very well that they largely allowed Trump to get his hands on their party by using those who marched in the Capitol. It is this white fringe, frustrated and mostly unable to accept the demographic evolution of the country that is the armed wing of the Great intimidator. When they hear the guru promise America her greatness. How many times has he said "America first" but it has become "America alone" They understand that he wants to make America white again. However, they will have to accept reality. Because the addition of color shades to America is here for good. In other words, they will have to forget the privileges of the past, and realize that the time is gone, when they did not need to compare themselves to those, they look down on to be successful in life.

Moreover, it is surprising to see how Donald J. Trump facilitated and encouraged this invasion of the Capitol by his followers; the armed marauders followed the orders as the Mob Boss indicated to them, a few hours before the intrusion of the Capitol, its army composed of members of the "Proud boy, Oath keepers, Qanon, Boogaloo Movement, and Wolverine Watchmen". What a disgrace it is this failed COUP, from a President treacherous for his country, but what a shame for Democracy.

What a beautiful parade it was, on this day in June 2020, in front of the "St John's Episcopal, Trump, a bible in his hand for this, mocked Black Lives Matter in the name of law and order, or the peaceful protestors were slaughtered. Yes, we have to talk about this bible; he has never read a bible in his life, and it was shown on the wrong side and especially this monster never goes to Church, Protesters against racism who, it is necessary underline it, were however far from being as insurrectionary as its army which seeks to change the popular will to offer it its uninhibited dream of owning a republic.

After the victory of Barack Obama in 2012, greatly facilitated by the vote of young people, women and cultural minorities, the Republican Party decided to do some introspection. At the heart of the major recommendations of this vast consultation was the need to reach out to cultural minorities, young people and women. The Republicans wanted to take this salutary turn, because relying on the traditional white vote reduced their leeway in this rapidly changing demographic America. The party was walking towards this path of wisdom when the Great Manitou Intimidator, who had perfected his skills in reality shows, landed there victoriously.

Faced with this aggressivity ready to do anything to keep power, even his detractors ended up closing ranks out of pure opportunism or cowardice.

Maleficence in exchange for privileges in the school yard. Sometimes, among the accomplices, there are some who feel uncomfortable, but the fear of suffering the wrath of the villain freezes them, they then swallow their indisposition and self-flagellate themselves for not having the courage of their convictions.

Alongside these passive or active accomplices, there are also righteous ones, like Senator John McCain who has always stood before the Great Bully. A righteousness he paid dearly, because Donald insulted him until his death, even long after his burial, he continued to spit his venom on his body, there is also Senator Mitt Romney, who honorably refused to be an accomplice in the president's mafia methods, this brave man even voted for his dismissal by clearly explaining that his grandchildren would never forgive him for having been on the wrong side of history, to satisfy personal political ambitions.

Apart from these rare exceptions, all the other Republican senators who did not see this January 6th happening are only hypocrites, liars, who do not want to recognize their great share of responsibility in the radicalization of this machine thirsty for the power which they have lost. Control. Indeed, many of them have spent the past four years making Trump believe that his flatulence smelled like vanilla and that he could claim all the rights. Why? To have privileges or not to attract his fury.

As a friend's grandfather said, if power grew on top of tall trees, some of these Republicans would lick chimpanzee asses to help them reach it faster.

These elected officials who are indignant at this attempt at sedition, have helped the Great intimidator to build this army of radicalized white marginalized people, who now seem ready to do anything to defend their guru, it is important to mention here, that these oddballs that we have seen on the flood are a crippled section of the radicals, whom the media overestimate. They are in no way representative of the 74,200 million people who are falsely thought they were Trump supporters because they voted for him. The vast majority of this electorate did not vote for the person who Trump is, but rather for the Republican vehicle he represented. Many voters simply pinched their noses before choosing him because right-wing politics are part of them, of their DNA.

Alongside his army of diehards, we can bet that the large mass of voters he considers his supporters, know that he has legally lost his elections. These people are by no means disciples of the guru, and would not go out in an alley to support this monster of ego, even if he had to go to Prison.

Do not forget that, Fox News Now is a Threat to National Security. The network's furthering of lies from foreign adversaries and flagrant disregard, for the truth have gotten downright dangerous.

Fox News is also an accomplice of theses domestic terrorists attacking the Capitol on Jan.6-2021. For a long time, day after day, they minimized this kind of action, repeated the lies of mob boss, and tried to overturn our Democracy, also inciting insurrection against the government of United States.

I do believe that it is time to formally accuse this institution of misfortune, which incites these people to violence, it's a disgrace.

Maybe one day not too far away, this media will be accused and guilty.

CHAPTER ONE

....

FRIEDRICH TRUMP'S FAMILY

We will get to know Donald Trump's descendants who came from Germany. The great-grandfather, Friedrich, was born in Kallstadt, Bavaria on March 14, 1869. Friedrich emigrated to the United States when he was sixteen on October 7, 1885. He landed in New York City in 1891 where he headed for the streets of gold in the Yukon, and then to Alaska, where he made a fortune by building restaurants under tents, small hotels as well as brothels. In 1901, he got married and went back to Germany. He came back to America later in 1905 and went back to Germany again. This time, the German authorities told Friedrich that he was not welcome because of circumstances that occurred a few years earlier when he had left Germany to avoid his military obligations.

He therefore returned to New York with his wife, Elizabeth Christ. They had been married on August 30, 1902, and finally settled in Woodhaven in Queens. He died on May 30,1918 of the Spanish flu. He was 49 years old. So, as you can see, Donald Trump has his ancestor's DNA since he also fraudulently avoided the Vietnam war.

Donald Trump was born on June 14, 1946, in New York City. His father, Frederick Christ (Fred), was born on October 11,1905, also in New York City. Fred died on June 25, 1999.

Donald's mother, Maryanne Macleod, was born on May 13,1912 in Scotland. She immigrated to the United States in 1930 where she raised five (5) children. Their children: Maryanne, born in April 1937; Fred, born in 1938, Elisabeth, born in 1942; Donald, born in 1946; and, Robert, born in 1948. Maryanne died on August 7, 2000, at the age of 88.

In 1977, Donald Trump married Ivana Zelnickova, a Czechoslovakian model. Together, they had three (3) children: Donald jr., born on December

31,1977; Ivanka, born on October 30, 1981; and, Eric, born on January 6, 1984. They were divorced in 1992.

On December 21,1993, he married Maria Maples. A daughter was born from this marriage, Tiffany, on October 13, 1993. He then divorced her in June 8,1999.

Donald was married again on January 22, 2005, to Melania Krauss, a model from Slovenia. They have a son, Baron, born on March 20, 2006.

Finally, we will see further, the rest of this story.

The enigma # 01: After two years at Fordham University, did Trump need special treatment to gain admission to Wharton?

The answer begins with James A. Nolan, the Penn admissions officer who interviewed Trump and ushered his application through the vetting process, which, he says, he did at the behest of Trump's older brother, Fred Trump Jr. Nolan grew up in Queens and had been friends with Fred since high school in the mid-1950s. During an interview at his apartment on Washington Square, Nolan told me he spent a lot of time in those days at the Trump McMansion in Jamaica Estates, which he described as "very big, with lots of bedrooms", and blackface lawn jockeys lining the approach. Both friends planned to enroll at Penn, but only Nolan got accepted. Ten years later, Nolan was working in Penn's admissions department — he would later become director of undergraduate admissions — when Fred called in a favor.

This was first revealed in Gwenda Blair's book: The Trumps: Three Generations That Built an Empire (Simon & Schuster, 2000). "Whether that was 100 percent why he got in, I don't know, but clearly it was helpful," Blair told me. Blair says that at Nolan's request she kept his identity a secret until earlier this summer, when Nolan granted interviews to the Washington Post and this magazine.

Now 80, Nolan says he found "no evidence" of Trump's alleged "super genius" at the time. Furthermore, he says, Wharton wasn't nearly as difficult to get into in the mid-'60s as it is today. Back then, according to Nolan, Penn was accepting 40 percent of all applicants, as opposed to its current cutthroat acceptance rate of seven percent. Not surprisingly, Trump remembers it differently. "I got in quickly and easily," he told the Boston Globe in 2015. "And it's one of the hardest schools to get into in the country — always has been."

Nolan says helping Trump is a big regret. "I wish I hadn't interviewed him," he says, breaking into the deep belly laugh of a man who knows that at his age, nothing he says can possibly hurt him. "In retrospect, I wish I hadn't done that."

The enigma #2: Did one of his Wharton professors repeatedly tell friends and associates that Donald Trump "was the dumbest goddamn student I ever had"?

The enigma #3: Was Donald Trump the proverbial Big Man on Campus at Penn?

Despite his braggadocio, Trump appears to have left no substantive mark in the collective memory of his graduating class. Efforts by media outlets — including the Washington Post, the Boston Globe, the Daily Pennsylvanian and this magazine — to locate Penn classmates with vivid memories of Trump's tenure proved largely fruitless. He was involved in no known extra-curricular activities, rarely socialized on campus, and didn't even submit a yearbook photo. One classmate, Louis Calomaris, told the Boston Globe that he remembered Trump standing up in class and declaring, "I'm going to be the king of New York real estate." prompting eye-rolls from his classmates. "Sit down, you [expletive]," Calomaris remembered thinking.

The enigma #4: Did Trump attempt to "date" Penn student Candice Bergen and get shot down?

Prior to flunking out in 1965, Ms. Bergen was the «It Girl» at Penn, elected both Homecoming Queen and Miss University. Her proto-screen-siren star power was apparently visible in the night sky from as far away as New York, because one evening, the phone in her dorm rang, and on the other end was one Donald Trump, pre-Wharton. "I was 18," Bergen told Harry Connick Jr. back in 2017. "He was a nice-looking guy, I mean, he was. And I was in college, and it's where he was going to be going to college.

The enigma Mid-sixties #5: Did Donald Trump finish first in his class at Wharton, as he bragged to multiple journalists over the years?

This assertion appeared in a fawning New York Times' profile of the Trump Organization published in 1973, the same year the Department of Justice sued Donald and his father Fred for housing discrimination for refusing to rent to people of color.

The claim was repeated in another doting profile of Trump in the New York Times in 1976. Noting that practically every article ever written about

Trump in the wake of the Times' profiles parroted the "first in his class" claim, the Times finally corrected the record

Trump himself finally copped to this in a 1988 New York magazine story written by Julie Baumgold. "Okay, maybe not 'first,' as myth has it," Baumgold wrote, "but he had 'the highest grades possible."

The enigma Mid-sixties #6: Did Trump donate $1.4 million to Penn over the years or merely pledge to do so? Did his pledges coincide with the enrollment applications of his children? Why doesn't his name appear prominently anywhere on Penn's campus?

Penn pleads the Fifth. "Thank you for your inquiry," says John H. Zeller, vice president for development and alumni relations. "We have a policy to not disclose or comment on any donors' history or support."

But a lot of the pledged donations seem to be made right around the time each of his kids was going to Penn or trying to get in.

The enigma Mid-sixties #7: Did Trump strike Don Jr. across the face in his freshman dorm room for attempting to wear a Yankees jersey to a baseball game with him?

That's the story recounted in a November 3 2016, Facebook post by Don Jr.'s former classmate Scott Melker:

Melker's post describes Donald Jr. as "a drunk in college," a young man who "despised his father, and hated the attention that his last name afforded him." It claims Don Jr.'s nickname was "Diaper Don" because he tended to "fall asleep drunk in other people's beds and urinate." (Melker's account was denied by the Trumps.)

The enigma Mid-sixties #8: What is known about Ivanka's Penn stint beyond the fact that after two years at Georgetown, she transferred to Wharton, where, unlike her father, she graduated cum laude, in 2004?

A rumor made the rounds on campus that a breakup drove her from Georgetown to Penn midstream, but she denied it in 2004 in Philadelphia.

The enigma Mid-sixties #9: What do we know about Tiffany's Penn years?

In 2012, Tiffany arrived at Penn on the heels of a brief but doomed bid at auto tuned pop stardom (google "Tiffany Trump" and "Like A Bird" if you're feeling sinister), as her father was waging his notoriously racist birther fake-news campaign. She double-majored in sociology and urban studies.

The enigma Mid-sixties #10: Did Michael Cohen threaten to sue Penn back to the Stone Age if it released Trump's grades?

Almost absolutely. In his televised testimony before the House Oversight & Reform Committee in February, Michael Cohen, who served as Trump's personal attorney and fixer from 2006 to 2018, said the following about his former boss:

When I say con man, I'm talking about a man who declares himself brilliant but directed me to threaten his high school, his colleges, and the College Board in order to never release his grades or SAT scores. As I mentioned, I'm giving the Committee today, copies of a letter I sent at Mr. Trump's direction threatening these schools with civil and criminal actions if Mr. Trump's grades or SAT scores were ever disclosed without his permission.

For reasons that are unclear, the House Oversight Committee only made public the letter sent to the president of Fordham University. But given that Cohen referred in his testimony to "a letter" — singular, not plural — that he says he sent to all the schools Trump attended, along with the College Board, which administers the SAT, and the fact that in the third paragraph of the letter sent to Fordham, Cohen refers to "all of the College Board employees" (presumably having neglected to customize the missive before sending), we can safely assume that all of Trump's academic institutions received the same letter. Amusingly, Cohen's letter concludes four paragraphs of dire threats, including liability "to the fullest extent of the law including damages and criminality" for anyone who dares to reveal Trump's grades, with the following:

P.S. Mr. Trump truly enjoyed his two years at Fordham and has great respect for the University.

TRUMP'S PROFESSOR 'DUMBEST STUDENT' EVER:

Despite the US president attesting to the fact that he finished "top of his class" at Wharton business school of the University of Pennsylvania, his former college professor, Professor William T. Kelley had another view. After Kelley's death, Frank DiPrima, a close friend of Kelley's, revealed that the professor felt the president was a fool. "Professor Kelley told me 100 times over three decades that 'Donald Trump was a fool.

DiPrima wrote for the Daily Kos. "I remember his emphasis and inflection — it went like this — 'Donald Trump was the dumbest goddam student I ever had'. DiPrima explained that Kelley told him this after Trump became a celebrity, but "long before" he was deemed a political figure. "Dr. Kelley often referred to Trump's arrogance when he told of this — that Trump came to Wharton thinking he already knew everything," Di Prima added.

DiPrima's revelation is the latest in the series of questions over the US President's academic record. According to The Daily Pennsylvania, Trump's name was not on the Wharton Dean's List in 1968, the year he graduated despite him allowing media to report for years that he graduated first in his class at Wharton. If he had performed as exceptionally well as is commonly believed, his name would have been present.

Recently, it was speculated that Rex Tillerson had called the president "a moron", although Tillerson himself refused to accept or deny these claims. Trump was deeply troubled at the possibility of having been called a moron; so much so that he even challenged Tillerson to compare IQ tests.

"Special Favor."

The alleged claim by Trump's professor is not the first of its kind. In 2001, Gwenda Blair, a biographer, wrote that Trump was admitted to Wharton on a "special favor" from a "friendly" admissions officer, allegedly known to Trump's older brother, Freddy. According to The Daily Kos, former classmates reported that Trump skipped classes and often spent his weekends in New York.

Louis Calomaris, who studied alongside Trump, claimed that the president was "loathe to really study much". He declared that Trump would come to seminars unprepared and did not "seem to care" about being ready for work. No matter how well Trump did in school or what his IQ is now, he is still currently one of the most powerful people in the world.

Looks like we may never know how smart he really is … unless maybe Tillerson gets back to him about that IQ test!

TRUMP WAS A NIGHTMARE LANDLORD IN THE 1980S:

March 28 2016

There's an episode in Donald Trump's past that shows just how far this supposed billionaire businessman will go to get his way.

It began in 1981. Trump bought a 14-story building on prime real estate facing New York City's Central Park.

His plan was to tear the building down and replace it with luxury condos. But first, he needed a small band of rent-stabilized tenants out of there.

To succeed, Trump played rough, according to lawsuits filed by the tenants. Renters said he cut heat and hot water, and he imposed tough building rules.

It went on for five years as Trump fought tenants, real estate lawyers, New York state regulators and city officials.

CNN Money reviewed 2,895 court documents -- most of them now only available on microfiche at New York state courts – a detail of that fight that's now largely forgotten.

The apartment building at 100 Central Park South, as seen in 2016, was the site of an epic battle between Trump and rent-stabilized tenants.

LEAKS, RATS AND BITTER COLD:

By 1981, Trump was already the epitome of American business bravado. At 35 years old, he had cut historic multi-million-dollar land deals, saved a blighted midtown Manhattan subway hub, and was in the process of erecting the black-framed glass behemoth of Trump Tower.

The next move in his real-life game of Monopoly came in July 1981, when he bought a hotel and its neighbor, a rent-stabilized building at 100 Central Park South.

Two months later, he applied for a demolition permit to blow it up. Trump fired the building manager and replaced him with Citadel Management. In his book, The Art of the Deal, Trump himself said he chose a company that "specialized in relocating tenants."

Just a few months later, on New Year's Eve, several tenants received identical "lease violation" warning letters. The previous building owner had given renters permission to knock down walls and renovate their apartment units. But Trump was reversing that exception, and renters had only 12 days to rebuild the walls -- or face eviction.

The renters hired a real estate lawyer known in New York City for being particularly aggressive. They sued Trump and his company, Park South Associates. CNN Money identified at least two instances in which New York state judges stepped in to put Trump's lease violation notices on hold.

This is what an eviction threat from Donald Trump looks like. (From a

1987 case involving an elderly couple living in the building at 100 Central Park South.)

In their 1982 lawsuits, the tenants said Trump had cut off their hot water and heat during New York's freezing winters and stopped all building repairs. One claimed he allowed "a rodent infestation of the premises." Another said he imposed burdensome new rules in an attempt to force them out.

For example, Trump's new building manager claimed there was a burglary in the building. Dentists with apartment offices were ordered to send patients to the garbage-filled service elevator, according to building management documents and a dentist's lawsuit that tried to fight it.

Dr. Michael Richman refused to comply with the new rule, complaining in court documents that Trump "mounted a campaign of harassment."

"Mr. Trump is willing to resort to any device or tactic to drive out the tenants from the building," he said.

One time, Trump sued a tenant for not paying rent -- even though the guy, Anderson Clipper, actually did. New York City Judge Jay Stuart Dankberg eventually blasted Trump for the "spurious and unnecessary" lawsuit, according to The New York Times. The judge dismissed the lawsuit, said Trump was trying to "harass" Clipper, and forced the developer to refund 5% of Clipper's rent.

"To most landlords happiness is having tenants who pay the rent each month without prodding or litigation," Dangberg wrote. "However, [Trump] is apparently searching for double happiness."

Clipper died this past October. His 72-year-old estranged wife, Nancy Clipper, didn't live with him at the Trump-controlled apartment building. But she remembers all he endured with Trump as his landlord: the lawsuits and the refusal to fix things.

"It was really a horrible experience," she recently told CNN Money. "He was insensitive, rude, and just a generally nasty man. I would never have considered him presidential."

Trump tells a very different story in his book, The Art of the Deal. He described the renters as privileged, rich "yuppies" who benefited unfairly from rent-control. The rent Trump collected barely covered expenses. That's why he installed cheaper light bulbs and cut back; he wrote.

To be fair, these people had an unbelievably sweet deal: low-rent homes a short stroll away from Broadway theaters and Carnegie Hall. Dr. Richman paid $700 a month for Apartment 5C. Fashion designer Arnold Scaasi paid $985 for his mind-blowing, six-bedroom with killer views of the park.

The building's superintendent, Anthony Ramirez, swore in court that Trump's building managers gave him explicit instructions.

"They didn't want any repairs done. No cleaning. No accepting of packages," Ramirez said, according to transcripts of a court hearing.

As a result, Scaachi's luxurious apartment was plagued by water leaks -- one that put at peril his art collection, which included a 1926 Picasso painting and works of art by Claude Monet and others.

A 10-month water pipe leak in Apartment 14B got so nasty that two brothers who grew up in there saw brown-and-white mushrooms sprouting from their bedroom carpet, according to court documents and recent CNN Money interviews.

"It felt like we were under attack," one of the brothers, now 57 and living north of the city, told CNN Money recently. "Trump did his best not to repair anything."

THEN IT GOT REALLY DIRTY:

Trump put out newspaper advertisements in 1982 and 1983 offering to shelter homeless people in the apartment building. The move was seen by tenants as a ruthless attempt to drive them out.

Trump denied that, telling The New York Times: "Some people think I'm just doing a number on the people in the building. That's not true. I just want to help with the homeless problem. It'll take two or three years to get everybody out, and in the meantime, I'll have more and more vacant apartments for the indigent."

But a top city official, Human Resources Administration deputy administrator Robert Trobe, told the Times that Trump's offer did "not seem appropriate."

There was alleged spying too. Trump's building manager told Ramirez, the superintendent, to monitor "the personal habits of the tenants" and "keep a list on the tenants' activities," according to his repeated sworn testimony in several transcripts.

Ramirez resisted:

"Sir, I have too many things on my conscience at this late stage in life, and I don't need any more headaches. I'm here to do my job and to do repairs to the building," Ramirez recalled telling a building management representative.

"What are you, Born Again Christian?" the manager replied.

In a sworn affidavit signed April 18 1985, Trump denied these complaints. First, Trump claimed he didn't directly run the building owner, Park South Associates (even though corporate documents show he owned 60 % of the company and was the only listed officer). Then he swore he kept the building in tip-top shape. Plus, a previous year's inspection by New York State's housing agency backed him up, finding that "all public areas were clean."

But in 1985, that same state agency went after Trump too. New York State's Division of Homes and Community Renewal sued, charging him with harassing tenants. Months later, the city of New York filed a similar suit.

There was a brief glimmer of peace that year. According to court documents, Trump and the leader of the tenants' association discussed a potential deal: The renters would team up and buy the building for $15 million -- and free themselves from their landlord.

But Trump used that opportunity to accuse the renters of shady behavior: using lawsuits of harassment to cover up their real mission.

Tenants were "waging a ceaseless guerrilla-type war... to coerce a bargain sale of the building," Trump's attorneys claimed in court documents. He sued them for $150 million.

It only escalated the legal battle. By 1986, Trump had spent more than $1 million fighting the tenants, according to his attorneys at the time. By comparison, he'd spent $160,000 in repairs over four years, according to statements filed by his legal team.

Trump finally settled with the tenants' association in 1986. He cut their attorneys a $550,000 check and agreed to let the housing agency monitor repairs for five years.

Filling a cancer patient's apartment with dust:

But the alleged harassment dragged on with one elderly couple, Alvin and Catalina Meyer. The elderly woman was dying of cancer and was plagued with emphysema -- so it was a particularly rude awakening when Trump's construction workers woke her up at 7 a.m. by drilling holes in the ceiling above her bed.

The construction crew had also set up a workstation in the apartment next door, and Mrs. Meyer complained of the dust in the air.

"I am a very sick woman battling for my life," she said in court papers. "I have begged for reasonableness. The landlord will not be reasonable."

After nearly a decade of nonstop fighting, tenants started turning on one another. Trump said he couldn't fix the building's heating system, because Meyer didn't give construction workers access to her apartment. Fellow tenants told Meyer to back down. Meyer's lawsuit fizzled out when her own attorney left her.

The fighting died down in the 1990s -- then popped up again in 2000 when 72-year-old Carmel Reingold in Apartment 2A sued Trump in the New York State court when he overcharged her $40,000 in rent over four years. He paid that money back.

In the end, no judge ever ruled that the tenants were being harassed. After all, he did settle. But Trump didn't get his way either. The building remains in place today. Trump's company owns 18 units, according to city records. Trump's son, Eric, owns a flat on the top floor. At least two renters actually bought their apartments. Most moved away.

But it remains a defining moment that shows his character, said Wayne Barrett, an investigative journalist in New York who documented the businessman's empire in the book: Trump: The Deals and the Downfall.

"This was a concrete choice he made, knowing he would disrupt the lives of many middle income, elderly people," Barrett said. "He has absolutely no excuse."

Trump never put in place a coronavirus program.

CHAPTER TWO

....

THE MAN WHO SHOWED TRUMP HOW TO EXPLOIT POWER AND INSTILL FEAR:

Donald Trump was a brash scion of a real estate empire, a young developer anxious to leave his mark on New York. Roy Cohn was a legendary New York fixer, a ruthless lawyer in the hunt for new clients.

They came together by chance one night at Le Club, a hangout for Manhattan's rich and famous. Trump introduced himself to Cohn, who was sitting at a nearby table, and sought advice: How should he and his father respond to Justice Department allegations that their company had systematically discriminated against black people seeking housing?

"My view is telling them to go to hell," Cohn said, "and fight the thing in court."

It was October 1973 and the start of one of the most influential relationships of Trump's career. Cohn soon represented Trump in legal battles, counseled him about his marriage and introduced Trump to New York power brokers, money men and socialites.

Cohn also showed Trump how to exploit power and instill fear through a simple formula: attack, counterattack and never apologize.

Since he announced his run for the White House a year ago, Trump has used such tactics more aggressively than any other candidate in recent memory, demeaning opponents, insulting minorities and women, and whipping up anger among his supporters.

By the 1970s, Cohn maintained a powerful network in New York City, using his connections in the courts and City Hall to reward friends and punish those who crossed him.

He routinely pulled strings in government for clients, funneled cash to politicians and cultivated relationships with influential figures, including

FBI Director J. Edgar Hoover, mafia boss Anthony "Fat Tony" Salerno and a succession of city leaders.

In the 1990s, a tragic character based on Cohn had a central place in Tony Kushner's Pulitzer prize-winning play, "Angels in America: A Gay Fantasia on National Themes."

Trump prized Cohn's reputation for aggression. According to a New York Times profile a quarter-century ago, when frustrated by an adversary, Trump would pull out a photograph of Cohn and ask, "Would you rather deal with him?" Trump remained friends with him even after the lawyer was disbarred in New York for ethical lapses. Cohn died in 1986.

When they met, Trump, 27, tall and handsome, was at the start of his career and living off money he was earning in the family business. Cohn, 46, short and off-putting, was near the peak of his power and considered by some to be among the most reviled Americans of the 20th century.

In interviews with The Post, Trump maintained that Cohn was merely his attorney, stressing that he was only one of many of Cohn's clients in New York. Trump also played down the influence of Cohn on his aggressive tactics and rhetoric, saying: "I don't think I got that from Roy at all. I think I've had a natural instinct for that."

"I don't feel I insult people. I try and get to the facts and I don't feel I insult people," he said. "Now, if I'm insulted, I will counterattack, or if something is unfair, I will counterattack, but I don't feel like I insult people. I don't want to do that. But if I'm attacked, I will counterattack."

Cohn himself once said he was "not only Donald's lawyer but also one of his close friends." Roger Stone, a political operative who met Trump through Cohn, said their association was grounded in business, but he also described the lawyer as "like a cultural guide to Manhattan" for Trump into the worlds of celebrity and power. "Roy was more than his personal lawyer," Stone told The Post. "And, of course, Trump was a trophy client for Roy."

Investigative reporter Wayne Barrett, who spent dozens of hours interviewing Cohn and Trump beginning in the 1970s, once wrote in "Trump: The Deals and the Downfall" that Cohn began to "assume a role in Donald's life far transcending that of a lawyer. He became Donald's mentor, his constant adviser."

Barrett now says Cohn's stamp on Trump is obvious. "I just look at him and see Roy," Barrett said in an interview. "Both of them are attack dogs."

In 1950, Cohn at age 23, was the lead prosecutor in what became known as the Atom Spy Case. A Jewish couple named Julius and Ethel Rosenberg were accused of conspiracy to commit espionage for the Soviet Union. After the two were convicted of passing atomic secrets to the Soviets, the judge left the courtroom and called Cohn from a phone booth on Park Avenue. As Cohn later wrote, the judge wanted "to ask my advice on whether he ought to give the death penalty to Ethel Rosenberg."

"The way I see it is that she's worse than Julius," Cohn told the judge, according to his autobiography. Both Julius and Ethel Rosenberg were executed in the electric chair. 1952

Settling back in New York, Cohn tapped his connections as he began building a private legal practice, documents show. Cohn often operated in the gray areas of the law. In the 1960s and early 1970s, he fought off four federal or state indictments for alleged extortion, bribery, conspiracy, perjury and banking violations. At the same time, he avoided paying state and federal income taxes and engaged in a variety of schemes to take advantage of wealthy clients, as shown by court records.

Cohn's brazenness seemed limitless. In 1969, while facing his third federal indictment, he wrote a confidential letter to J. Edgar Hoover, the director of the FBI. Cohn included affidavits, legal motions, news articles and other material outlining his defense.

Hoover wrote back eight days later: "Your generous comments regarding me are indeed gratifying."

In October 1973, when Trump and Cohn first met at Le Club, the lawyer was instantly recognizable, with piercing blue eyes, heavy eyelids and a perpetual tan. James D. Zirin, a New York lawyer who later wrote about Cohn, recalled him as "the strangest-looking man I ever met," with a face "contorted in a perpetual ugly sneer that seemed to project an air of unbridled malevolence." Trump, not yet a household name, knew about Cohn's reputation as a legal knife fighter.

At the time, Trump and his father, Fred, were facing Justice Department allegations that they had systematically discriminated against black people at their family-owned or -managed apartment complexes across New York City. Cohn agreed to represent the Trumps — his way. That meant hitting back hard while shaping public opinion. On December 12 1973, Donald Trump, his father and Cohn called a news conference at the New York Hilton hotel. They said they were suing the government for $100 million in damages relating to the Justice Department's "irresponsible and baseless" allegations.

A federal judge dismissed the countersuit. And two years later, after a string of theatrics and unfounded allegations by Cohn — including the claim that a Jewish prosecutor had used Nazi Gestapo tactics — Donald and Fred Trump settled the case without admitting guilt.

Following Cohn's lead, Donald Trump declared victory.

Cohn began advising Trump on major real estate deals and other matters. Trump once said that Cohn represented him in two libel cases against journalists. Although Trump said the legal work cost $100,000, he said it was worth the money because "I've broken one writer," according to a statement he once gave to Barrett, who was a veteran investigative reporter for the Village Voice. Trump did not name the writer.

Cohn often provided counsel for free, collecting money when he needed it. That included help on Trump's personal matters, such as his marriage to Ivana Zelnickova in 1977. She was a model in Canada who claimed to be a former member of the Czech national ski team. After they had dated for months, Trump rented a two-bedroom apartment on Fifth Avenue and began making arrangements for their wedding. Cohn urged Trump to create a prenuptial agreement.

Ivana balked when she learned what Cohn included in the document. His proposal called on her to return any gifts from Trump in the event of a divorce. In response to her fury, Cohn added language that allowed her to keep her own clothing and any gifts. With Trump's consent, he also included a "rainy day" certificate of deposit worth $100,000. She would be allowed to begin tapping that fund one month after the wedding, according to Barrett's book. During one of the negotiating sessions, held at Cohn's townhouse office, the lawyer wore a bathrobe.

As Cohn helped arrange Trump's marital circumstances, he also helped the 30-year-old would-be tycoon to gain access to Manhattan's drug-fueled disco scene. Trump maintained a reputation as a strait-laced teetotaler, but he loved to be in the mix late at night, especially among beautiful women, according to his own accounts.

In April 1977, Trump and Ivana went to the opening night of a club called Studio 54. The owners were impresarios named Steve Rubell and Ian Schrager, and their lawyer was Roy Cohn.

The city had never seen anything quite like Studio 54, a freewheeling club that offered up celebrity, glitter and debauchery. It attracted city leaders, Hollywood stars and a Techni-color cross section of other straight, gay and bisexual partyers.

Trump was a regular at the club. "I'd go there a lot with dates and with friends, and with lots of people," Trump said in an interview. "Roy would always make it very comfortable."

Cohn also lobbied against gay rights legislation in New York City. He once called a lawyer's sponsor on the City Council and offered a profane warning: "You've got to get off this fag stuff, it's very harmful to the city and it's going to hurt you," Cohn said in a phone call that Zion overheard. "These fucking fags are no good, forget about them."

Connections:

Stone stood for some time in the townhouse's waiting room. When Stone was finally admitted, Cohn was sitting at a dining-room table, in a silk bathrobe, Stone told The Post. On the table were three strips of bacon and a square of cream cheese. Cohn ate the food with his fingers.

Sitting at the table was a heavyset man.

"Mr. Stone, I want you to meet Tony Salerno," Cohn said.

There Stone was, standing before the future boss of the Genovese crime family.

"So, Roy says we're going with Reagan this time," Salerno said.

Cohn and Salerno listened to Stone's pitch. Then Cohn recommended that Stone reach out to Trump.

"You need to meet Donald and his father," Cohn said, as Stone recalls it now. "They'd be perfect for this. Let me set up a meeting for you."

"I'm proud of my sister. She's done a great job," Trump said in an interview. "I just don't comment on that."

One of Trump's early ambitious real estate ventures was Trump Tower, a concrete-and-glass skyscraper on Fifth Avenue. Starting in 1978, Trump began moving to acquire the site between East 56th and East 57th streets and, with Cohn's help, strengthening his ties to the city leaders and others who would decide the project's fate. Their efforts included a stream of campaign contributions by both men to public officials.

Trump became a generous campaign contributor himself. He eventually gave $150,000 in just one year to local candidates in New York. State officials later said Trump had "circumvented" state limits on individual and corporate contributions by spreading out payments through Trump subsidiaries, but they did not formally accuse Trump of wrongdoing.

Testifying under oath about his giving, Trump said, "Well, my attorneys basically said that this was a proper way of doing it."

To thrive in this milieu, Trump also had to work with unions and companies known to be controlled by New York's ruling mafia families, which had infiltrated the construction industry, according to court records, federal task force reports and newspaper accounts.

Cohn represented some of the mafia figures who had sway over Trump projects. S&A Concrete, which supplied building material for the Trump Plaza on Manhattan's East Side, was owned in part by Salerno, the Genovese family mobster and Cohn client, court records show.

Mob-friendly labor leaders dominated local construction unions. At the head of Teamsters Local 282 was John Cody. A House of Representatives investigation found he "was universally acknowledged to be the most significant labor racketeer preying on the construction industry in New York." Without Cody's support, projects were liable to stall.

Cody claimed Cohn as a friend. Cody also said he worked with Trump — with Cohn serving as intermediary. "I knew Trump quite well," Cody told Barrett. "Donald liked to deal with me through Roy Cohn."

"Since 1950 — the year I prosecuted the Rosenberg atom-spy trial at age 23 with the magnificent investigative help of the Bureau, up to the present, 34 years later, I have had a first-rate relationship with and in respect for the Bureau," Cohn wrote on March 11 1985, according to documents obtained by The Post.

The next year, Salerno and 14 others were indicted on an array of criminal charges, including conspiracy, extortion and "infiltration of ostensibly legitimate businesses involved in selling ready-mix concrete in New York City," the federal indictment said. One of Trump's projects was mentioned in the indictment. Salerno and others eventually went to prison on federal charges including racketeering and bid-rigging.

"Roy understood the value of the tabloids," Stone said in an interview. "He did business at this dining-room table in the dining room at his brownstone. He would call reporters and dictate their copy with you sitting there. He would just dictate it."

Cohn had his setbacks. Zion wrote that Cohn had personally chartered a 747 for a group of male friends to travel to Europe. The group trashed the plane, and Cohn never paid the charter bill. The airline sued Cohn successfully but could not get any money from him. An executive aware of the close ties between Trump and Cohn called Trump to see whether he would pay. Trump declined.

Trump knew Cohn had a shady side, saying "he could be a nasty guy."

"I don't kid myself about Roy. He was no Boy Scout," Trump wrote in "Trump: The Art of the Deal." "He once told me that he'd spent more than two thirds of his adult life under indictment for one charge or another. That amazed me. I said to him, 'Roy, just tell me one thing. Did you really do all that stuff?' He looked at me and smiled. 'What the hell do you think?' he said. I never really knew."

In the fall of 1984, Cohn became ill. A year later, he started treatment at the Clinical Center at the National Institute of Health in Bethesda, Md. He maintained that he had liver cancer. But he was suffering from the effects of the HIV virus. As he struggled to stay alive, Trump pulled back from his friend for a spell. Cohn was thrown off balance by this apparent betrayal. "I can't believe he's doing this to me," Cohn said, according to Barrett's account. "Donald pisses ice water."

Before the appellate division made its ruling in 1986, a host of prominent people testified to Cohn's good character. Among them was Trump, who had resumed his visits to Cohn and, that spring, had invited him to his Mar-a-Lago estate in Florida.

On June 23 1986, Cohn was disbarred. "For an attorney practicing for nearly 40 years in this State, such misconduct is inexcusable, notwithstanding an impressive array of character witnesses who testified in mitigation," the court said.

Cohn died six weeks later, on August 2 1986. He was 59.

His friends held a memorial service for him. Trump stood silently in the back.

One year after his death, Trump professed admiration for Cohn.

"Tough as he was, Roy had a lot of friends," Trump wrote in "The Art of the Deal," "and I'm not embarrassed to say I was one."

"But with all of that being said, he did a very good job for me as a lawyer," Trump said. "I get a kick out of winning, and Roy would win."

Trump never put in place a coronavirus program.

Chapter Three

....

THE MANY SCANDALS OF
TRUMP, A CHEAT SHEET:

One of the women who accused trump of sexual misconduct has sued him for defamation after he labeled her claims false.

January 23 2017

Donald Trump is now president and not just a private citizen, but that doesn't mean he's free of the controversies that dogged him in his former life.

Last week, a few days before Trump's inauguration, former Apprentice contestant, Summer Zervos, sued him in New York State, accusing the president of defamation. Zervos, who is represented by the famous lawyer Gloria Allred, was one of the several women who accused Trump of sexual assault or misconduct prior to the election. She claims that he kissed her and pressed his genitals against her non-consensually. Trump denied those claims, saying all of the women who had accused him had made their stories up. So Zervos sued him for defamation.

The 2016 presidential campaign saw a long string of stories showing scandals involving Trump, both large and small—from questionable business dealings to allegations of sexual assault. While they did not derail his presidential hopes, many of them remain live issues as Trump begins his transition to the White House.

The breadth of Trump's controversies is truly huge, ranging from allegations of mafia ties to unscrupulous business dealings and from racial discrimination to alleged marital rape. They stretch over more than four decades, from the mid-1970s to the present day. To catalogue the full sweep of allegations would require thousands of words and lump together the trivial with the truly scandalous. Including business deals that have simply failed, without any hint of impropriety, which would require thousands more. This is a snapshot of some of the most interesting and largest of those scandals.

SEXUAL-ASSAULT ALLEGATIONS:

Where and when: Various, 1970s to 2005.

The dirt: Even before the release of a 2005 video in which he boasted about sexually assaulting women "Grab them by the pussy. You can do anything," he said, as well as "I just start kissing them. It's like a magnet. Just kiss. I don't even wait. And when you're a star they let you do it. You can do anything"—there's a long line of allegations against Trump. Jill Harth says Trump assaulted her in the 1990s. Trump's ex-wife Ivana Trump once suggested he had raped her, though she has since recanted her story. Former Miss Utah Temple Taggart said he kissed her on the lips inappropriately. But since the release, more women have come forward. Two told The New York Times that Trump had assaulted them, one saying he tried to put his hand up her skirt on a flight in the 1970s and another saying he forcibly kissed her. A Florida woman says Trump groped her. A former People reporter recounted an alleged assault at his Mar-a-Lago debate, and says he told her, "You know we're going to have an affair, don't you?" Several former teen pageant contestants said Trump walked in on them while they were naked or partially dressed.

The upshot: Trump denies all of the allegations. In the sexual-assault cases, Trump faces the difficulty that he, in some cases, bragged openly about just the behavior of which he has accused—whether grabbing or forcibly kissing. Trump has demanded a retraction from the Times, and has threatened to sue several outlets. The paper, in a letter, refused. A woman, who brought a rape case against Trump, (twice) withdrew her suit in November, but in January, Summer Zervos sued Trump for defamation, after he labeled her claims of sexual assault false.

THE BEAUTY PAGEANT SCANDALS:

Where and when: Various, 1992 to the present

The dirt: The Boston Globe's Matt Viser reports on the mess of the American Dream pageant in 1992. After years of attending beauty pageants—Trump seems to have always enjoyed the company of beautiful, scantily clad women—he decided he wanted to get in on the business himself, meeting with George Houraney and Jill Harth, a couple who ran the American Dream pageant. It was an ill-fated effort. Harth and Houraney alleged that Trump started making passes at her almost immediately. On one occasion, Trump allegedly asked them to bring some models to a party. Harth alleges that Trump groped her at the party. In a limo afterward, another model said she heard him say that "all women are bimbos" and most are "gold diggers." Trump reportedly joined another model in bed, uninvited, late at night. On other occasions, he forced Harth into bedrooms and made passes at her, she said. But after the contest, Trump broke off dealings. Harth sued Trump, alleging sexual misbehavior, while the couple together, sued him for breach of contract. In the suit, they also alleged that Trump had kept black women out of the pageant.

The upshot: The couple settled with Trump for an unannounced sum, and Harth dropped her suit. Trump has denied all the allegations. But it wasn't Trump's last turn in the pageant business. A few years later, he bought the Miss Universe pageant, which also includes Miss USA and Miss Teen USA. "Honestly, when I bought [Miss Universe], the bathing suits got smaller and the heels got higher and the ratings went up," he boasted to Vanity Fair later. In 2012, he won a $5 million suit against a former contestant who claimed the contest was rigged. By 2015, he operated Miss Universe as a joint venture with NBC, but after he slurred Mexican immigrants at his campaign launch, Univision and NBC both announced they would not air the pageant. Trump bought out NBC's share, and then promptly sold the company. He sued Univision but settled in February. The terms were undisclosed.

RACIAL HOUSING DISCRIMINATION:

Where and when: New York City, 1973-1975

The dirt: The Department of Justice sued Trump and his father Fred in 1973 for housing discrimination at 39 sites around New York. "The government contended that Trump Management had refused to rent or negotiate rentals 'because of race and color," The New York Times reported. "It also charged that the company had required different rental terms and conditions because of race and that it had misrepresented to blacks that apartments were not available." Trump called the accusations "absolutely ridiculous."

The upshot: The Trumps hired attorney Roy Cohn, who had worked for

Joe McCarthy and whom Michael Kinsley once indelibly labeled "innocent of a variety of federal crimes." They sued the Justice Department for $100 million. In the end, however, the Trumps settled with the government, promising not to discriminate and submitting to regular review by the New York Urban League—though crucially not admitting guilt. The Times much more on the long history of allegations at Trump-owned properties

MAFIA TIES:

Where and when: New York and Atlantic City, 1970s?

The dirt: Trump has been linked to the mafia many times over the years, with varying degrees of closeness. Many of the connections seem to be the sorts of interactions with mobsters that were inevitable for a guy in the construction and casino businesses at the time. For example, organized crime controlled the 1980s New York City concrete business, so that anyone building in the city likely brushed up against it. There have been a string of other allegations, too, many reported by investigative journalist Wayne Barrett. Cohn, Trump's lawyer, also represented the Genovese crime family boss Tony Salerno. Barrett also reported a series of transactions involving organized crime, and alleged that Trump paid twice market rate to a mob figure for the land under Trump Plaza in Atlantic City. Michael Isikoff has also reported that Trump was close to Robert LiButti, an associate of John Gotti, inviting him on his yacht and helicopter. In one case, Trump's company bought LiButti nine luxury cars.

The upshot: Though Trump has been questioned in court or under oath about the ties; he's never been convicted of anything. A New Jersey Division of Gaming Enforcement report after Barrett's 1992 book on Trump generally found no mafia-related wrong-doing on Trump's part. Trump Plaza was fined $200,000 for keeping black employees away from LiButti's table, at his behest, and for the gift of the cars, though Trump personally was not penalized.

TRUMP UNIVERSITY:

Where and when: 2005-2010, online

The dirt: In 2005, Trump announced an eponymous "university" to teach his real-estate development secrets. Students ponied up as much as

$35,000—some after being suckered in by slick, free "seminars"—to learn how to get rich. One ad promised they would "learn from Donald Trump's handpicked instructors, and that participants would have access to Trump's real estate secrets." In fact, Trump had little to do with the curriculum or the instructors. Many of the "students" have since complained that Trump University was a scam. At one time, it had some prestigious instructors, but over time the "faculty" became a motley bunch of misfits. (It was also never really a "university" by any definition, and it changed its name to the "Trump Entrepreneur Initiative," because, as it happened, the school was violating New York law by operating without an educational license.)

The upshot: The school shut down in 2010. In November 2016, Trump agreed to settle a series of lawsuits related to the school for $25 million. Trump did not admit any wrongdoing as part of the settlement. But he had insisted for months that he would not settle the suit because he expected to win. For a time, he appeared to have been trying to intimidate plaintiffs, including countersuing one for $1 million (a favorite Trump litigation tactic) and refusing to let her withdraw from the suit. His lawyers cited positive reviews, but former students say they were pressured to give those. Trump also mounted a length attack on the judge, claiming his ethnicity made him biased. Trump has been widely repudiated across the board, with fellow Republicans openly calling him racist.

TENANT INTIMIDATION:

Where and when: New York City, 1982-1986

The scoop: In 1981, Trump scooped up a building on Central Park South, reasoning that the existing structure was a dump, but the land it was on would be a great place for luxury condos. Trump's problem was that the existing tenants were—understandably and predictably—unwilling to let go of their rent-controlled apartments on Central Park. Trump used every trick in the book to get them out. He tried to reverse exceptions the previous landlord had given to knock down walls, threatening eviction. Tenants said he cut off heat and hot water. Building management refused to make repairs; two tenants swore in court that mushrooms grew on their carpet from a leak. Perhaps Trump's most outlandish move was to place newspaper ads offering to house homeless New Yorkers in empty units—since, as Trump wrote in *The Art of the Deal*, he didn't intend to fill units with permanent residents anyway. City officials turned him down, saying the idea did not seem appropriate. Typically, Trump also sued tenants for $150 million when they complained.

The upshot: Trump gave in. He settled with tenants and agreed to being monitored. The building still stands today, and his son Eric owns a unit on the top floor.

THE FOUR BANKRUPTCIES:

The Four Bankruptcies: now six and a seventh pending, and some more to come in 2021-2022

Where and when: 1991, 1992, 2004, and 2009

The dirt: Four times in his career, Trump's companies have entered into bankruptcy. (Now six)

In the late 1980s, after insisting that his major qualification to build a new casino in Atlantic City was that he wouldn't need to use junk bonds, Trump used junk bonds to build Trump Taj Mahal. He built the casino, but couldn't keep up with interest payments, so his company declared bankruptcy in 1991. He had to sell his yacht, his airline, and half his ownership in the casino.

A year later, another of Trump's Atlantic City casinos, the Trump Plaza, went bust after losing more than $550 million. Trump gave up his stake but otherwise insulated himself personally from the losses, and managed to keep his CEO title, even though he surrendered any salary or role in day-to-day operations. By the time all was said and done, he had some $900 million in personal debt.

Trump bounced back over the following decade, but by 2004, Trump Hotels and Casino Resorts were $1.8 billion in debt. The company filed for bankruptcy and emerged as Trump Entertainment Resorts. Trump himself was the chairman of the new company, but he no longer had a controlling stake in it.

Five years later, after the real-estate collapse, Trump Entertainment Resorts once again went bankrupt. Trump resigned from the board, but the company retained his name. In 2014, he successfully sued to take his name off the company and its casinos—one of which had already closed, and the other near closing.

The upshot: Trump is very touchy about any implication that he personally declared bankruptcy, arguing—just as he explains away his campaign contributions to Democrats—that he's just playing the game: "We'll have the company. We'll throw it into a chapter. We'll negotiate with the banks. You know, it's like on The Apprentice. It's not personal. It's just business. Okay? If you look at our greatest people, Carl Icahn with TWA and so many others. Leon Black, Linens-n-Things and others. Henry Kravis. A lot of them, everybody. But with me it's Ok, you did— this is a business thing. I've used the laws of this country to reduce debt."

THE UNDOCUMENTED POLISH WORKERS:

Where and when: New York City, 1980

The dirt: In order to construct his signature Trump Tower, the builder first had to demolish the Bonwit Teller store, an architecturally beloved Art Deco edifice. The work had to be done fast, and so, managers hired 200 undocumented Polish workers to tear it down, paying them substandard wages for backbreaking work—$5 per hour, when they were paid at all. The workers didn't wear hard hats and often slept at the site. When the workers complained about their back pay, they were allegedly threatened with deportation. Trump said he was unaware that illegal immigrants were working at the site.

The upshot: In 1991, a federal judge found Trump and other defendants guilty of conspiring to avoid paying union pension and welfare contributions for the workers. The decision was appealed, with partial victories for both sides, and ultimately settled privately in 1999. In a February GOP debate, Marco Rubio brought up the story to accuse Trump of hypocrisy in his stance on illegal immigration. Meanwhile, Massimo Calabresi testified under oath shows that Trump was aware of illegal immigrants being employed there.

Trump never put in place a coronavirus program

CHAPTER FOUR

....

ALLEGED MARITAL RAPE:

Where and when: New York City, 1989

The dirt: While married to Ivana Trump, Donald Trump became angry at her—according to a book by Harry Hurt, over a painful scalp-reduction surgery—and allegedly forcibly had sex with her. Ivana Trump said during a deposition in their divorce case that she "felt violated" and that her husband had raped her. Later, Ivana Trump released a statement saying: "During a deposition given by me in connection with my matrimonial case, I stated that my husband had raped me. On one occasion, in 1989, Mr. Trump and I had marital relations in which he behaved very differently toward me than he had during our marriage. As a woman, I felt violated, as the love and tenderness, which he normally exhibited towards me, was absent. I referred to this as a 'rape,' but I do not want my words to be interpreted in a literal or criminal sense."

The upshot: When The Daily Beast reported on the incident, Trump's right-hand man Michael Cohen threatened reporters and claimed—incorrectly—that a man cannot legally rape his wife. The case is one of several cases where Trump has been accused of misogyny, including his comments about Megyn Kelly early in the primary campaign or his fury at a lawyer who, during a deposition, asked for a break to pump breast milk. "You're disgusting," Trump said, and walked out. (Wayne Barrett collects some lowlights here.)

BREAKING RULES:

Where and when: New York and New Jersey, various

The dirt: Trump has been repeatedly fined for breaking rules related to his operation of casinos. In 1990, with Trump Taj Mahal in trouble, Trump's father Fred, strolled in and bought 700 chips worth a total of $3.5 million. The purchase helped the casino pay debt that was due, but because Fred Trump had no plans to gamble, the New Jersey gaming commission ruled that it was a loan that violated operating rules. Trump paid a $30,000 fine; in the end, the loan didn't prevent bankruptcy the following year. As noted above, New Jersey also fined Trump $200,000 for arranging to keep black employees away from Mafioso Robert LiButti's gambling table. In 1991, the Casino Control Commission fined Trump's company another $450,000 for buying LiButti nine luxury cars. And in 2000, Trump was fined $250,000 for breaking New York state law in lobbying to prevent an Indian casino from opening in the Catskills, for fear it would compete against his Atlantic City casinos.

The upshot: Trump admitted no wrongdoing in the New York case. He's now out of the casino business.

ANTITRUST VIOLATIONS:

Where and when: New Jersey, 1986

The dirt: In 1986, Trump decided he wanted to expand his casino empire in Atlantic City. His plan was to mount a hostile takeover of two casino companies, Holiday and Bally's. Trump started buying up stock in the companies with an eye toward gaining control. But Bally's realized what was going on and sued him for antitrust violations. "Trump hopes to wrest control of Bally's from its public shareholders without paying them the control premium they otherwise could command had they been adequately informed of Trump's intentions," the company argued.

The upshot: Trump gave up the attempt in 1987, but the Federal Trade Commission fined him $750,000 for failing to disclose his purchases of stock in the two companies, which exceeded minimum disclosure levels.

CONDO HOTEL SHENANIGANS:

Where and when: New York, Florida, Mexico, mid-2000s

The dirt: Trump was heavily involved in condo hotels, a pre-real-estate crash fixation in which people would buy units that they'd only use for a portion of the year. The rest of the time, the units would be rented out as hotel rooms, with the developer and the owner sharing the profit. The result has been a slew of lawsuits by condo buyers who claim they were bilked. Central to many of these are the question of what Trump's role in the projects was. In recent years, Trump often essentially sold his name rights to developers—he gets a payoff, and they get the aura of luxury his name imparts.

The upshot: In the case of Trump SoHo, in Manhattan, Trump's partners turned out to have a lengthy criminal past. Trump said he didn't know that, but—atypically—settled a lawsuit with buyers (while, typically, not admitting any wrongdoing). n 2013, he settled a suit with prospective buyers who lost millions when a development in Baja Mexico went under. Trump blamed the developers again, saying he had only licensed his name.

REFUSING TO PAY EVERYBODY:

Where and when: various, 1980s-present

The dirt: Contractors, waiters, dishwashers, and plumbers who worked at Trump projects say that his company stiffed them for work, refusing to pay for services rendered. USA Today did a lengthy review, finding that some of those contracts were for hundreds of thousands of dollars, many owed to small businesses that failed or struggled to continue because of unpaid bills. (Trump was also found to have improperly withheld compensation in the undocumented Polish worker controversy.)

The upshot: Trump offered various excuses, including shoddy workmanship, but the scale of the problem—hundreds of allegations—makes that hard to credit. In some cases, even the lawyers Trump hired to defend him have sued him for failing to pony up their fees. In one lawsuit, a Trump employee admitted in court that a painter was stiffed because managers determined they had "already paid enough." The cases are damaging because they show Trump not driving a hard bargain with other businesses, but harming ordinary, hard-working Americans. More recently, several contractors filed $5 million in liens against Trump's new hotel in Washington, alleging he did not pay them for services rendered.

TRUMP INSTITUTE:

Where and when: Boca Raton and elsewhere, 2005?

The dirt: Around the same time Donald Trump was operating Trump

University, the allegedly fraudulent real-estate seminar for which he's now being sued, he also franchised his name to Irene and Mike Milin, serial operators of get-rich-quick schemes. Unlike Trump University, Trump did not own the company. Instead, he licensed his name, appearing in an infomercial and promising falsely that he would hand-pick instructors. (He made a similar promise with Trump University) As Jonathan Martin reports, the course materials at Trump Institute consisted in part of textbooks that were plagiarized.

The upshot: The Milins were forced to declare bankruptcy in 2008, in part because of the law-enforcement investigations and lawsuits against their company. Trump Institute continued on for a few years afterwards. A Trump aide says he was unaware of the plagiarism, but said he stood by the curriculum.

BUYING UP HIS OWN BOOKS:

Where and when: various, 2016

The dirt: The Daily Beast noticed, in FEC filings, that the Trump campaign spent more than $55,000 buying his own book, Crippled America: How to Make America Great Again. (The book has since been retitled Great Again: How to Fix Our Crippled America, for the paperback edition.) That means Trump used donor money to his campaign to buy a book, sending the cash back to himself. Copies were given to delegates at the Republican National Convention.

The upshot: The maneuver could break FEC rules, campaign expert Paul S. Ryan told the Beast: "its fine for a candidate's book to be purchased by his committee, but it's impermissible to receive royalties from the publisher... There's a well-established precedent from the FEC that funds from the campaign account can't end up in your own pocket." The Huffington Post also noticed that Trump jacked up rent for campaign offices when he stopped funding his own campaign.

UNDOCUMENTED MODELS:

Where and when: New York, 1999?

The dirt: Former models who worked for Trump Model Management say that they, and others, worked for the agency in the United States despite not having proper permits. Some of them worked on tourist visas, either never getting the correct permits or else getting them only after working in the U.S. illegally for months.

The upshot: The story is embarrassing for Trump, who has argued that U.S. immigration laws should be much more strictly enforced. Some models also received H-1B visas, a special type of permit for workers in specialized industries—a program that Trump has criticized on the campaign trail this year.

THE TRUMP FOUNDATION:

Where and when: Various, 1988-present

The dirt: Though Donald Trump often promises to give to charity, his foundation has proven rather skimpy on the gifts over the years—and when it has given, the money has often come from other pockets than Trump's, including outside donors and even NBC. In the mid-2000s, Trump reconfigured the charity as a pass-through, soliciting donations from others and then giving the money away as though from himself. It appears that the foundation did not have the requisite legal permission from New York State to gather donations. In a few cases, the foundation also reported making donations it had not made.

There's special scrutiny on one $25,000 donation it did give to a group supporting Florida Attorney General Pam Bondi, which arrived just days before she quashed an investigation into Trump University and the Trump Institute. Trump also appears to have used $258,000 in foundation money, most of it given by other donors and not himself, to settle legal disputes, including donations to charity in lieu of paying fines. Trump directed more than $2 million in income to the foundation, and if he didn't pay taxes on them—his campaign for the most part refused to say—it would be illegal tax-dodging.

The upshot: The foundation appears to have broken IRS rules on "self-dealing" by paying to resolve the legal disputes as well as buying a portrait of Trump and a Tim Tebow helmet that went back to the Trump family. In November, in tax filings posted online, the Trump Foundation said it had violated self-dealing rules in 2015 and in previous, indeterminate years. On the donation, Trump and Bondi both say there was no quid-pro-quo, but the donation was an illegal one for a charitable nonprofit, and the foundation had to pay a $2,500 fine. Liberal watchdog group Citizens for Responsibility and Ethics in Washington charges other laws may have been broken as well. New York Attorney General Eric Schneiderman has reportedly launched an investigation into the foundation. Schneiderman has also informed the foundation that it is in violation of rules on fundraising and ordered it to quit.

TRUMP FLAWS ARE IMPRESSIVE (44):

Mr. Hoax, he suffers from chronic psychosis paranoia.

Mr. Hoax is an impostor, "With the Russians' interference in the 2016 election". Also, he hired The Firm REDFINCH to rig the election system CNBC drudge poll to favor him.

Mr. Hoax is the biggest pathological liar we have ever seen.

Mr. Hoax, he suffers from Narcissism and, most of the time, also from Histrionism (The apprentice), at a very high level.

Mr. Hoax is the commander-in-chief but he has his own army (Proud boys). (Wolverine Watchmen, Qanon) (Boogaloo movement) (8chan) Oath Keepers and the Three Percenters.

He is a notorious Womanizer.

Master in bankruptcy.

Evil-doer. A person who commits profoundly immoral and malevolent deeds.

Master in fraud and cheating.

Master of chaos.

Crook. A person who is dishonest or a criminal, he is not to be trusted.

Hypocrite. Two-faced person, and Sneaky.

Despot. A ruler or other person who holds absolute power, typically, who exercises it in a cruel or oppressive manner.

Racist. A person who is prejudiced against or antagonistic toward people on the basis of their membership in a particular racial or ethnic group, typically one that is a minority or marginalized.

Monster. A person who is aroused by horror, is cruel, his perversity. A person who is aroused by a deep antipathy, some defect, some vice, which it presents to an extreme degree.

Rapist. A person who rapes, transgresses, sexually without consent.

Psychopath. A person suffering from chronic mental disorder, with abnormal or violent social behavior.

Predator. Person or group that ruthlessly exploits others. He is always looking for prey.

Con man. A man who cheats or tricks someone by gaining their trust, and persuades them to believe something that is not true.

Godfather. A man who is influential or pioneering in a movement or organization.

Mob boss. A tightly knit group of trusted associates, as of a political leader.

Asshole. A fool-stupid moron.

Dumbass. A congenital idiot, who lacks common sense. A foolish or stupid person: A dumb-ass is someone who holds a stupid, illegitimate or completely baseless opinion.

Scumbag. A Dysphemism for a base, despicable, dirty person; also, a term of vulgar abuse, a bastard beast, finally, a person who cheats the most vulnerable.

Humbug. To engage in a hoax or deception, fake, forgery, sham, misinformation.

Mean. An unkind man, spiteful, or unfair.

Vile. Extremely unpleasant, corrupt, depraved indifference to human life.

Obnoxious. A nasty, unpleasant person.

Nefarious. A wicked or criminal person.

Villainous. One who takes pleasure in causing pain? Beastly, vicious, inhuman, heartless.

Sociopath. A person with a personality disorder, manifesting itself in extreme antisocial attitudes, and behavior and a lack of conscience.

Egotistical. Excessively conceited or absorbed in oneself, self-centered. Selfish, arrogant.

Charlatan, A person falsely claiming to have a special knowledge or skill. A fraud or a cheater.

Tyrant. Intimidator, authoritarian; harsh, and pushy.

Bully. To persecute or oppress somebody.

Mischievous child. A person causing or showing a fondness for causing trouble in a playful way.

Islamophobe. A person with a dislike of or prejudice against Islam or Muslims, especially as political force.

Xenophobe. A person having a dislike of or prejudice against people from other countries.

Chauvinist Pig. A person showing or relating to excessive or prejudiced loyalty or support for a particular group or cause.

Deity, "He takes himself for God». One day in a rally he said (I am the chosen one).

Demagogue "A demagogue" is diplomacy's worst enemy.

He doesn't have any empathy for anyone.

Illuminated fascist, a disgusting rotten fool.

With his behavior he is the biggest traitor since the civil war.

The republicans and 95 % of his base are partners in crime through their behavior (Accomplice Puppet).

All these people are accomplice in some criminal conspiracy.

They are a bunch of puppets and cowards at the White House. I suggest you look at yourself in the mirror before you go to bed at night,

This pyromaniac will set the USA on fire like Nero did with Rome in the year 64 of our era. So, it is absolutely necessary that this monster does not get a second term, otherwise the unthinkable may happen.

He has no knowledge of the etiquette to respect during formal meetings with people, so he is ignorant, and without manner; we remember July 13th 2018, this President broke royal protocol by arriving late to meet Queen Elisabeth, failing to bow, and walking in front of her, what a disgrace.

We also remember May 25 2017 at the new NATO headquarters in Brussel, this President shoved the PM of Montenegro, Mr. Dusko Markovic. He was once later, but above all a grotesque manner from a President.

HE IS RIDDLED WITH FLAWS.

He is completely unencumbered by the truth, the need to tell it or accept it. He will do and say anything he believes will help him. He has no greater guiding principles. He is not bound by ethics or morals. This guy has no Boundary

"Access Hollywood" tapes, on which Trump bragged about groping, also said, "grab them by the pussy they like that", and sexually assaulting women,

It is extraordinary that as a party nominee using vulgar, violent language he seems to reduce an entire gender to sexual anatomy.

No one is as shameless a showman as Trump. He was in survival mode. Nothing was too far; nothing was too crass.

Then Trump said on the debate stage: "Nobody has more respect for women than I do." Really.

He will never admit to any fault. He will lie and lie and lie and lie some more. And the people who support him will stick with him every step of the way. Be prepared for Trump to do anything and everything to win reelection in November 2020. A man who can dismiss a recording of his own voice bragging about assaulting women is capable of anything.

As you will see later, at the end of December 2020, and the beginning of January 2021. Trump and his traitors will undermine our democracy and attempt a "coup d'état" shame on them. Remember their faces.

Trump never put in place a coronavirus program.

CHAPTER FIVE

....

IN THIS COUNTRY WE HAVE A
TENDENCY TO FORGET:

Donald Trump is not encumbered with doubts about what he creates around himself, he is proud of his monster; he prides himself on his anger and his destruction and, if he cannot imagine his love, he believes with all his heart in his rage. He is a Monster without conscience.

Donald Trump understands nothing about history, constitutional principles, geopolitics, and diplomacy and has never been encouraged to cultivate this knowledge. He has never listened to anyone in the White House, let alone scientists.

But to better understand this fanatic, at home during his childhood, he made his mother sometimes mad. He did nothing but tortured his brother, Freddy, stole his toys. He never did his household chores or anything that was asked of him. He was a Sagouin who never picked up what he lay around despite his mother's threats.

Finally in 1959, with Donald's bad behavior at school, the brawls, the brutalities, the insolence with the teachers, of Kew-Forest, he was sent to the New York Military Academy to get him in line. This private boarding school for boys was recognized as a reformatory.

A few years later, around 1966, Donald wanted to leave Fordham for Wharton School to help his reputation. But, knowing full well that his IQ was not the highest, and that Maryanne had done his homework for him all along, in the past, he now needed help. So, he hired a friend, Joe Shapiro, who was good at exams, to take the SAT's - the national assessments in his stead. Donald paid his buddy handsomely on top of that to make sure his project was a success. He asked a friend of his brother's, James Nolan, who worked in the admissions office, if he could say a word in his favor. With his shenanigans,

Donald got what he wanted, once again, cheating. And that is what he will do throughout his life, today he is a master at cheating.

It was around 1980, with the losses Donald had accumulated through his mistakes that his father realized that the monster he had created was at large.

It is entirely possible that in the late 1960s and early 1970s Fred did not appreciate the extent of Donald's incompetence; but over time Fred had to play along since it was, he who was the one who had taught him to play it; to bend the rules, to lie, to cheat; all of which was legitimate in business, by embezzling subsidies.

For the construction of the Grand Hyatt and the others, Trump hired undocumented migrants, not paying or underpaying them; as well as staff of his Golf clubs, with the help of the Italian Mafia union in New York, who were his friends. What hypocrisy! 35 years later he was talking about Mexicans and all the other immigrants saying that they were undocumented job thieves, rapists and so on.

With Donald Trump's multitude of bankruptcies, even though he inherited nearly a billion dollars from his father, it is an understatement to say that he was not cut out for running business at all.

In 2020 we know he is a master fraudster, so let's go back in time to show you how far Donald Trump can be a crook. Nearing the end of his life, Fred was living with dementia and Donald imagined writing a codicil, with the help from lawyer, Irwin Durben, and accountant, Jack Mitnick, former employees of Fred's. A codicil that would give him full control over the inheritance, including the real estate empire. So, according to some sources, the whole family would end up begging. This scheme was stopped just in time, for a while.

In an article, Adam Serwer of ATLANTIC wrote that for Trump, the end the game is cruelty. Trump's cruelty serves, in part, to distract the world, and his own, from the extent of his failures.

It is also through cruelty that he exercises his power. He has always brandished it against those weaker than himself or against those whose duty or dependence was hindered. The servants of the state and even the advisers, who he placed, himself, in the White House, cannot defend themselves when attacked by him.

Through his cruelty, his catastrophic decisions, and his disastrous inaction, he literally killed people. While millions of lives were at stake, he took no responsibility for the COVID19 pandemic, even though he was responsible, according to some sources, for 89% of the deaths, on account of his behavior; with the masks, not listening to scientists, and mainly for promoting the idea that this pandemic was a hoax of the Democrats. But, especially since February 2020 and even today, at the time of this writing, December the 30 2020, Trump speaks only of his re-election. And especially playing golf; this bully played 312 times since 2016, as people are dying of hunger, shame on you.

Speaking of Trump's cruelty, let's not forget the children, caged and separated from their parents at the border, I remember that time well. I was certain that the cruelty and incompetence of this demagogue was going to kill.

So, Trump in his rage, can only do one thing: collectively punish Americans, with the story about the famous respirators. Too bad for the dead! He is a born killer and there will be many deaths because of his deplorable appetite for revenge. What Trump sees as fair retaliation in this context is no more and no less a mass murder.

THE NEW YORK RUSSIAN GANGS' PART 1:

The brotherhood.

Unless you've been living in a cave for the past two years, you will have heard the words 'Trump' and 'Russia' in the same sentence at least once. As furious debate around Russia's alleged election interference burgeons with each new Mueller indictment, fresh issues, like shadowy Russian donors to Trump's suspiciously large inauguration fund, continually rear their heads. But some would argue, Trump's flirtation with Russia began long before his election campaign; long before Putin came to power; long, even, before the Soviet Union collapsed.

Russian criminals used trump tower, in New York, as a "money-laundering cathedral":

In his new documentary, Active Measures, Jack Bryan argues Trump was compromised decades ago through his financial ties to the Russian Mafia; a criminal organization which, in the words of House of Trump, House of Putin author, Craig Unger, is "an adjunct of the Russian Government". The argument goes that following a series of bankruptcies when Trump was around $4 billion in debt, Russian criminals effectively bought him, and in return used Trump Tower, in New York, as a "money-laundering cathedral". Since the 1980s, at least 13 people with proven or suspected Russian mafia links have owned or lived in Trump Tower apartments, or other Trump properties. Some have even conducted criminal operations out of hem.

THE NEW YORK RUSSIAN GANGS' PART 2:

Our feature on the Russian gangs of New York explores the links between the Russian Mafia and the Kremlin.

The Soviet Union's collapse, in 1991, prompted an influx of thousands of powerful criminals from all over the USSR, known collectively as the 'Russian Mafia' to the United States. Once again, many of these new arrivals settled in South Brooklyn. More deadly and organized than their predecessors, these newcomers maintained close ties with their counterparts in Moscow and elsewhere in the former Soviet Union.

The arrival of Vyacheslav Ivankov (aka "Little Japanese"), in 1992, was symbolic. Identified by Russian police as a Vor v Zakone. He was also, apparently, killing too many people back home, and considered a liability. The story goes that he was met by a fellow Vor at JFK Airport, who handed him $1.5 million in cash in a suitcase. Ivankov took over all Russian organized crime in New York, apparently with little opposition. (Former New York boss, Boris Nayfeld was convicted of drug trafficking in 1994.)

Over the next three years, Ivankov helped move New York's Russian mob from local business to a global brand. Under his leadership, the new influx of criminals (labelled the 'first team' by New York crime-fighting agencies) expanded into high stake drug trafficking, money laundering, extortion and prostitution. The FBI believes Ivankov recruited two 'combat brigades' of Special Force veterans of the Soviet War in Afghanistan to run the mafia's protection racket and kill his enemies. In 1994, the US Justice Department elevated the Russian Mafia to a top investigative priority, alongside the Sicilian and American Mafias, Asian organized crime groups and Colombian drugs cartels. The FBI established a specialist Russian squad in New York, a few months later.

Ivankov was convicted of a million-dollar extortion attempt in 1996 and sentenced to 9 years in prison. Following prison time in the US, he was extradited to Russia to face murder charges in 2004, where he was acquitted and freed, but was assassinated in 2009.

Prior to his arrest, the FBI uncovered alleged links between Ivankov and New York art dealer, Felix Komarov, who lived on the 31st floor of the Trump

Plaza. It was alleged that Komarov, who was never charged and has denied any wrongdoing, had been laundering money for Ivankov. Ivankov himself, was living in Trump Tower at the time of his arrest; though there is evidence Trump knew him personally.

When Russia's economy collapsed in 1998, money was moved even more aggressively out of Russia, and many mobsters attempted to raise capital through North American stock.

The mob was believed to have laundered up to $10 billion through the bank of New York:

"Boss of bosses", Semion Mogilevich, made US history from his Eastern Europe hub in 1999, when one of the largest money laundering operations ever uncovered in the country was traced back to him. The mob was believed to have laundered up to $10 billion through the Bank of New York. Mogilevich successfully evaded justice and continues to live openly in Moscow today.

In April 2013, the FBI indicted Alimzhan Tokhtakhounov (aka "Little Taiwanese") over a sophisticated money-laundering, gambling and extortion ring, run out of 63-A Trump Towers. Tokhtakhounov, meanwhile, had moved back to Russia a decade earlier, where he was accused of rigging an ice-skating contest at the 2002 Winter Olympics, and so, once again, escaped US authorities. Other members of the racket included billionaire art dealer, Hilel "Helly" Namad, living on the 51st floor of Trump Towers, who also pleaded guilty and served five months of a one-year sentence. Seven months after evading justice, Tokhtakhounov was to be found in the VIP section of Moscow's Miss World pageant, close to Trump himself, in November 2013.

Trump never put in place a coronavirus program.

CHAPTER SIX

....

TRUMP THE SNEAKY RAPIST:

'You can do anything': in a 2005 tape, trump brags about groping, kissing women.

October 7, 2016

Editor's note: This post contains language that is crude and explicit and that many will find offensive.

Just two days before Donald Trump and Hillary Clinton were set to meet for their second presidential debate; more damaging audio of the GOP nominee using crude language about women and how he would hit on them surfaced.

After an uproar over the tape, Trump pulled out of an event in Wisconsin on Saturday at which he was to appear with House Speaker, Paul Ryan. Trump also posted a video to social media saying the remarks didn't reflect his true character.

October 8: Trump tells the Washington Post he will not withdraw from the race amid multiple Republicans calling for him to drop out.

On Friday afternoon, the Washington Post published a clip of Trump on a hot mic before an interview with Access Hollywood. In chatting with then-host Billy Bush, who is now co-host of NBC's *Today* show, Trump talked about kissing women and grabbing them between their legs (using far cruder language) without permission, because he's "attracted" to them like a "magnet."

"Grab them by the pussy":

When you're a star," he said, "they let you do it. You can do anything."

The interview occurred before Trump was set to film a cameo on the soap opera Days of Our Lives, and he said, laughing, that he needed "some Tic Tacs, just in case I start kissing her."

In talking about kissing women, Trump boasted: "I'm automatically attracted to beautiful — I just start kissing them. It's like a magnet. Just kiss. I don't even wait. And when you're a star, they let you do it. You can do anything."

"Grab them by the pussy. You can do anything," the Republican nominee continued, using vulgar slang for the female anatomy.

Access Hollywood has this description of the scene:

"There were seven other people on the bus with Mr. Trump and Billy Bush at the time," host Natalie Morales said of the incident, noting that the camera crew, Trump's security guard and his publicist were all present. She revealed that Nancy O'Dell, currently Entertainment Tonight co-host, was the woman identified on the tape as "Nancy" that Trump had been captured speaking crassly about."

"I moved on her and I failed": Trump told Bush — who is the nephew of former President George H.W. Bush and cousin of former President George W. Bush and former 2016 candidate Jeb Bush — about a time he unsuccessfully tried to seduce a married woman.

"I moved on her, and I failed," Trump said. "I'll admit it. I did try and fuck her. She was married." He continued, "I moved on her very heavily."

"I moved on her like a bitch," he said, "but I couldn't get there. And she was married. Then, all of a sudden, I see her — she's now got the big phony tits and everything. She's totally changed her look."

Trump apologizes in video message:

In the video Trump released early Saturday morning he said, «Anyone who knows me knows these words don't reflect who I am. I said it, I was wrong and I apologize."

He said spending time with people during his campaign travels has changed him. "I pledge to be a better man tomorrow and will never let you down," said Trump.

That's despite Trump's having been divorced twice and admitting to his own adultery. At the time of this 2005 recording, Trump had just married his third (and current) wife, Melania.

"I am sickened by what I heard today. Women are to be championed and revered, not objectified. I hope Mr. Trump treats this situation with the seriousness it deserves and works to demonstrate to the country that he has greater respect for women than this clip suggests. In the meantime, he is no longer attending tomorrow's event in Wisconsin."

Trump said he would be represented in Wisconsin by his running mate Mike Pence. Trump said he would spend the day in New York preparing for Sunday's debate with Clinton, aided by Republican National Committee Chairman Reince Priebus, New Jersey Gov. Chris Christie and Sen. Jeff Sessions, R-Ala.

Priebus, who has defended Trump after past controversial statements, issued a short but direct statement:

"No woman should ever be described in these terms or talked about in this manner. Ever."

This is far from the first time Trump has come under fire for using offensive language about women. Last fall, he criticized Fox News host Megyn Kelly for her tough questions during the first GOP primary debate and said she had "blood coming out of her wherever."

During the first general-election debate last week, Trump said actress Rosie O'Donnell "deserves" past insults he has made calling her a "pig" with a "fat ugly face."

And when Clinton brought up how he had mocked a former Miss Universe, Alicia Machado, after she had gained weight, Trump doubled down on his comments for days.

Reactions from around the political scene.

Many GOP leaders and lawmakers condemned Trump's,

Here is a list of women who have been assaulted

Ivana Trump (1989)

Ivana Trump and Donald Trump married in 1977. Ivana stated in a deposition taken in 1989, during their divorce proceedings, that Donald had visited her plastic surgeon following which he had expressed anger and ripped out hair from her scalp. Donald said the allegation was "obviously false". The book Lost Tycoon: The Many Lives of Donald Trump (1993), by Harry Hurt III, described the alleged attack as a "violent assault" during which Donald attacked Ivana sexually. According to the book, Ivana later confided to some of her friends that Donald had raped her. In a statement given just before the publication of Hurt's book, and included in the book, Ivana said:

On one occasion during 1989, Mr. Trump and I had marital relations in which he behaved very differently toward me than he had during our marriage. As a woman, I felt violated, as the love and tenderness, which he normally exhibited towards me, was absent. I referred to this as a "rape", but I do not want my words to be interpreted in a literal or criminal sense.

The Trumps' divorce was granted in December 1990 on grounds that Donald's treatment of Ivana, including his affair with Marla Maples, was "cruel and inhuman". According to Trump's lawyer, Jay Goldberg, this was based on Trump having been seen in public with Marla Maples in 1990. Their settlement had a confidentiality clause preventing Ivana from discussing the marriage or the divorce. In 1992, Trump sued Ivana for not honoring a gag clause in their divorce agreement by disclosing facts about him in her best-selling book, and Trump won a gag order.

Jill Harth (1992)

Jill Harth alleged that Trump assaulted her several times. Harth has stated that in December 1992, while dining with Trump and her then-boyfriend George Houraney, Trump attempted to put his hands between her legs. Harth and Houraney visited Trump's Mar-a-Lago estate in Florida in January 1993 for a contract-signing celebration. Trump, according to Harth, offered her a tour before pulling her into the empty bedroom of his daughter, Ivanka. "I was admiring the decoration, and next thing I know he's pushing me against a wall and has his hands all over me. He was trying to kiss me. I was freaking out." Harth says she desperately protested against Trump's advances and eventually managed to run out of the room. She and her boyfriend left rather than stay the night, as they had intended. After she became engaged, Harth alleges, Trump began to stalk her.

Harth filed a lawsuit in 1997 in which she accused Trump of non-consensual groping of her body, among them, her "intimate private parts", and "relentless" sexual harassment. The suit was withdrawn after Houraney settled with Trump for an undisclosed amount in a lawsuit that claimed Trump had backed out of a business deal. She still claims to have been sexually assaulted and although he was never violent with her, she says his actions were "unwanted and aggressive, very sexually aggressive".

Following the incident, Harth said she received "a couple years of therapy". In 2015 she contacted Trump's campaign to get a job as a makeup artist and sell her men's cosmetic product line. She later said, "Yes, I had moved on but had not forgotten the pain [Trump] brought into my life. I was older, wiser. Trump was married to Melania and I had hoped he was a changed man."

She worked at one of Trump's rallies as a makeup artist. Of the experience, she said: "I'm a makeup artist. The guy is a mess, OK? He really needed my services, and I'm a makeup artist that needs a job. Why, if I was on friendly terms, wouldn't I try to get that job?"

Harth's lawsuit was first published in February 2016 by LawNewz.com. Her case was first published in May 2016 in The New York Times article "Crossing the Line". Trump characterized her story in the Times as "false, malicious and libelous" and he "strongly denies the claims". Harth stood by her charges in a July 2016 interview with The Guardian. In October 2016, she said that, if sued by Trump, she intends to counter-sue.

E. Jean Carroll (1995 or 1996)

On November 4, 2019, writer E. Jean Carroll filed a lawsuit against Trump, accusing him of defamation by claiming she lied. The author, who had first publicly disclosed the alleged sexual assault by Trump in June, said Trump's reaction to the accusation has directly harmed her career and reputation. Carroll said she was filing this lawsuit on behalf of each woman who has faced harassment, assault, or belittlement.

In September 2020, the Justice Department filed a court motion seeking to take over Trump's defense, arguing he had acted "within the scope" of the presidency when he called Carroll a liar.

Attorney general Bill Barr asserted the move was a routine application of the Westfall Act that permits the Justice Department to defend federal employees against civil liability for acts conducted in the normal course of their duties. Barr stated the White House had requested the Justice Department action and noted that taxpayers would pay any judgment should Carroll win the case.

Summer Zervos (2007)

Summer Zervos was a contestant on the fifth season of The Apprentice, which filmed in 2005 and aired in 2006. Subsequently, she contacted Trump in 2007, about a job after the show's completion, and he invited her to meet him at The Beverly Hills Hotel. Zervos said that Trump was sexually suggestive during their meeting, kissing her open-mouthed, groping her breasts, and thrusting his genitals on her. She also said that his behavior was aggressive and not consensual. Zervos is being represented by attorney Gloria Allred.

John Barry, her cousin and a Trump supporter, said Zervos talked to her family and friends about Trump, promoting his candidacy and stating how Trump had helped her out in her life. Barry said that during the presidential primary campaign, Zervos invited Trump to her restaurant, and he declined. In October 2016, the Trump presidential campaign released an email by Zervos, sent to Trump's secretary in April 2016, in which she stated: "I would greatly appreciate reconnecting at this time. He will know my intentions are genuine." Zervos said she had intended to confront Trump and give him the "opportunity to clear the air". On January 17, 2017, Zervos filed a defamation lawsuit against Trump, arising from his statement that she had lied about the allegations. Marc Kasowitz is defending Trump in the case. Zervos filed a subpoena for "all documents concerning any woman who asserted that Donald J. Trump touched her inappropriately".[61] On March 21, 2018, a New York Supreme Court judge decided to allow a defamation lawsuit against the President to go forward. On June 4, 2018, Manhattan Supreme Court Justice Jennifer Schecter ruled that Trump must be deposed by January 31.

Alva Johnson (2019)

On February 25, 2019, Alva Johnson filed a lawsuit against Trump, alleging he had forcibly kissed her at a rally in Florida in August 2016 while she was working on his 2016 presidential campaign. Johnson said two people—including Pam Bondi, then the attorney general of Florida—saw the kiss, but both denied it. According to an interview with Teen Vogue, Johnson decided to stop working for the Trump campaign after the media started covering the Access Hollywood tape. She declared sick days until she could speak to a lawyer.

OTHER INCIDENTS:

In 1992, Trump appeared on NBC News' show A Closer Look, hosted by Faith Daniels. During the show, Daniels said Trump (divorced at the time) agreed to make an appearance because: "You kissed me on the lips in front of the paparazzi, and I said, 'That'll cost you. I'm booking you on the show'." Trump replied that the kiss was "so open and nice", and that he thought Daniels' husband "had his back turned at the time". Trump invited NBC News to film a party he threw for himself and Jeffrey Epstein at Mar-a-Lago, where they joined various NFL cheerleaders; the kiss incident occurred there. NBC News revealed footage of the party in July 2019, showing Trump, Epstein and the cheerleaders. At one point during the video, Trump grabbed a woman around her waist, pulled her against his body, and patted her buttocks. At another point, Trump appears to tell Epstein: "Look at her; back there ... She's hot."

for the Presidency, saying "Can you imagine how controversial I'd be? you think about (Bill Clinton) with the women. How about me with the women? Can you imagine?"

A 2002 article in New York magazine quoted Trump talking about Jeffrey Epstein: "I've known Jeff for fifteen years. Terrific guy. He's a lot of fun to be with. It is even said that he likes beautiful women as much as I do, and many of them are on the younger side. No doubt about it, Jeffrey enjoys his social life."

In 2008, Epstein pleaded guilty to charges involving child prostitution. In 2019, he was charged with child sex trafficking, he died in his cell before facing trial.

Trump never put in place a coronavirus program.

CHAPTER SEVEN

....

MY PERSONAL OPINIONS:

This predator is always looking for prey. All that moves, he has to pursue it and see what he can do; he eats it right away without preparation or without thinking about it; he has all the time in the world and everything belongs to him. As he said above, "He owned the beauty pageants". This monster is a mess. And a rapist.

PUBLIC ALLEGATION SINCE 2016

In addition to the "unwanted sexual attention", the lawsuit also alleged that Johnson was "a victim of race and gender discrimination through unequal pay". In response, White House press secretary Sarah Huckabee Sanders called the lawsuit "absurd on its face".

In May 2016, The New York Times published the article "Crossing the Line: How Donald Trump Behaved with Women in Private". For the article, Times reporters Michael Barbaro and Megan Twohey conducted 50 interviews with women who had known Trump socially, during their professional career, or while modeling or competing for a beauty pageant title.

The interactions occurred in his offices at Trump Tower, at his homes, at construction sites and backstage at beauty pageants. They appeared to be fleeting, unimportant moments to him, but they left lasting impressions on the women who experienced them.

Recording controversy and the second 2016 presidential debate:

Billy Bush was recorded having "an extremely lewd conversation about women" with Trump in 2005.

Two days before the second 2016 presidential debate, the 2005 Access Hollywood tape was released, which records Trump having "an extremely lewd conversation about women" in which he described being able to kiss and grope women because he was "a star": "You know I'm automatically attracted to beautiful—I just start kissing them. It's like a magnet. Just kiss. I don't even wait. And when you're a star, they let you do it, you can do anything ... grab them by the pussy. You can do anything". Many attorneys and media commentators have said Trump's statements described sexual assault.

During the second debate, Anderson Cooper asked Trump if he understood that he had bragged about sexually assaulting women. Cooper used the Justice Department's sexual assault definition to include "any type of sexual contact or behavior that occurs without the explicit consent of the recipient". Trump denied having said that he had sexually assaulted women. He claimed the comments were merely "locker room talk", then, after being asked three times whether he had ever kissed or groped any person without consent, he said "no I have not". Several of his subsequent accusers said this was the moment at which they were motivated to come.

In 1992, Trump appeared on NBC News' show A Closer Look, hosted by Faith Daniels. During the show, Daniels said Trump (divorced at the time) agreed to make an appearance because: "You kissed me on the lips in front of the paparazzi, and I said, 'That'll cost you. I'm booking you on the show'." Trump replied that the kiss was "so open and nice", and that he thought Daniels' husband "had his back turned at the time". Trump invited NBC News to film a party he threw for himself and Jeffrey Epstein at Mar-a-Lago, where they joined various NFL cheerleaders; the kiss incident occurred there. NBC News revealed footage of the party in July 2019, showing Trump, Epstein and the cheerleaders. At one point during the video, Trump grabbed a woman around her waist, pulled her against his body, and patted her buttocks. At another point, Trump appears to tell Epstein: "Look at her; back there ... She's hot."

for the Presidency, saying "Can you imagine how controversial I'd be? you think about (Bill Clinton) with the women. How about me with the women? Can you imagine?"

A 2002 article in New York magazine quoted Trump talking about Jeffrey Epstein: "I've known Jeff for fifteen years. Terrific guy. He's a lot of fun to be with. It is even said that he likes beautiful women as much as I do, and many of them are on the younger side. No doubt about it, Jeffrey enjoys his social life."

In 2008, Epstein pleaded guilty to charges involving child prostitution. In 2019, he was charged with child sex trafficking, he died in his cell before facing trial.

Trump never put in place a coronavirus program.

CHAPTER EIGHT

....

TRUMP AND EPSTEIN:

When asked about Jeffrey Epstein in the Oval Office on July 23, 2019, President Trump seemingly went back on his earlier remarks, stating: "I had a falling out a long time ago with him. I don't think I've spoken to him in 15 years." He added that he was also "not a fan" of Epstein, but didn't specify the cause of their falling out.

The two were also involved in the same lawsuit filed in 2016, where an unnamed accuser alleged, she was sexually assaulted by both. Trump and Epstein in 1994 — when she was 13 years old — at Epstein's New York home. The court documents describe the assault as "acts of rape, sexual misconduct, criminal sexual acts, sexual abuse, forcible touching, assault and battery," among others.

HOW SEX TRAFFICKER JEFFREY EPSTEIN CONNECTED TO PRESIDENT TRUMP:

May 27, 2020

Roughly a year after Jeffrey Epstein was charged for multiple counts of child sex trafficking, the disgraced billionaire and convicted sex offender's many links to the fashion and media industries have come to light.

Epstein, who died in an apparent suicide on August 10, 2019, was arrested and charged on July 6, 2019 for one count of sex trafficking of minors and one count of conspiracy to engage in sex trafficking of minors between 2002 and 2005 in New York and Florida. He was facing a maximum prison sentence of 45 years.

Here, WWD (Women's Wear Daily) looks at Epstein's close ties within the fashion and media industries, including those with President Trump,

In 2015, Epstein accuser, Virginia Roberts Giuffre, claimed in court documents that are part of the Crime Victims' Rights Act that Brunel, a French model agent, helped supply Epstein with underage girls from around the world by recruiting them as models through the agency. The lawsuit is ongoing.

Giuffre also filed a civil suit against socialite Ghislaine Maxwell in 2015, who had also been accused of enlisting underage girls under the ruse of modeling assignments. Giuffre claims she was recruited as a sex slave for Epstein at the age of 15 — where she states she was forced into sexual activities— when she worked as a spa attendant at President Trump's Mar-a-Lago resort. In 2017, the civil suit was settled between both parties.

When asked about Epstein at the Oval Office on Tuesday, President Trump seemingly went back on his earlier remarks, stating: "I had a falling out a long time ago with him. I don't think I've spoken to him in 15 years." He added that he was also "not a fan" of Epstein, but didn't specify the cause of their falling out.

The two were also involved in the same lawsuit filed in 2016, where an unnamed accuser alleged, she was sexually assaulted by both Trump and Epstein in 1994 — when she was 13 years old — at Epstein's New York home. The court documents describe the assault as "acts of rape, sexual misconduct, criminal sexual acts, sexual abuse, forcible touching, assault and battery," among others.

Three months later, the victim dropped the case voluntarily…

According to court documents that were part of lawsuits, Epstein was once a member of Trump's Mar-a-Lago resort in South Florida, but was later barred by Trump for allegedly sexually assaulting an underage girl at the exclusive club. The two men ate dinner at one another's homes and Trump flew on Epstein's private airplane.

Despite the praise of Epstein by Trump and the social interactions, a Trump attorney has denied that the two men were friends or had a relationship. He told reporters over the weekend that he did not "know anything about" Epstein's alleged arrest.

FOR A PERSON WITH NARCISSISM:

1. Have (constant fantasies of unlimited success) of (unlimited power) and (splendor).
2. Believe himself (special and unique). (In his head) there are no two people like him.
3. To have one (grandiose sense of own importance) and one (total disregard for all who are not like him).
4. Have an (excessive need to be admired).
5. To think that everything is due him, even without reason.
6. Using the other to achieve his ends. (He uses it and he throws it away after use). He explained.
7. Have a total lack of empathy. (He does not see the suffering of the other, he does not see the needs or the feelings or what the other needs.
8. Envy of others and firmly believe that (everyone else envies him as well), (he believes he is the most envied being in the world), said the Psychologist.
9. Behaves (arrogantly and haughtily).

Many women are now familiar with the word 'narcissism,' but not always totally aware of the specifics of the disorder. The word 'narcissism' is tossed around a lot as a catch-all phrase for people who are conceited or aloof. But narcissism is more than a case of conceit. It is a pathological and incurable disorder.

Narcissism is a brutal way for women to learn about dangerous and destructive men. By the time a woman realizes a man is narcissistic, she has been pounded into the emotional dirt.

Many women find fascination with men who seem self-assured, but this is merely the mask of narcissism, which hides an emotionally undeveloped little boy seeking the attention NOW that he didn't get as a child.

But all the attention he has sucked out of women never fills the broken vessel of his soul. All the attention never stays in him. It spills out only for him to seek MORE and MORE from anyone whom he can get it from. Dr. Sam Vaknin refers to this as the 'narcissistic supply'—the need for a constant stream of affirmations, attention, and admiration from a constant supply of givers.

Narcissists are rarely happy with only one stream of attention. They seek it from friends, strangers, co-workers, family, and anyone else they can tap into, which is also why narcissists are rarely faithful—all this attention-seeking leads to more focused admiration via sexual contact.

Trump never put in place a coronavirus program

CHAPTER NINE

....

TRUMP'S MOB CONNECTIONS:

There's a reason why Trump's behavior is so "Mafia-like."

SEPTEMBER 27, 2019

The comparison is fitting, considering Trump is known to have multiple ties to mobsters. Trump himself was quoted saying that he was tentative to sign on to participating in the reality show "The Apprentice" due to the number of "mobsters" frequenting his place of work.

"I don't want to have cameras all over my office, dealing with contractors, politicians, mobsters and everyone else I have to deal with in my business," Trump told a panel at the Museum of Television and Radio in Los Angeles, in 2004. "You know, mobsters don't like, as they are talking to me, having cameras all over the room. It would play well on television, but it doesn't play well with them."

Trump's behavior and language have also been likened to that of mobsters by several news outlets, who have noted that his speech is often peppered with terms typically used by members of the mob, like late Gambino family boss John Gotti. The president's former attorney, Michael Cohen, who is currently serving a three-year sentence in federal prison for tax evasion and campaign finance violation, has also remarked that Trump operates "much like a mobster would," in February, while testifying before the House Oversight and Reform Committee.

Perhaps it's common when working as a major real estate developer and landlord in New York City to brush up against mob-connected figures. The Five Families of New York have historically been influential in the city's construction unions and private waste management companies, for example. Even so, Trump's history of friendly – and sometimes ethically dubious – interactions with mobsters are remarkably long and complex.

To break it down, we've compiled a list of the president's most notable Mafia connections:

THE LATEST CONSPIRACY THEORY MEMBERS:

Ralphe, Paulo, Jodye. And Marjory.

These ignorant people are complicit, and inciting to violence. For them the sky is red, 09-11, and the pentagon wasn't attacked, and Pearl-Harbor in December 1941, also NASA never sent a rocket to the moon, January 6, 2021 was a tourist vacation tour, and finally, Biden didn't win the 2020 election, believe it or not, most of the Trump enablers think that's true. Hello!! Is everything going well in your bird brain on the second floor? And for those who don't know, the size of small bird brain is the size of a grain of rice.

Trump the Imposter President. Lost the house, lost the senate. Twice impeached, one term, and finally, lost the Presidential election, the worst President ever.

When McCarthy answered a journalist, lately, it seems that he had one deaf ear, which he used by saying, that he did not read or he did not hear all kinds of stupidity, from his dear girlfriend with her big mouth full of green Mamba snake, (oh Green like the snake). Also, she likes to speak via a mail-box slot. Tell me Mr. McCarthy, are as old as her, that Qnon ignorant 6–8-year-old, or maybe she's ready for the asylum.

THE TRUTH:

I wonder if there are still people who believe in the truth in this country.

In businesses, employees speak the truth to power when they deliver unwelcome facts to their bosses. In government, appointed officials do that when they tell elected leaders something they don't want to hear.

But in a democracy, the people are the ultimate source of power. Our elected officials work for us, and they fail us when they decline to tell us truths that we, the people, don't want to hear. Even worse, they fail us when they set up false expectations we desperately want to believe.

Telling the public only what it wants to hear is no way to keep democracy going. If the GOP continues to promote disinformation and false narratives, as it usually has been doing, it is designed to undermine our democracy.

The twin words (truth and lies) are not known to 40% of Republicans, because most of those people in elementary schools who owned a dictionary were missing 2 pages in which the words truth and lie were written. I therefore suggest that they either go back to school or else stop spreading all kinds of conspiracy theories across the USA. Even after January 6, when we have all the evidence, with over 800 arrests of those guilty who confessed, that they had been sent to the Capitol by their mob boss. So, the new demagogue by the name of Ron, where were you on January 6, and are you going to show yourself, you hypocrite, liar, and thug, maybe you live on another planet, or in a fantasy world, I wonder why the FBI doesn't arrest you and send you to jail, or the asylum for those who lack neurons on the second floor. You have to stop all these spreaders of fake news. This guy is peddling ridiculous conspiracy theories...

Trump never put in place a coronavirus program

CHAPTER TEN

WHAT HYPOCRISY IS THIS
SECOND AMENDMENT:

In the United States of America, the right to self-defence has been enshrined in the Second Amendment of the Constitution since 1791, which I think is archaic, this law should be changed.

Since the start of 2017 there have been 307 shootings with 13,158 gun-related deaths in this country. Then you have the NRA who has the nerve to say that it is not guns that kill but people. What hypocrisy! This stupid association which was founded in 1871 and encourages people to walk in the streets with guns in search of bison or any other prey. It feels like the Far West of the years 1700 to1800.

The NRA financed the GOP's Marco for his campaign to the amount of $ 3.3 million, so we can easily say that this gentleman has hands stained with blood. The same goes for the leaders of this association. Why? Because they are complicit in these crimes.

I know you are going to tell me that you have the law to protect you, but this is just hogwash. We are the only country in the world with this stupid killer law. The proof is that you are the number one on this killer track record in the world.

You notice that I am talking about you in the second person plural, and not about us in the first-person plural. Why do I mention this small detail? I never bought a rifle and neither did my family or my close friends. We have no weapons. There is a saying that goes: Those who play with fire eventually burn themselves. So, we are not part of you.

According to the known records, there are 357,000 firearms of all types in circulation in the United States. They are not in danger of disappearing anytime soon.

If, one day, you dream of living in harmony with yourselves and your neighbors, it will be because you will have decided, by voting, to force your elected officials to change this situation; it is on the elections ballot that this can be done.

If, one day, that happens, then you will be able to have a party, like the one that took place on December 16th 1773. I am speaking of the tea party in the bay of the city of Boston; and this time it will be by lighting fires on the beaches or elsewhere, nationwide, by burning all these weapons, and celebrating the abolition of this plague. I am allowing myself to dream… it's free.

Don't forget it's always you, you and you.

THE SECOND AMENDMENT:

(Amendment II) to the United States Constitution protects the right to keep and bear arms. It was ratified on December 15 -1791.

To me this law is archaic. At the time, this law was established for the cowboys, who shot on anything and anyone, and things haven't changed much since.

On the other hand, if you tell me that this law is to control the human race, then I say this Second Amendment is for MASS CARNAGE. Every time there is a MASS SHOOTING, for, and only for a short period of time, what we see on multiple media are people crying, crying, and crying. 95% of the people are for regulations on gun control. Nothing is being done, nothing, nothing, and nothing.

Really, first this is bullshit, hypocrisy, and lies. And nothing will be done, because of the fact that weapons are part of the American homo-sapiens genes. That's all.

Secondly, we have this killer association: the NRA. They are complicit in all the MASS SHOOTINGS, in the USA? And, by the way, who else has this stupid cowboy law, no others country in the world has this butcher law.

Thirdly, New Zealand, a few weeks after the mass shooting of 51 Muslims in Christchurch, banned the semi-automatic AR-15 rifle. But you should ask yourself why did they solve this problem so quickly? Guess what? Easy, this country doesn't have a crazy killer association the likes of the NRA.

Finally, why is it easier to buy guns than to vote? This question is for the GOP. According to some sources, since this country doesn't have this deep desire to solve the problem of their deadly toys, the days to come will not be easy. In the near future, by the year 2050, the prognosis of gun-related deaths in the USA will be around one million per year.

America, wake up:

A TRUE PARADISE, REALLY:

We, as Americans, have been involved in all kinds of wars for over 160 years, and this is on a global scale for a variety of reasons.

I think we should ask ourselves the following question today: have all of those millions of deaths really won us anything positive? Surely. The question arises for the poor people of this country who go to the front lines in wars and surely not to the companies which manufacture all this panoply of destructive weapons. There are also our elected officials who applaud and allow themselves to pass laws, to receive bribes. All this is pure hypocrisy; these people are bandits of the worst kind.

They don't give a <u>damn about these deaths</u>. All they care about is the famous dollar sign. Since this world of dollars only lives for these dirty sheets of paper, we should honor them by adding a small spot of two red C / M whose components are the following "54% plasma & 45% red blood cells and 1% white blood cells".

The United States is first on the list of countries that have intervened in various conflicts since our country has existed. I will name, below, only the main interventions the Americans were involved in or intervened in, in 51 different conflicts, for a total of 1,354,664 dead.

You must agree with me, enough is enough, there is no more room in our graveyards for our heroes, yes, our heroes but, for the demagogue monster Trump, they are losers.

It is remembered that Donald's grandfather, Friedrich was born in the Bavarian town of Kallstadt; he immigrated to the United States in 1885 to avoid military service and his grandson Donald did the same, to avoid the war of Vietnam by being given a paper by his father's pediatrician, Dr Larry Braunstein. So, where losers or coward are concerned, he's the master, and he's not shy about making fun of our heroes. Shame on you Mr. Dictator, you are a rat and all rats deserve to d...

I chose only one conflict from this list where I approve of the American intervention in the conflict. The threat of the Nazis, who were close to finalizing their nuclear research on the atomic bomb, had to be eliminated.

But the inevitable could not be contained, since Nazism was imported right here on our American soil, this ideology is on the doorstep of our residences, also in some of our institutions, and unfortunately in all the government infrastructure which is promoted by the greatest traitors that the United States has ever had until now, and this traitor, is called Donald Trump, former president impostor, and he has the help of a certain person of FOXNEWS and also most of the GOP, who incite the population to violence.

Finally, I am tired of hearing the media repeating this sentence every day, that our country is the best in the world in which we can live, it is a free country. Oh, yes? Really? What hypocrisy! We are in the twentieth row; there is nothing to freak out about! All the countries of Western Europe, Australia, England, and Canada, our mind-boggling neighbor, and many other small, no-fuss republics, are all much more civilized in internal politics, than we are.

Not all residents of the countries mentioned above need to look over their shoulders when walking on the sidewalk for fear of being attacked, or sometimes shot at point blank range by killer police, especially if you are a non-white person. Also, Domestic terrorist and other.

If, sometimes, Americans really want to make sure that they are number one in the world for a good country to live in, then we are going to have to forget about these current laws. Some of these laws are outdated and archaic. Firstly, the second amendment must be amended from top to bottom; secondly, we must abolish this association of killers: the NRA, which has 3 principal directors, who have their hands soiled with blood every day since there are daily gun-related deaths. Thirdly, all establishments selling weapons must be eliminated. Fourthly, the government must buy back all these weapons, to put them to recycling. Fifthly, only the police and the army should possess these weapons. Sixthly, that the other weapons, for the hunters, are always stored and checked in at the police stations in their respective regions.

This is all utopian, so, from 2050 onwards there will be 1 million gun-related deaths per year in the United States, because, generally speaking, we don't give a damn about death in the United States. Why? Because guns here in the USA are a toys or trophies that we cherish more than anything, we fondle and admire them. I have often seen owners of these famous toys; all smiles embracing their pieces of deadly destruction and telling themselves that this phenomenon only exists here in the United States.

This is why we are No. 1 in the world in the field of human butchery. We should all cry out our discontent together, in tune with our rulers. All policies combined, that this butchery must end once and for all. This is my dearest wish, for this country, before it becomes a banana republic.

Trump never put in place a coronavirus program

CHAPTER ELEVEN

NATIONAL ENQUIRER ADMITS TO 'CATCH AND KILL' PAYMENT TO EX-PLAYMATE:

DECEMBER 12, 2018

AMI told prosecutors it had worked with Trump's campaign to pay for and suppress the story of a sexual affair to 'prevent it from influencing' US election

The publisher of the National Enquirer had said it coordinated with Donald Trump's presidential campaign to pay a Playboy model $150,000 in hush money, placing the president and his inner circle in further legal peril.

American Media Inc. (AMI) told prosecutors it had worked "in concert" with Trump's campaign when it bought Karen McDougal's story of a sexual affair with Trump, which it suppressed "to prevent it from influencing the election".

From fixer to inmate: Michael Cohen reckons with his 'blind loyalty' to Trump.

The publisher revealed details of the so-called "catch and kill" deal for McDougal's story in an agreement with federal authorities that means the company will not face charges, prosecutors in Manhattan announced on Wednesday.

The agreement raises the possibility that Trump's presidential campaign, which is currently making early preparations for his re-election bid, could be indicted for violating campaign finance laws through its involvement in the payout.

An unidentified member of the campaign who was involved in the arrangement with AMI could also be vulnerable to prosecution. Michael Cohen, Trump's former lawyer and legal fixer, previously pleaded guilty to involvement in the scheme.

Cohen previously testified that he had arranged the payment to McDougal, along with a $130,000 payout to buy the silence of the porn star Stormy Daniels, at the direction of Trump. The president has denied involvement in the payments.

US law bars corporations from spending money to influence elections in coordination with a candidate or campaign. Prosecutors said that AMI's payment to McDougal amounted to a secret in-kind contribution to Trump's campaign.

But Wednesday's agreement – struck in September but kept secret until now – means that federal prosecutors in New York now have testimony from two witnesses, Cohen and AMI, that the Trump payments were made to women in a deliberate attempt to influence the 2016 election.

The agreement said that in August 2015, Cohen and "at least one other member of the campaign" met AMI's chief executive David Pecker, who "offered to help deal with negative stories" about Trump during the presidential campaign.

In August 2016, AMI paid McDougal $150,000 for the rights to the story of "her relationship with 'a then-married man'," according to prosecutors, which was "substantially more money than AMI otherwise would have paid".

The deal said AMI would feature McDougal on magazine covers, but AMI actually had no intention of publishing her story.

Prosecutors said that, following Trump's election victory, AMI published articles by McDougal in some of its other magazines, including OK! and Star, in an attempt to keep her from talking publicly about the $150,000 deal.

SEX, LIES AND TABLOIDS: HUSH PAYMENTS TO WOMEN THAT SPELL DANGER FOR TRUMP:

Karen McDougal and Stormy Daniels: two women who may pose the biggest danger to Donald Trump.

An unknown number of years ago, documents relating to Donald Trump began to land in the safe. Trump was a longtime friend of the Enquirer publisher, David Pecker, a fellow New Yorker who was a frequent guest at Trump's Mar-a-Lago resort in Florida, including at Trump's wedding to Melania Knauss. When the actress Cameron Diaz threatened to sue the Enquirer in 2005 over an allegation of an affair, Trump went in to bat for Pecker.

The launch of Trump's presidential campaign in June 2015 did not stop the accumulation of documents. On the contrary, Trump's political career made his secrets more precious – or so he seemed to believe. At least two major documents landed in the safe in late 2016, it appears, just weeks before Trump was elected.

The documents were agreements with two women who alleged affairs with Trump early in his marriage to Melania. The first, former Playboy model Karen McDougal accepted a cash payment from a magazine publisher for exclusive rights to her story, which has not yet been printed. The second, adult film-maker and actor Stormy Daniels was represented by the same lawyer as McDougal and had a similar story to tell.

As for Trump, the man handling the hush agreements was Michael Cohen, a personal injury lawyer and taxi business owner who had been plying his unique skills on Trump's behalf since 2007. Cohen was a child of Long Island, New York, who grew up reading The Art of the Deal and aiming for the big time.

It points a finger directly at the president.

In the plea deal, Cohen's legal team agreed with prosecutors that the hush payments violated federal laws restricting direct corporate donations to political candidates and limiting individual gifts to $2,700 per cycle.

The payment to McDougal was $150,000. Daniels got $130,000.

Cohen told the court that Trump directed him to make the payments, implicating the president in the crime. As Lanny Davis, Cohen's lawyer put it: "If those payments were a crime for Michael Cohen, then why wouldn't they be a crime for Donald Trump?"

The Cohen plea deal "raises the stakes very significantly for the president himself"', said Ryan Goodman, a law professor at New York University.

"I do think that the most important new development of the last few months is the Michael Cohen guilty plea," said Goodman, "because it points a finger directly at the president for criminal liability, and it comes out of the SDNY office" (the US attorney's office for the southern district of New York) "which is not something that the president could even begin to control in the same way that he or his appointees could try to control the [special counsel Robert] Mueller investigation."

Most analysts agree that Trump is not likely to be charged with a crime during his time in office. Trump himself has asserted his innocence, tweeting: "The only thing that I have done wrong is to win an election that was expected to be won by Crooked Hillary Clinton and the Democrats."

But the prospect of a president known for misogynistic behavior being laid low by a serial adultery scandal is laden with irony, said Juliet Williams, a professor of gender studies at the University of California, Los Angeles and contributing co-editor of Public Affairs: Politics in the Age of Sex Scandals.

It's like one tiny straw of hay in a giant haystack of bad behavior

"Here's candidate Trump running for office, blatantly misogynistic, not afraid to get on a stage and criticize women for their appearance, known to speak in vulgar terminology – and also running on a platform that is widely characterized by opponents as anti-woman. And all of that is out there."

The calculation to pay off Daniels and McDougal was made under pressure. A month before the election, the Trump campaign was hit by the release of an Access Hollywood videotape in which Trump could be heard saying that one of his techniques for approaching women was to "grab'em by the pussy".

Karen McDougal and Stormy Daniels both alleged affairs with Trump early in his marriage to Melania.

To pay Daniels, Cohen set up Essential Consultants LLC, a shell company he told the bank was part of his real estate business. Instead, he deposited $130,000 in the company account which then was wired to Daniels' lawyer.

In other words, there is a direct link between Trump sitting on a tour bus counseling Billy Bush to "Grab 'them by the pussy", and Trump on the run from his own justice department.

"Weissenberg's cooperation takes the Mueller and SDNY investigations out of some of the penny ante stuff in play so far and into the heart of the Trump Organization and President Trump's business history," O'Brien tweeted. "The game gets started here."

"So that a person is not afraid to stand on a stage and talk about his penis size and deride his opponent for her face, but he is afraid that somebody might know that he committed adultery."

HERE'S WHAT THE THREE WOMEN ACCUSING BRETT KAVANAUGH HAVE SAID:

September 27, 2018

As President Donald Trump's next pick for the United States Supreme Court, Brett Kavanaugh, heads into hearings on Thursday, the allegations about his behavior in the past will be at the top of their minds for many.

Christine Blasey Ford releases full statement ahead of Senate Judiciary hearing

As of Wednesday, three women -- Julie Swetnick, Christine Blasey Ford and Deborah Ramirez -- have come forward to accuse the nominee of either sexual misconduct or sexual assault.

Here's a look at what each of them has said about what allegedly happened:

Dr. Christine Blasey Ford:

Who she is: Ford is a research psychologist and clinical psychology professor who is now based in California. She is married with two children. She knew Kavanaugh when they were both in high school in suburban Maryland, outside of Washington, D.C., in the early 1980s. Ford attended an all-girls school and Kavanaugh attended an all-boys school.

What to know about the allegations: Ford said that Kavanaugh sexually assaulted her when she was 15. She said that at a small gathering at a home, she was on her way to the restroom when she was pushed into a bedroom and found herself with Kavanaugh and a friend, Mark Judge. She said that both boys were drunk, while she had consumed one beer.

Ford said that Kavanaugh pinned her to a bed and that he and Judge were laughing. Ford said she tried to get away but Kavanaugh's weight was too heavy. She said she tried to scream for help but Kavanaugh put his hand over her mouth.

"It was hard for me to breathe, and I thought that Brett was accidentally going to kill me," she wrote of that moment.

When she learned of Kavanaugh's potential nomination, she initially reached out confidentially to her congresswoman in California, Democratic Rep. Anna Eshoo, but her identity has since been made public.

Sen. Orrin Hatch said that he believes Ford could have "mistaken" Kavanaugh for someone else, but a childhood friend of hers found the thought insulting.

"It's really a way of dismissing her and suggesting that her memory isn't clear," Samantha Guerry told ABC News. "I think that when you have someone's hand over your mouth and you think that you might die by accident you know who you're dealing with."

"While I am frightened, please know, my fear will not hold me back from testifying and you will be provided with answers to all of your questions," she wrote in a letter to the Republican committee chairman Sen. Chuck Grassley. "I ask for fair and respectful treatment.

Deborah Ramirez:

Who she is: Ramirez knew Kavanaugh when they were classmates at Yale University. After college, Ramirez would go on to work for an organization that supports victims of domestic violence, according to a report published in The New Yorker.

What to know about the allegations: Ramirez said that, at a party where both she and Kavanaugh were drinking, Kavanaugh exposed himself near her face. Ramirez said there was unwanted contact as she tried to push him away.

Ramirez initially told the New Yorker that she wasn't sure of Kavanaugh's involvement in the incident but, after days of reflection, she said she was confident of her recollection. The allegations were sent to Democratic senators by a civil-rights lawyer, according to the report, which also said that Ramirez was hesitant to come forward.

In a statement to KGO-TV, Kavanaugh's first-year roommate, James Roche, described Ramirez as an honest person and Kavanaugh as someone who could become belligerent when drunk.

"Based on my time with Debbie, I believe her to be unusually honest and straightforward and I cannot imagine her making this up," he wrote. "Based on my time with Brett, I believe that he and his social circle were capable of the actions that Debbie described."

Julie Swetnick:

Who she is: Like Ford, Swetnick said she knew Kavanaugh in high school in the 1980s. According to a sworn statement released by her lawyer, Michael Avenatti, Swetnick is a longtime government worker. She has worked for the Department of Homeland Security and the Justice Department, and she now has active security clearances with the U.S. Department of Treasury and the IRS, according to the sworn statement.

What to know about the allegations: Swetnick said that she was the victim of a gang rape at a party, and that Kavanaugh was one of the teens present at the party

"During the incident, I was incapacitated without my consent and unable to fight off the boys raping me. I believe I was drugged using Quaaludes or something similar placed in what I was drinking," the statement reads.

In her statement, Swetnick wrote that, at other parties, she witnessed a "train" of boys, including Kavanaugh, lined up outside of bedrooms for what she believed were gang rapes on more than one occasion.

What Brett Kavanagh says?

Kavanaugh has strongly denied the allegations from both Ford and Ramirez. In a new statement on Wednesday, Kavanaugh responded to Swetnick's accusations, saying, "This is ridiculous and from the Twilight Zone. I don't know who this is and this never happened."

Like Ford, Kavanaugh released his statement ahead of Thursday's hearing. In it, he again denies the allegations made by Ford.

"I am not questioning that Dr. Ford may have been sexually assaulted by some person in some place at some time. But I have never done that to her or to anyone. I am innocent of this charge," he wrote.

Among those who have stood behind Kavanaugh are President Trump and Senate Majority Leader Mitch McConnell, tell me who your friends are, and I'll tell you wo you are.

TRUMP IS A MASTER HATEMONGER:

He has skillfully tuned into feelings of resentment on the part of substantial numbers of white Americans by openly denigrating immigrants as 'rapists' and 'murderers' and labeling the press as 'the enemy of the people'. Anyone who has dared to question his inflated narcissistic self-image has been vilified. But hate-mongers are threatening the very foundations of democracy.

DONALD TRUMP 2016 PRESIDENTIAL CAMPAIGN WERE A LIE:

June 16, 2015, Trump came down the golden escalator at the Trump Tower, and announced his White House run it's not a surprise to learn that the first words Donald Trump 2016 Presidential campaign were a lie, and four years later 30,573 lies, more than 50 false or misleading claims a day, and today he continues to lie as always lying, lying is in his DNA, why not because he knows his followers are naïve and stupid, remember one day he said, he could kill someone on 5th avenue, and they wouldn't blame me, as you can see these people are ignorant.

Trump never put in place a coronavirus program

CHAPTER TWELVE

....

HOW TRUMP FRAUDULENTLY BECOME THE 45TH PRESIDENT OF THE UNITED STATES 2016:

Here are the Chief Architects who designed the monster, and, subsequently, the one who became the 45th President of the United States, and finally the one we knew in 2020, the biggest cheater in our country.

Please believe me, I do not denigrate the fact that this person was and is a very good communicator. To indoctrinate 40% of his supporters, with his 4,000 lies, since he has been in power, it takes a certain rigor for that to happen. As Hitler did with the population of Germany in the years 1928-1945.

So, you are going to tell me how to deprogram all his subjects who are hooked to a macabre ideology of a guru. It remains to be seen, how our elected officials will proceed in the future; will they be liars of the worst kind, like those who are currently members of the Republican Party. If so then, good luck, to our democracy.

So, I'll start with the first Architect who fraudulently allowed Trump to become the 45th President of the United States.

Felix Sater:

The enigmatic businessman at the heart of the Trump-Russia inquiry.

Felix Sater, a Moscow-born businessman now at the center of the Trump-Russia affair, says he lives by a simple code: "Screw me once, shame on you; screw me twice, shame on me for letting it happen."

As the Trump presidency finds itself increasingly hemmed in by an investigation into possible collusion between the Trump campaign and the Kremlin, and as key protagonists hire their own lawyers and reportedly make their own arrangements with prosecutors, they are words likely to become ever more relevant to those caught in the whirlpool.

Sater – a former Trump associate whom the president had, in recent years, trouble recalling – repeated the motto more than once in exchanges with the Guardian, while asking for fair coverage of his past. He insists it has sustained him through a convoluted and colorful life that led him from Moscow to Wall Street to prison to the freewheeling world of international real estate deals, secret arrangements with US law enforcement and intelligence agencies – and ultimately, to Trump Tower.

Whatever the truth of Donald Trump's relationship with the Kremlin and Vladimir Putin, Sater is likely to end up being part of the story. He surfaced this week in leaked emails that he sent in 2015 to Trump's lawyer, claiming he could engineer Putin's support for a Trump Tower in Moscow and thus, somehow, a victory in the US presidential election.

"Our boy can become president of the USA and we can engineer it," Sater said, according to one of the emails, leaked to the New York Times. "I will get all of Putin's team to buy in on this, I will manage this process."

Sater's links to Trump's circle can be traced back to not long after he came to the US as a child. His father, Mikhail Sheferovsky (who changed the family name after arriving in New York) became a local crime boss in Brighton Beach and Sater grew up on that side of Brooklyn, where he got to know another teenager in the neighborhood, Michael Cohen, a Long Island boy who would go on to become Trump's personal lawyer and vice-president of the Trump Organization. Named later the Trump Fixer.

Three decades later, it was Cohen that Sater contacted when he thought he could win Putin's backing for a Moscow real estate deal and Trump's presidential run.

Sater first came directly into Trump's orbit when he teamed up with one of his neighbors, another Soviet-born striver, Tevfik Arif, a Kazakh developer who set up the Bayrock real estate firm in 2001 with offices in Trump Tower. Sater rose to become managing director, and Bayrock went into partnership with Trump to build the Trump Soho hotel.

Trump, Arif and Sater were masters of ceremonies at the official opening in Manhattan in September 2007, and pictures of the event show them basking together in the glow of the publicity.

Sater was forced out of the limelight not long after, when details of his criminal record appeared. His first career as a stockbroker had come to a sudden end when he was jailed for slashing a man with the stem of a shattered margarita glass. When he emerged from a year in prison ("the worst time in my life", he told Talking Points Memo), he got involved in a mob-run stock exchange scam, persuading gullible customers to buy worthless shares.

The government's lawyer Todd Kaminsky told the court that Sater, referred to throughout the proceedings as John Doe, and had provided cooperation that "was of an extraordinary depth and breadth, almost unseen, at least in this United States attorney's office".

Kaminsky added that "unlike some cooperators who cooperate within one type of organized crime family or over one type of crime, Mr. Doe's cooperation runs a gamut that is seldom seen".

"It involves violent organizations such as al-Qaida, it involves foreign governments, it involves Russian organized crime. And, most particularly, it involves various families of La Cosa Nostra. By that, specifically, I mean an individual on the ruling board of the Genovese crime family, a captain in the Bonanno crime family, a soldier in the Gambino crime family, the list goes on and on."

"Sater added: "That work went into high gear after September 11, when America was attacked."

His government service ended in 2009, when he was finally sentenced for the securities fraud charges more than a decade earlier, paying a $25,000 fine and spending no time in jail. By now, however, his criminal past had been exposed. But there was still one Manhattan high-roller willing to make use of Sater's particular skills.

Sater told New York magazine: "I stopped by to say hello to Donald, and he says, 'You got to come here.'"

The Trump Organization insisted that Sater was never an employee but he worked out of Trump Tower and carried a now infamous business card identifying him as "senior advisor" to Trump.

"Donald wanted me to bring deals to him. Because he saw how many I put on the table at Bayrock," Sater said.

What Sater did for Trump from that time on is part of the puzzle that entwines Trump with Moscow. What is known is that he was involved in the abortive attempt to secure Trump a slice of the Moscow real estate market and that he took part in an effort, also involving Michael Cohen, to promote a Moscow-backed peace plan in Ukraine that would have left Crimea in Russian hands on a long-term lease, and potentially to the removal of the Ukrainian president, Petro Poroshenko.

Among the many unknowns is the question of whether he returned to his collaboration with the FBI. The Financial Times reported that he is cooperating with an international investigation into Kazakh money-laundering, but he did not say whether he is talking to Robert Mueller, the special counsel looking into possible Trump-Kremlin collusion.

As Sater predicted in an email to the Guardian: "There are many additional stories that will be coming out about me in the future, much timelier and more important than 20-year-old stock cases."

HIRED A FIRM TO RIGG THE POLLS:

And now, with the second Architect who fraudulently allowed Trump to become the 45th President of the United States, Michael Cohen "the fixer" with the Trump Organization. By the beginning of 2014, Trump was seriously considering running for President, but at the time, CNBC was conducting an online poll to determine the twenty-five most influential business people alive in order to celebrate the twenty-fifth anniversary of the network. Trump was one of the two hundred businessmen listed as contenders.

The Trump organization discovered that he was, at that time, near the bottom of the list, around 187th out of 200. Upon Trump's request, his Fixer was asked to find out what could be done.

The Fixer, Michael Cohen, called a friend, John Gauger, the same day. Gauger was, at that time the chief of information at Liberty University and he also had a side business, called Red finch Solution LLC, which provided services for search engine optimization and internet reputational management.

A few days later, Mr. Gauger came back with a plan: "The algorithmic code". His plan was to manipulate the vote by inserting IP addresses, which needed to be bought at the cost of 7,500 $. Everything was going well and after a few days, Trump was in the first 29 ranking. But Trump, with is ego, wasn't happy. He called in his fixer. "What can we do?" he asked. The fixer said, "You need to purchase more IP addresses to get back in the game." Trump said, "Ok let's do it. Buy another 7,000 $ of IP addresses, and make sure that I make it to the top ten." The fixer returned to his office to call Mr. Gauger again and his team of techies fed the fake IP "votes" into the poll.

Gauger altered the algorithm and more votes were cast. When the poll closed, Trump was on the list, as promised by Gauger. The next morning everyone was euphoric in the Trump offices until the following day, when Trump discovered that CNBC claimed to have reserved the right to remove anyone they wanted from the list, and they had unilaterally, <u>removed his name from the list.</u>

CNBC Staff must have thought there was <u>something cooking out there</u> with the Trump ranking, but Trump wanted to fight back. He wanted to take action against them so he decided to complain and asked them to restore his rightful slot.

But, in the meantime, afraid they were going to be found out, the Trump organization waited until the next day to see what was going to happen.

CNBC executives immediately saw that <u>something fishy was happening</u> with Trump's votes. Under normal circumstances, it is impossible to go from rank 185 to rank 9 in only a few days; impossible! So, Trump threatened to sue them. Immediately, the chaos settled, in his favor, by cheating again. Later that week, when the fixer dropped <u>John Gauger an invoice</u>, it already proved him to be the cheater. He said to leave it, <u>"we'll deal with it later».</u> Knowing Trump as well as he did, <u>the fixer knew he wasn't going to pay up this invoice</u>; as usual this monster is cheating.

Trump never put in place a coronavirus program

72

CHAPTER THIRTEEN

DOES DONALD TRUMP'S FOREIGN POLICY ACTUALLY MAKE SENSE:

July 15, 2018

It's entirely logical for narcissists to seek alliances with authoritarian leaders.

President Vladimir Putin and President Donald Trump meet in Hamburg, Germany on July 7, 2017.

After leaving allies rattled at the NATO Summit in Brussels and dodging mass protests in the UK, Donald Trump is now traveling on to meet with Vladimir Putin in Helsinki—a meeting he has said "may be the easiest of all." Trump's boorish behavior in Brussels fits a now well-established pattern of attacks on democratic allies and praise for authoritarian leaders that has left the rest of the world struggling to make sense of his seemingly incomprehensible conduct. Viewed from the perspective of Trump's possible mental state, however, his foreign policy makes perfect sense.

From the beginning of his involvement in politics, Trump's behavior has prompted questions about the state of his mental health. During the 2016 presidential election campaign, three psychiatrists wrote to then-President Barack Obama warning that Trump's "widely reported symptoms of mental instability—including grandiosity, impulsivity, hypersensitivity to slights or criticism, and an apparent inability to distinguish between <u>fantasy and reality</u>—lead us to question his fitness for the immense responsibilities of the office."

After Trump was sworn in as President, 27 psychologists and mental health professionals published a book called "The Dangerous Case of Donald Trump," in which the authors expressed their collective professional opinion "that anyone as mentally unstable as this man simply should not be entrusted with the life-and-death powers of the presidency."

While a range of conditions have been mooted by mental health professionals as possible explanations for Trump's disturbing behavior, the condition that most concerns these psychiatrists is a disorder known as 'malignant narcissism.' This disorder combines extreme narcissistic behavior and acute paranoia with the absence of conscience that is usually exhibited by psychopaths.

It's entirely logical for narcissists to seek alliances with authoritarian leaders.

President Vladimir Putin and President Donald Trump meet in Hamburg, Germany on July 7, 2017.

After leaving allies rattled at the NATO Summit in Brussels and dodging mass protests in the UK, Donald Trump is now traveling on to meet with Vladimir Putin in Helsinki—a meeting he has said "may be the easiest of all." Trump's boorish behavior in Brussels fits a now well-established pattern of attacks on democratic allies and praise for authoritarian leaders that has left the rest of the world struggling to make sense of his seemingly incomprehensible conduct.

During the 2016 presidential election campaign, three psychiatrists wrote to then-President Barack Obama warning that Trump's "widely reported symptoms of mental instability—including grandiosity, impulsivity, hypersensitivity to slights or criticism, and an apparent inability to distinguish between fantasy and reality—lead us to question his fitness for the immense responsibilities of the office."

After Trump was sworn in as President, 27 psychologists and mental health professionals published a book called "The Dangerous Case of Donald Trump," in which the authors expressed their collective professional opinion "that anyone as mentally unstable as this man simply should not be entrusted with the life-and-death powers of the presidency."

While a range of conditions have been mooted by mental health professionals as possible explanations for Trump's disturbing behavior, the condition that most concerns these psychiatrists is a disorder known as 'malignant narcissism.' This disorder combines extreme narcissistic behavior and acute paranoia with the absence of conscience that is usually exhibited by psychopaths.

One of the distinguishing traits of malignant narcissism, as the psychiatrists' letter to President Obama noted, is a hypersensitivity to slights or criticism, which results in what is known as 'narcissistic rage' towards anyone who disagrees. When exhibited by someone in a position of power, this would be manifested as a kind of fury towards one's political opponents, the press and the courts, together with active measures to curtail their dissent.

A paranoid leader would therefore recoil from alliances and seek to fortify their territory against internal and external threats. Leaders who combine both extreme narcissistic and paranoid traits characteristically hold deeply racist beliefs, viewing others unlike themselves as not only inferior but also as existential threats to this territory, or to 'the nation' and 'our values.'

TRUMP RHETORIC FRESHLY CONDEMNED AFTER MASS SHOOTINGS:

April 8, 2019

2020 candidates and other politicians battle over the president's words about minorities, while the Justice Department pursues the El Paso killings as domestic terrorism.

The Justice Department, on Sunday, said it was treating a mass shooting in Texas as domestic terrorism, while 2020 candidates and politicians across the spectrum, frustrated by a string of deadly shootings, battled over President Donald Trump's rhetoric on minorities and whether it is encouraging violence.

Democratic candidates were unsparing in assessing blame, with former Rep. Beto O'Rourke of Texas leading the way. He said, on Sunday, that responsibility for the shooting in his hometown of El Paso the day before — one of two in 24 hours that left at least 29 dead — fell on President Donald Trump and his racial rhetoric, accusing the president of "encouraging" such acts of violence.

In addition to shoring up gun control laws, O'Rourke said in an interview on CNN's "State of the Union," "we have to acknowledge the hatred, the open racism that we're seeing," adding that "there is an environment of it in the United States."

Nearly half a dozen other presidential contenders — including Rep. Tim Ryan of Ohio, Sen. Cory Booker of New Jersey, Mayor Pete Buttigieg of South Bend, Ind., and Julián Castro, the only Hispanic candidate in the 2020 Democratic field — also placed blame on Trump for his rhetoric.

"He is ripping at our nation," Booker said on CNN, repeatedly using the word "failing" and saying the president "must be held responsible."

On Saturday afternoon, a gunman opened fire outside a Walmart in a busy shopping center in El Paso, which sits just across the border from Mexico and has a large Latino population. Police say that the attack killed at least 20 and wounded two dozen others. The suspect, identified as 21-year-old Patrick Crusius, is in custody.

Hours later, a mass shooting in Dayton, Ohio, left nine dead and injured dozens. Police have identified that shooter, who was killed by responding officers, as 24-year-old Connor Betts. Authorities have not determined a motive for that attack. The killings Saturday and Sunday came less than a week after three were killed and a dozen others wounded when a gunman opened fire at a garlic festival in Gilroy, California.

O'Rourke, who left the presidential campaign trail to return home in the wake of the El Paso shooting, repeatedly accused Trump of using language more commonly found during Hitler's Third Reich, but also said that the president's rhetoric was commonly found on the internet and even Fox News.

"He is encouraging this," O'Rourke told host Jake Tapper of CNN. "He doesn't just tolerate it; he encourages it, calling immigrants rapists and criminals and seeking to ban all people of one religion."

"Anybody who has the ability to see and hear and understand what the president has been doing since he started his campaign in 2015 knows that division and bigotry and fanning the flames of hate has been his political strategy," he said on ABC's "This Week."

O'Rourke outlined a litany of instances by the president in which he has derided minorities or immigrants, including Trump's call to ban Muslims from entering the U.S. during the 2016 presidential campaign, his assertion that there were "very fine people" on both sides of a 2017 neo-Nazi rally in Charlottesville, Va., that turned violent, and Trump's more recent attacks on lawmakers of color.

The David Dukes of the world support him," he said on "State of the Union," referring to Trump's endorsement from the grand wizard of the Ku Klux Klan. "They said he's going to implement their agenda. That's all you need to know."

Trump made to Republican senators early in his term in which he referred to majority-black countries as "shithole countries" and wondered why the U.S. didn't have more immigrants from majority-white countries...".

Ivanka Trump, the president's daughter and adviser, similarly condemned the attacks, writing that "white supremacy, like all other forms of terrorism, is an evil that must be destroyed."

Congressional leaders also railed against Trump's heated rhetoric, with Senate Minority Leader Chuck Schumer (D-N.Y.) echoing pleas for Majority Leader Mitch McConnell (R-Ky.) to call senators back from their August recess to pass background-check legislation.

In a statement, Schumer also took a swipe at the president: "When President Trump spends more time and energy denouncing Rep. Elijah Cummings and Baltimore than he does denouncing right-wing extremists who often traffic in hate and white nationalism, it shows his priorities are un-American and way off balance."

"McConnell made no mention of the calls, which he is unlikely to heed, in a tweet calling the attacks "sickening." What do you expect from that two faced.

WITH THEIR SILENCE REPUBLICANS ARE COMPLICIT IN TRUMP'S RACISM:

July 2019

The next time a Republican tries to tell you that he or she is an heir to the legacy of Abraham Lincoln, defender of the union and freer of the slaves, remind them, in no uncertain terms that, in 2019, when the GOP had a chance to stand up to the worst kind of bigotry and un-American behavior, the self-styled "Party of Lincoln" was conspicuously and shamefully silent.

In the wake of President Donald Trump's despicable and racist tweets telling four minority women members of Congress — all American citizens, all duly elected representatives of hundreds of thousands of American citizens of all races, colors, and creeds — to "go back" to where they came from, Capitol Hill Republicans surrendered whatever tattered remnants of their spines remained and were complicit in the face of the worst kind of anti-American bigotry.

Senate Majority Leader Mitch McConnell, R-Ky., who suddenly found himself in the middle of an actual re-election challenge, declined to comment on Trump's tweets.

All four of the women targeted by Trump — U.S. Reps. Alexandria Ocasio-Cortez, D-N.Y.; Rashida Tlaib, D-Mich; Ilhan Omar, D-Minn;

and Ayanna Pressley, D-Mass — pushed back during a Capitol Hill news conference on Monday night, according to the Washington Post.

"I encourage the American people and all of us, in this room and beyond, to not take the bait," Pressley said. "This is a disruptive distraction from the issues of care, concern and consequence to the American people that we were sent here with a decisive mandate from our constituents to work on."

But some Republicans not only took the bait — they swallowed it: hook, line, and sinker.

House Minority Leader Kevin McCarthy, R-Calif., told the Washington Post that Trump "is not a racist," and instead was speaking out of "frustration." Asked if he believed that Omar, who is a naturalized American citizen, should return to Somalia, where she was born, McCarthy said, "No, they're Americans. Nobody believes somebody should leave the country. They have a right to give their opinion. "This guy is a two-face.

Actually, Mr. Minority Leader, that is precisely what the president of the United States, the leader of the free world and an unvarnished racist, actually believes, if you are not happy here, you can leave! It is your choice and your choice alone. This is about love for America. Certain people HATE our Country," Trump tweeted again Monday in a hateful tirade.

Trump's comments "were not based on any religious preference, on any skin color," but rather on frustration over "having a crisis at the border and having a whole lot of people weigh in and yet not really putting action to those words," he said.

Maybe he forgot that. Maybe someone should remind him.

Trump never put in place a coronavirus program.

CHAPTER FOURTEEN

THE MUELLER REPORT HAS BEEN SUBMITTED — HERE ARE ALL THE MAJOR PLAYERS CAUGHT UP IN THE RUSSIA-TRUMP SAGA:

The Special counsel Robert Mueller submitted his final report into his nearly two-year-long investigation into Russian interference in the 2016 US election and the Trump campaign's contacts with Russia, to Attorney General William Barr on March 22nd.

Mueller's investigation led to the indictments of 34 people and three Russian companies. At least one person was convicted in court. Five individuals caught up in the investigation became cooperating witnesses three of whom are from the Trump campaign.

The Mueller probe ensnared some of the most important people in President Donald Trump's orbit, including his campaign chairman, Paul Manafort, his longtime friend and occasional adviser, Roger Stone, and his former personal lawyer and "fixer," Michael Cohen.

Donald Trump Jr:

Donald Trump Jr., the president's eldest son, played a crucial role in the Russia saga at several key points in the campaign.

On May 21, Alexander Torshin, a former Russian senator from Putin's party and a current senior official at Russia's central bank, told Bloomberg he had dinner with Trump Jr., at the annual convention for the National Rifle Association.

In early June 2016, Donald Jr. was then contacted by Rob Goldstone, a music publicist, on behalf of one of his clients, the Russian pop artist Emin Agalarov, whose father is a prominent real-estate developer with ties to Putin.

Goldstone said Agalarov could provide "very high level and sensitive information" that would "incriminate Hillary" and was a part in "Russia and its government's support for Mr. Trump."

On June 7, Trump promised "a major speech about Hillary Clinton's crimes." Two days later on June 9, Trump Jr., along with Jared Kushner and Paul Manafort, met_with_Natalia_Veselnitskaya, a top Russian lawyer and lobbyist.

Shortly before the election, Wikileaks contacted Trump Jr. several times to request him and his father to tweet out links to Wikileaks stories about Hillary Clinton and other topics, which they did.

Jared Kushner:

Jared Kushner, a current top White House adviser and Trump's son-in-law, was involved in some of the crucial points of Trump campaign's contacts with Russia.

Kushner was present for the 2016 Trump tower meeting. Additionally, during the presidential transition period, he engaged Russia's ambassador to the US, Sergei Kislyak, in an effort to create a secure communications backchannel between the Trump transition and the Kremlin.

Kushner reportedly proposed using Russian diplomatic facilities and resources to create the backchannel, which is not known to have actually materialized. Regardless, the meeting, which was also reportedly attended by Gen. Michael Flynn, was probed by congressional investigators and the Mueller probe.

Roger Stone:

Roger Stone, a longtime Trump ally and occasional campaign adviser, became a central figure in the Mueller probe over his extended contacts with Russian hacker Guccifer 2.0, and WikiLeaks, the self-styled transparency group accused of disseminating hacked emails to interfere in the 2016 election.

Stone was arrested and charged with one count of obstruction of justice, five counts of making false statements to Congress, and one count of witness-tampering in January and plans to plead not guilty.

In the weeks that followed, Stone and Guccifer exchanged several messages on Twitter in which Guccifer expressed admiration for Stone and offered to assist the Trump campaign.

Attorney General Jeff Sessions:

Jeff Sessions, Trump's former attorney general, was on the receiving end of heavy criticism and ire from Trump and his allies for recusing himself from overseeing the Mueller probe due to his contacts with Russians during the 2016 campaign.

First, Sessions and Jared Kushner met with Russian ambassador Sergey Kislyak at a reception before Trump gave a speech on foreign policy at the Mayflower Hotel.

In the speech, which was edited by George Papadopoulos, Trump vowed to improve relations with Russia by collaborating on "shared interests."

Ambassador Kislyak said he and Sessions discussed policy matters related to Russia, which Sessions denied. US intelligence officials later described them as having had a "substantive conversation."

Sessions, who was a US senator from Alabama at the time, also met with Kislyak in his Senate office in September; a meeting which was not disclosed until March 2017, after his confirmation hearing to the position of attorney general.

Michael Flynn:

Gen. Michael Flynn, who briefly served as a national security adviser during the first days of the Trump administration, became a cooperating witness in the Mueller probe in December 2017 when he pleaded guilty to one count of lying to the FBI regarding his contacts with Kislyak.

The special counsel's indictment of Flynn said he contacted Kislyak requesting that Russia "vote against or delay" a UN resolution regarding Israeli settlements in Palestinian territory in December 2017.

Flynn also called Kislyak multiple times on December 29, the day President Barack Obama announced sanctions against Russia and the expulsion of Russian intelligence operatives from the US in response to Russian hacking and interference in the 2016 election.

The special counsel's indictment says Kislyak reached out to Flynn on December 31 to inform him that the Kremlin had decided not to impose retaliatory sanctions against the US "at the Trump team's request."

George Papadopoulos:

George Papadopoulos, a 28-year-old energy consultant, joined the Trump campaign as a low-level national security adviser, but ended up taking on an outsize role in trying to facilitate communications between the Trump campaign and Russia, and ended up inadvertently being the impetus for the FBI investigation into the Trump campaign.

Papadopoulos maintained communications over the course of several months with Joseph Mifsud, a Russia-linked Maltese academic who made efforts to broker Kremlin access to the Trump campaign.

In May, Papadopoulos told the Australian diplomat Alexander Downer

About Russia's dirt on Clinton while they were drinking at a swanky bar in London.

Papadopoulos pleaded guilty to lying to the FBI about the nature of his contacts with Mifsud and became a cooperating witness in the Mueller probe. In September, he was sentenced to 14 days in prison and 200 hours of community service.

Natalia Veselnitskaya:

Russian lawyer Natalia Veselnitskaya speaks during an interview with The Associated Press in Moscow, Russia on April 22, 2018.

In what is now known as the infamous "Trump Tower meeting," Donald Trump Jr, Jared Kushner, and Paul Manafort met with Russian attorney and Kremlin affiliate Natalia Veselnitskaya, as well as four other people affiliated with Russia at Trump Tower in Manhattan.

The Trump campaign attended the meeting under the impression that they would receive the damaging information about Hillary Clinton that Donald Jr. was promised by Rob Goldstone.

Subsequent reporting, however, suggests Veselnitskaya was in fact working on behalf of the Kremlin at the time. A memo she brought with her to the meeting almost identically matched one written by Russia's chief prosecutor.

Joseph Mifsud:

Papadopoulos' main contact was Joseph Mifsud, the director of the London Academy of Diplomacy, a for-profit college program that was later shut down. Mifsud boasted of having "substantial connections to Russian officials," according to court documents.

He also introduced Papadopoulos to Ivan Timofeev, a Director at the Kremlin-linked Russian International Affairs Council who claimed to have ties to Russia's foreign ministry.

Paul Manafort:

Paul Manafort was found guilty 21 august 2018 on two counts of bank fraud, five counts of tax fraud and one count of failing to disclose foreign bank accounts.

Paul Manafort, a longtime political operative and lobbyist for Ukraine's Party of Regions, served as Trump's campaign chairman, with him and his deputy Rick Gates leading the effort to ensure Trump's nomination at the Republican National Convention.

Earlier this month, Manafort was sentenced to seven and a half years in prison after being charged in two separate cases. In August, he was convicted on eight counts of tax and bank fraud, and later pleaded guilty to one count of conspiracy and one count of lying to investigators.

Manafort had frequent correspondence and in-person meetings with Konstantin Kilimnik, a political operative and former member of Russian intelligence. Kilimnik was a long-time associate of Manafort's, who worked for several years in Ukraine and Eastern Europe as a political consultant and financier.

Paul Manafort had, over a period of months, corresponded with Kilimnik on the subject of giving "private briefings" on the Trump campaign to Oleg Deripaska, the oligarch to whom Manafort owed tens of millions of dollars.

The emails between Manafort and Kilimnik suggested that Manafort sought to take advantage of the influence he had through his role on Trump's campaign, which was unpaid, to make up for a significant financial debt he owed to Deripaska.

TRUMP SAYS "RUSSIA, IF YOU'RE LISTENING" WAS A JOKE. THERE'S TAPE TO PROVE OTHERWISE:

July 2016

Trump is layering lie upon lie to rewrite the history of his encouragement of Russian hackers.

September 29, 2020 Trump accused reporters this weekend of mischaracterizing comments he made in July 2016 publicly encouraging Russian hackers to attack Hillary Clinton. But the way he described those comments is completely at odds with reality, and there's video to prove it.

"Do you remember when I said, 'Russia, if you're listening, find her emails,' or whatever the hell I said. 'Find her emails,' and then we all laughed together, 25,000 people in a stadium," Trump said at a rally in Middletown, Pennsylvania, on Saturday. "They cut it off exactly before we all started to laugh together, right? And for two years they've been saying, 'He dealt with Russia. He asked Russia to please get her emails,' or whatever the hell we were asking ... the whole place cracks up with me ... this is how dishonest these people are."

Trump made the remarks in question during his first campaign, saying, "Russia, if you're listening — I hope you are able to find the 30,000 emails that are missing. I think you will probably be rewarded mightily by our press. Let's see if that happens."

Jim Acosta of CNN, the reporter who asked the question that prompted Trump to say "Russia, if you're listening" at the July 2016 news conference, tweeted on Tuesday morning that "the reporters at the news conference didn't laugh. And Trump didn't appear to be joking."

Trump is spitting on his supporters and telling them it's raining:

Reckoning the incident has become a staple of Trump's campaign speeches. On September 19 in Fayetteville, North Carolina, for instance, Trump brought it up and claimed "everybody laughed" and "it was a joke," then added the lie about it happening at a rally for the first time over the weekend.

Even if Trump didn't mean for his comments to be taken seriously, Russian hackers apparently did. According to Robert Mueller's indictment of 12 Russian military intelligence officials, on the same day Trump made those comments, Russian hackers "attempted after hours to spear phish for the first time email accounts at a domain hosted by a third-party provided and used by Clinton's personal office.

Trump made it clear in the years since that he doesn't think foreign interference in American elections is a bad thing, insofar as it helps him. In October 2019, Trump flatly told reporters that he thought the Chinese and Ukrainian governments "should investigate the Bidens." Those comments were widely condemned but were defended as just a joke by Republican members of Congress like Kevin McCarthy the two-sided face and Roy Blunt, even though footage of the comment showed Trump was serious.

Trump's comments about the July 2016 news conference were especially shameless, but they were far from the only brazen lies he pushed in Middletown. He told his supporters that just prior to the coronavirus hitting the US, "we were coming together ... I was getting calls from stone-cold, hard-liner Democrats," even though in reality he had just been through an impeachment trial. He claimed 35,000 people attended his Friday evening rally in Newport News, Virginia, but local reports indicate there were around 4,000.

NEW INFORMATION:

The Washington Post reported in May 2017, for example, that Trump had revealed highly classified information to the Russian foreign minister and the Russian ambassador to the United States during a White House meeting, jeopardizing a valuable source of intelligence on the Islamic State.

LESS FOR THE CONSTITUTION:

No one in living memory has done less to "preserve, protect and defend the Constitution" than Donald Trump.

Trump has willfully and repeatedly violated this promise.

He has called neo-Nazis and other right-wing domestic terrorists "very fine people". White supremacists and other members of the new right claim him as an inspiration and a hero. The ku klux klan, nazis and other hate-mongers see Trump — quite correctly — as their ally and champion. Donald Trump rode the racist conspiracy theory known as "birtherism" to the White House. He and his republican party are leading a multi-spectrum assault on the civil and human rights of non-whites in America and around the world.

Donald Trump has repeatedly, flagrantly and consistently violated the sacred oath he took on January 20, 2017. In betraying that oath, Donald trump has done something even worse — he has betrayed the American people and placed the survival of our republic in danger. Trump never put in place a coronavirus program.

CHAPTER FIFTEEN

....

TRUMP A COWARD LEADING
COWARDS MARCH 5- 2020

He's a liar.

U.S. President Donald Trump delivers his State of the Union address at the US Capitol in Washington, D.C., on February 4.

Who could it possibly be? Here's a little help:

He's a liar. A pretender. Fabricator. Alternative Facts Creator. Con artist. Unapologetic. Snake oil salesman. Creates diversions to divert attention away from reality. Narcissistic. Will blame anyone but himself for a problem or mistake. Bullying is an effective tactic.

He uses his lies as a coat of armor to become someone he's not. He'll fight like hell not to be exposed. Disagreeing with him is not accepted. Do you need more help?

As if this isn't enough, what's even scarier is the control he has over other branches of our government. He's got the Republicans in both houses on their knees. It's doubtful how many of them can spell the word "integrity." Survival is the word of the day.

Watching members of Congress in action, one got the impression that they were sitting on chairs of nails. No sooner had they sat down, they jumped up to applaud, cheer and whistle. The bigger the lie, the louder their response.

What's most bothersome is that these marionettes, in their response, are complicit in his lies. By their response, they are endorsing everything he said. His lies are now their lies.

If that doesn't make your palms perspire, there's very little hope for our country. According to the Los Angeles Times, here are some of the facts he stated that are not factual:

"Since my election, we have created 7 million new jobs." He claimed the success was possible because he had "reversed the failed economic policies" of the Obama administration.

Some 6.7 million new jobs were created during his first 35 months in office, according to the Bureau of Labor Statistics. This compares with nearly 8 million created in the final 35 months of the Obama administration.

To continue, the nation enjoyed 110 months of job growth, two-thirds of them under President Barack Obama.

The manufacturing sector actually has been in a recession. About 12,000 such jobs were lost in December alone.

Mark Zandi of Moody's Analytics said the nation has about 200,000 factories, a figure that hasn't changed appreciably since 2013.

So, the question is, "How can we trust this group," whose job, in addition to other things, is to monitor the executive branch of government? This groups who rolls over and kisses the ring of the president. Who gives him Carte Blanche?

This group who is supposed to be responsible for declaring war. How many of them would you trust in a foxhole with you? Cowardly is. Cowardly does:

ALWAYS KEEP IN MIND:

March 28, 2020

Trumps proclaims to be the "greatest president ever," "a stable genius" and the "smartest man on the face of the earth.

"In his own mind, he is more like a persona than a person, more like a primal force or superhero, rather than a fully realized human being,"

He doesn't convey any sense of humanity.

"The features of Trump's" strange personality — his orientation to love, his proclivity for untruth, his narcissistic goal agenda, his authoritarian sentiments in his mind, must be fully appreciated and understood.

President Trump and others have repeatedly downplayed the threat of covid-19 by comparing its lethality to seasonal influenza, which claims tens of thousands of lives in the United States every year. But covid-19 may be many times as lethal for an infected person as the seasonal flu.

TRUMP IN CONNECTION WITH VIOLENCE, THREATS, AND ALLEGED ASSAULTS:

May 30, 2020

Threats: update 2015:

Megyn Kelly was the moderator from Fox news at the debate in August 2015 in Cleveland Ohio. Mrs. Kelly said to Trump and quote, 'You call women you don't like "fat pigs, dogs, slobs," and disgusting animals.

The Trump supporters (Killers) were threatening her later in front of her hotel; she was terrified, and could not go to her studio to do the show on Fox news; she, a mother of 3 children's.

Do you know Trump's answer, when the fixer reported the case to him? 'She came after me', Trump replied, 'if you come after me, I will come after you 10 times harder'. That was the answer from this President; can you imagine? He could not care less about this woman's life.

From that moment on, I said to myself, if this monster one day becomes the president of United States, we are going to have a big problem. And indeed! We have the problem which has been going on for over 4 years now, and it's not over yet. As we speak, in December 2020, this predator, mobster, is constantly in motion and always looking for prey.

President Donald Trump insists he deserves no blame for the divisions in America

President Donald Trump has repeatedly distanced himself from acts of violence in communities across America, dismissing critics who point to his rhetoric as a potential source of inspiration or comfort for anyone acting on even long-held beliefs of bigotry and hate.

"I think my rhetoric brings people together," he said last year, four days after a 21-year-old allegedly posted an anti-immigrant creed online and then allegedly opened fire in a Walmart in El Paso, Texas, killing 22 and injuring dozens of others.

But a nationwide review conducted by ABC News has identified at least 54 criminal cases where Trump was invoked in direct connection with violent acts, threats of violence or allegations of assault.

After a Latino gas station attendant in Gainesville, Florida, was suddenly punched in the head by a white man, the victim could be heard on a surveillance camera recounting the attacker's own words: "He said, 'This is for Trump.'" Charges were filed but the victim stopped pursuing them.

When police questioned a Washington state man about his threats to kill a local Syrian-born man, the suspect told police he wanted the victim to "get out of my country," adding, "That's why I like Trump."

Reviewing police reports and court records, ABC News found that in at least 12 cases, perpetrators hailed Trump in the midst or in the immediate aftermath of physically assaulting innocent victims. In another 18 cases, perpetrators cheered or defended Trump while taunting or threatening others. And in another 10 cases, Trump and his rhetoric were cited in court to explain a defendant's violent or threatening behavior.

Thirteen cases identified by ABC News involved violent or threatening acts perpetrated in defiance of Trump, with many of them targeting Trump's allies in Congress. But the vast majority of the cases – 41 of the 54 – reflected someone echoing presidential rhetoric, not protesting it.

ABC News could not find a single criminal case filed in federal or state court where an act of violence or threat was made in the name of <u>President Barack Obama or President George W. Bush.</u>

The perpetrators and suspects identified in the 54 cases are mostly white men – as young as teenagers and as old as 75 – while the victims largely represent an array of minority groups – <u>African-Americans, Latinos, Muslims and gay men</u>.

"Any public figure could have the effect of inspiring people," FBI Director Chris Wray told a Senate panel last year. "But remember that the people who commit hate fueled violence are not logical, rational people.".

Nevertheless, Trump has said he deserves "no blame" for what he calls the "hatred" seemingly coursing through parts of the country. And he told reporters that he is "committed to doing everything" in his power to not let political violence "take root in America".

Trump never put in place a coronavirus program.

Chapter Sixteen

HERE ARE THE 54 CASES
IDENTIFIED BY ABC NEWS:

August 19, 2015: In Boston, after he and his brother beat a sleeping homeless man of Mexican descent with a metal pole, Steven Leader, 30, told police "Donald Trump was right, all these illegals need to be deported." The victim, however, was not in the United States illegally. The brothers, who are white, ultimately pleaded guilty to several assault-related charges and were each sentenced to at least two years in prison.

December 5, 2015: After Penn State University student Nicholas Tavella, 19, was charged with "ethnic intimidation" and other crimes for threatening to "put a bullet" in a young Indian man on campus, his attorney argued in court that Tavella was just motivated by "a love of country," not "hate." "Donald Trump is running for President of the United States saying that, 'We've got to check people out more closely'," Tavella's attorney argued in his defense. Tavella, who is white, ultimately pleaded guilty to ethnic intimidation and was sentenced to up to two years in prison.

April 28, 2016: When FBI agents arrested 61-year-old John Martin Roos in White City, Oregon, for threatening federal officials, including then-President Barack Obama, they found several pipe bombs and guns in his home. In the three months before his arrest, Roos posted at least 34 messages on Twitter about Trump, repeatedly threatening African Americans, Muslims, Mexican immigrants and the "liberal media," and, in court documents, prosecutors noted that the avowed Trump supporter posted this threatening message to Facebook a month earlier:

June 3, 2016: After 54-year-old Henry Slapnik attacked his African-American neighbors with a knife in Cleveland, he was sentenced to more than five years in prison. He told police, "Donald Trump will fix them because they are scared of Donald Trump".

August 16, 2016: In Olympia, Washington, 32-year-old Daniel Rowe attacked a white woman and a black man with a knife after seeing them kiss on a popular street. When police arrived on the scene, Rowe professed to be "a white supremacist" and said "he planned on heading down to the next Donald Trump rally and stomping out more of the Black Lives, and he was sentenced to more than four years in prison.

September 1, 2016: The then-chief of the Bordentown New Jersey, police department, Frank Nucera, allegedly assaulted an African American teenager who was handcuffed. Federal prosecutors said the attack was part of Nucera's "intense racial animus," noting in federal court that "within hours" of the assault, Nucera was secretly recorded saying "Donald Trump is the last hope for white people."

September 2016: After 40-year-old Mark Feigin of Los Angeles was arrested for posting anti-Muslim and allegedly threatening statements to a mosque's Facebook page, his attorney argued in court that the comments were protected by the First Amendment because Feigin was "using similar language and expressing similar views" to "campaign statements from then-candidate Donald Trump."

October 10, 2016: Police in Albany, New York, arrested 55-year-old Todd Warnken for threatening an African-American woman at a local grocery store "because of her race", according to a police report. Warnken allegedly told the victim, "Trump is going to win, and if you don't like it, I'm gonna beat your ass you n----r," the police report said.

October 13, 2016: After the FBI arrested three white Kansas men for plotting to bomb an apartment complex in Garden City, Kansas, where many Somali immigrants lived, one of the men's attorneys insisted to a federal judge that the plot was "self-defensive" because the three men believed "that if Donald Trump won the election, President Obama would not recognize the validity of those results.

November 3, 2016: In Tampa, Florida, David Howard threatened to burn down the house next to his "simply because" it was being purchased by a Muslim family, according to the Justice Department. He later said under oath that while he harbored a years-long dislike for Muslims, the circumstances around the home sale were "the match that lit the wick."

November 10, 2016: A 23-year-old man from High Springs, Florida, allegedly assaulted an unsuspecting Hispanic man who was cleaning a parking lot outside of a local food store. "[H]e was suddenly struck in the back of the head," a police report said of the victim. "[The victim] asked the suspect why he hit him, to which the suspect replied, 'This is for Donald Trump.'

November 12, 2016: In Grand Rapids, Michigan, while attacking a cab driver from East Africa, 23-year-old Jacob Holtzlander shouted racial epithets and repeatedly yelled the word, "Trump," according to law enforcement records. Holtzlander, who is white, ultimately pleaded guilty to a charge of ethnic intimidation, and he was sentenced to 30 days in jail.

November 16, 2016: Police in San Antonio, Texas, arrested 32-year-old Dusty Paul Lacombe after he and a companion assaulted a black man at a convenience store. According to a police report, Lacombe "stepped out of a vehicle and walked to the [victim] and stated he was a Trump supporter and swung at him several times".

January 25, 2017: At JFK International Airport in New York, a female Delta employee, wearing a hijab in accordance with her Muslim faith, was "physically and verbally" attacked by 57-year-old Robin Rhodes of Worcester, Mass., "for no apparent reason," prosecutors said at the time.

February 19, 2017: After 35-year-old Gerald Wallace called a mosque in Miami Gardens, Florida, and threatened to "shoot all", he told the FBI and police that he made the call because he "got angry" from a local TV news report about a terrorist act.

February 23, 2017: Kevin Seymour and his partner Kevin Price were riding their bicycles in Key West, Florida, when a man on a moped, 30-year-old Brandon Davis of North Carolina, hurled anti-gay slurs at them and "intentionally" ran into Seymour's bike, shouting, "You live in Trump country now".

May 3, 2017: In South Padre Island, Texas, 35-year-old Alexander Jennes Downing of Waterford, Connecticut, was captured on cellphone video taunting and aggressively approaching a Muslim family, repeatedly shouting, "Donald Trump will stop you!" and other Trump-related remarks.

May 11, 2017: Authorities arrested Steven Martan of Tucson, Arizona, after he left three threatening messages at the office Rep. Martha McSally, R- another he Ariz. In one message, he told McSally he was going to "blow your brains out," and in told her that her "days are numbered."

May 23, 2017 George Jarjour and his brother, Sam Jarjour, were getting gas at a station in Bellevue, Washington, when 56-year-old Kenneth Sjarpe started yelling at them to "go back to your country," according to a police report. Sjarpe then drove his truck toward the brothers, rolled down his window, and declared, "Fuck you, you Muslims," and "I'll fucking kill you," he was sentenced to six months behind bars.

October 22, 2017: A 44-year-old California man threatened to kill Rep. Maxine Waters, D-Calif., for her frequent criticism of Trump and her promise to "take out" the president. Anthony Scott Lloyd left a voicemail at the congresswoman's Washington office, declaring: "If you continue to make threats towards the president, you're going to wind up dead, Maxine. Cause we'll kill you."

February 21, 2018: A federal grand jury in Washington, D.C., indicted a former U.S. diplomat – William Patrick Syring, 60, of Arlington, Virginia – on several counts for threatening employees of the Arab American Institute. He had previously served nearly a year in prison for threats he had made in emails and voicemails to the same organization in 2006, but soon after serving his time he began emailing the organization again. In January 2017, a week after Trump was inaugurated, Syring sent one email saying: "It's time for ethnic cleansing of Arabs in America. He was sentenced to five years in prison.

June 8, 2018, Federal authorities arrested Nicholas Bukoski of Anne Arundel County, Maryland, for threatening to kill Sen. Bernie Sanders, I-Vermont, and Sen. Kamala Harris, D-California. "You wouldn't want to be caught off guard when I use my second amendment protected firearms to rid the world of you," Bukowski wrote to Sanders via Instagram on March 24, 2018. Two minutes later, he wrote to Harris saying he will "make sure you and your radical lefty friends never get back in power ... because you won't make it to see that day."

August 2018: After the Boston Globe called on news outlets around the country to resist what it called "Trump's assault on journalism," the Boston Globe received more than a dozen threatening phone calls. "You are the enemy of the people," the alleged caller, 68-year-old Robert Chain of Encino, California.

October 4, 2018: The Polk County Sheriff's Office in Florida arrested 53-year-old James Patrick of Winter Haven, Florida, for allegedly threatening "to kill Democratic office holders, members of their families and members of both local and federal law enforcement agencies," according to a police report. In messages posted online, Patrick detailed a "plan" for his attacks, which he said he would launch if then-nominee Brett Kavanagh was not confirmed as a Supreme Court justice, His trial is pending.

Late October 2018: Over the course of a week, Florida man Cesar Sayoc allegedly mailed at least 15 potential bombs to prominent critics of Trump and members of the media. Sayoc had been living in a van plastered with pro-Trump stickers, and he had posted several pro-Trump messages on social media. He was sentenced to 20 years in prison.

October 21, 2018: While Bruce M. Alexander of Tampa, Florida, was flying on a Southwest Airlines flight from Houston, Texas, to Albuquerque, New Mexico, he assaulted a woman by "reaching around the seat" in front of him and "offensively touching" her, he acknowledged in court documents. When federal authorities then arrested him, he "stated that the President of the United States says it's ok to grab women by their private parts."

December 4, 2018: Michael Brogan, 51, of Brooklyn, New York, left a voicemail at an unidentified U.S. Senator's office in Washington insisting, "I'm going to put a bullet in ya. ... You and your constant lambasting of President Trump. Oh, reproductive rights, reproductive rights."

January 17, 2019: Stephen Taubert of Syracuse, New York, was arrested by the U.S. Capitol Police for threatening to kill Rep. Maxine Waters, D-Calif., and for threatening to "hang" former President Barack Obama. Taubert used "overtly bigoted, hateful language" in his threats, according to federal prosecutors. He was sentenced to nearly four years in prison.

January 22, 2019: David Boileau of Holiday, Florida, was arrested by the Pasco County Sheriff's Office for allegedly burglarizing an Iraqi family's home and "going through" their mailbox, according to a police report. "He also stated if he doesn't get rid of them, Trump will handle it." Boileau, 58, has since pleaded guilty to a misdemeanor charge of trespassing, and he was sentenced to 90 days in jail.

February 15, 2019: The FBI in Maryland arrested a Marine veteran and U.S. Coast Guard lieutenant, Christopher Paul Hasson, who they said was stockpiling weapons and "espoused" racist and anti-immigrant views for years as he sought to "murder innocent civilians on a scale rarely seen in this country. Hasson ultimately pleaded guilty to federal weapons-related charges, and he was sentenced to more than 13 years in federal prison.

March 16, 2019: Anthony Comello, 24, of Staten Island, New York, was taken into custody for allegedly killing Francesco "Franky Boy" Cali, the reputed head of the infamous Gambino crime family. Comello's defense attorney, Robert Gottlieb, said Comello suffered from mental defect and was a believer in the "conspiratorial fringe right-wing political group" Qanon.

April 5, 2019: The FBI arrested a 55-year-old man from upstate New York for allegedly threatening to kill Rep. Ilhan Omar, D-Minn., one of the first two Muslim women elected to the U.S. Congress. She is an outspoken critic of Trump, and Trump has frequently launched public attacks against her and three other female lawmakers of color. Two weeks before his arrest, Patrick Carlineo Jr. allegedly called Omar's office in Washington labeling the congresswoman a "terrorist" and declaring: "I'll put a bullet in her fucking skull." He has since pleaded guilty to the charge and was sentenced to one year in prison.

April 13, 2019: 27-year-old Jovan Crawford, of Gaithersburg, Maryland, and 25-year-old Scott Roberson Washington, D.C., assaulted and robbed a black man wearing a red "Make America Great Again" hat while walking through his suburban Maryland neighborhood. Before punching and kicking him, "The two suspects harassed [the victim] about the hat and asked why he was wearing it. rawford and Roberson have since pleaded guilty to assault charges. They were each sentenced to at least one year in prison.

April 18, 2019: The FBI arrested John Joseph Kless of Tamarac, Florida, for calling the Washington offices of three prominent Democrats and threatening to kill each of them. At his home, authorities found a loaded handgun in a backpack, an AR-15 rifle and hundreds of rounds of ammunition. Kless admitted that in a threatening voicemail targeting Rep. Rashida Tlaib, D-Mich., he stated: "You won't fucking tell Americans what to say, and you definitely don't tell our president, Donald Trump, what to say." " Kless was sentenced to one year behind bars.

April 24, 2019: The FBI arrested 30-year-old Matthew Haviland of North Kingstown, Rhode Island, for allegedly sending a series of violent and threatening emails to a college professor in Massachusetts who publicly expressed support for abortion rights and strongly criticized Trump. In one of 28 emails sent to the professor on March 10, 2019, Haviland allegedly called the professor "pure evil" and said "all Democrats must be eradicated," insisting the country now has "a president who is taking our country to a place of more freedom rather than less." He is awaiting sentencing.

June 5, 2019: The FBI arrested a Utah man for allegedly calling the U.S. Capitol more than 2,000 times over several months and threatening to kill Democrat lawmakers, whom he said were "trying to destroy Trump's presidency." "I am going to take up my second amendment right, and shoot you liberals in the head," 54-year-old Scott Brian Haven allegedly stated in one of the calls on October 18, 2018, according to charging ls were made during periods of documents. He was sentenced to time served.

August 3, 2019: A gunman opened fire at a Walmart in El Paso, Texas, killing 22 people and injuring 24 others. The FBI labeled the massacre an act of "domestic terrorism," and police determined that the alleged shooter, 21-year-old Patrick Crusius, posted a lengthy anti-immigrant diatribe online before the attack. Crusius has been charged with capital murder by the state of Texas.

August 16, 2019: The FBI arrested Eric Lin, 35, of Clarksburg, Maryland, for sending threatening and hate-filled messages over Facebook vowing to kill a Miami-area woman and "all Hispanics in Miami and other places," as the Justice Department described it. FBI said. In June 2019, Lin allegedly wrote: "In 3 short years your entire Race, your entire culture will perish."

August 21, 2019: Nathan Semans of Humphreys County, Tennessee, was arrested by state law enforcement for allegedly emailing a threat to a local TV station that demanded the station broadcast a certain story. "Look if you don't run the story, I'm going to the state capital to blow someone's brains out," the email stated. The email then added in part: "I don't look good at the moment cause the tyranny of what Trump did … I'm sick of this nonsense and bologna hanging around that Trump's [sic] the perfect American, hallelujah against Trump."

October 7, 2019: A woman driving in Moorhead, Minnesota, called police after 27-year-old Joseph Schumacher of North Dakota allegedly rolled down his window and "began yelling at the female expressing his dislike for the political bumper sticker [she] had displayed on her car," according to police reports. Schumacher then allegedly pointed to the "Trump Pence" bumper sticker on his own vehicle "and further expressed his difference in national political views" before "brandishing a pistol" inside his vehicle.

October 25, 2019: The FBI arrested Jan Peter Meister of Tucson, Arizona, for threatening to kill House Intelligence Committee chairman Adam Schiff, D-California. Three weeks earlier, he left a voicemail at Schiff's office in Washington, D.C, promising to "blow your brains out." "He strongly dislikes the Democrats.

November 1, 2019: Clifton Blackwell, 61, of Milwaukee was arrested by local police after allegedly throwing acid on a Peruvian-American's face and accusing him of being inside the United States illegally. Before attacking the victim outside of a Mexican restaurant, Blackwell allegedly asked the victim "Why did you invade my country?" and "Why don't you respect my laws?" and the victim suffered second-degree burns on his face and neck. He pleaded not guilty and is awaiting trial.

February 19, 2020: The FBI arrested Salvatore Lippa II, 57, of upstate New York for allegedly threatening to kill Sen. Charles Schumer, D-New

York, the top Democrat in the Senate, and Rep. Adam Schiff, D-California, the chairman of the House Intelligence Committee. In late January, he left a voicemail at Schiff's office in Washington, D.C., calling Schiff a "scumbag" and threatening to "put a bullet in your [expletive] forehead," according to charging documents. Lippa has been charged with threatening to kill a U.S. official.

April 30, 2020: A Pennsylvania man who fled Cuba nearly two decades ago, Alazo Alexander, allegedly opened fire on the Cuban embassy in Washington, D.C. After his arrest, Alexander told authorities he had heard voices in his head and believed certain Cubans were trying to kill him, so he "wanted to get them before they got him," It's unclear if he's entered an initial plea.

Trump never put in place a coronavirus program.

CHAPTER SEVENTEEN

....

HERE ARE THE ACCOMPLISHMENTS OF THE TRUMP ADMINISTRATION:

September 14, 2020

They cut taxes for the wealthiest, which increased income equality adding over a billion dollars to the deficit. Their priorities were with the rich vs. the rest of us.

The Trump team had inefficient negotiations with China by going it alone rather than with all the nations involved in the TPP. This led to needless farm bankruptcies and harmed manufacturing. The results vs. the cost are not a win.

They consistently ignored medical and environmental science causing loss of life and economic devastation. They refused to model good life saving measures during the Pandemic. This administration's environmental policies are counter to what science says is needed.

The Trump administration divided our country so we cannot agree on the facts even after 50+ court rulings. They have lost the respect of our European Allies.

The Trump administration has demonstrated disregard for the human condition for policies on race, sexual orientation, immigration, poverty, hunger, disabilities, religion, and healthcare.

DONALD TRUMP AND THE BANALITY OF EVIL:

Emptiness, lack of character and a fundamental unwillingness to take responsibility lurk at evil's core.

OCTOBER 27, 2020

Despite our best intentions, Trump's name is on everyone's lips, yet I have no interest in the sordid details of his psyche. His pathologies are a matter of indifference. It's clear to me that he's a violent, dangerous lunatic. His desperate attempts to win attention and adulation likely stem from abuse he suffered as a youth.

Whatever action Trump takes is almost guaranteed to be idiotic, not just run-of-the-mill idiotic but epically, spectacularly so. Commenting on his actions reduces you to his level. Regardless of how many words you use, the verdict is clear: "Trump…bad." But this gets us nowhere.

However, thinking about Trump does teach us something useful: profound evil can coexist with deep mediocrity. Trump is responsible for an incredible amount of suffering and death, but when I watch him on television, I feel a surprising lack of emotion. We could chalk it up to my privilege, my insulation from the direct consequences of Trump's actions, or to psychological burnout, psychic defense mechanisms, or a pervasive cynicism verging on nihilism.

Beneath the bullying, blustering, and casual cruelty; beneath the mangled syntax and rhetorical excess; beneath the torrent of lies, the shocking vapidity and astonishing stupidity, one senses a radical vacuum. Trump perfectly mirrors an age of spectacle, presenting us with deconstructed fascism. His incessant harangues, evacuated of all substance, are a stream-of-consciousness scream of rage and discontent. He says something. He contradicts it. He performs as a demagogue yet lacks the true air of command. He is a post-modern 'wannabe' dictator.

His attention span is minimal, yet he has none of the traditional gifts of the leader, like extraordinary stamina, a herculean work ethic, strategic vision, and the keen selection of capable advisors. He is a bloviating buffoon, careening from one absurdity to the next, anticipating what nonsense Fox churns out about him next.

There is a peculiar disconnect between the evils his administration has directly wrought, internment camps on the southern border, incitement of racist and anti-Semitic violence, hundreds of thousands of senseless coronavirus deaths, instances of corruption too numerous to list, and the hollowness of the man and his sycophants.

Evil has at least two aspects. There is the evil of individuals: hideous, painfully personal acts of violence committed by specific people. And then there is systematic evil: the enormity of cruel systems which deprive people of their liberty, their human rights, and their very reason for being. These systems' refusal to entertain any appeal to humanity is perhaps what distinguishes them most of all. But the particular terror of evil is the way the evildoer's humanity, his frailty, foibles, and bodily existence, is eradicated.

What's more, treating evil as if it consists only or chiefly of acts of commission rather than in acts of omission means that we are poorly positioned to recognize the evil of the Trump administration's coronavirus negligence. Neglect has never been treated with the same seriousness as affirmative action. But we're not ready to recognize that evil individuals often don't match the simplistic, psychopathic, and cartoonish maleficent profile that we've been trained to recognize.

Hannah Arendt, the theorist, philosopher, author, and originator of the phrase "the banality of evil," teaches us that before Adolf Hitler attained frightening amounts of power, his physical tics were widely derided, and even regarded as comical. Writing about the Nazi war criminal Adolf Eichmann, Arendt remarked on "the dilemma between the unspeakable horror of the deeds and the undeniable ludicrousness of the man who perpetrated them." Later, in 1965, she observed that:

Trump's clownish antics and the abnegation of responsibility so characteristic of his administration are perfectly consonant with this vision of the evildoer. Emptiness, a lack of character, and a fundamental unwillingness to take responsibility for oneself lurk at evil's core.

Systematic evil may subsume individual evildoers in a chain of command and obedience, but the individuals involved have usually forfeited their personhood from the start.

Hitler, who was fully aware of this interdependence, expressed it once in a speech addressed to the SA [the Nazis' paramilitary gang]: 'All that you are, you are through me; all that I am, I am through you alone.' |

In the same way, Trump is inextricable from the mob he has spawned. He lives for their applause. Without it, he is lost, but he doesn't know why he seeks their plaudits. He enriches himself and his cronies, but his riches far exceed the sum that anyone can spend in a lifetime. Trump and his friends seek power, but to what end? Corporations' profits are already sky-high, and they are destroying the planet that produces their profits and gives wealth its meaning. Even if neo-fascists achieved complete dominion over the United States, they have no grand plan for what they would do after that. This is what Arendt meant when she wrote of evil that:

Nothing meaningful justifies the Trumpian incarnation of evil, just as nothing meaningful underlays its predecessors. One hopes that his desperate existential quest won't drag us all even further into the depths. Mocking Trump is a predictable response - he is a tempting target for derision. But ridicule can't mean inaction. We have been warned: evil can come in masquerade.

TIME MAGAZINE NOBEL PRIZE FOR SURE IT'S NOT FOR A DICTATOR:

October 2020

Trump says he deserves the Nobel peace prize.

Who was he talking about?

Although he did not name the Nobel Peace Prize winner or the country, it is clear that Mr. Trump was referring to Ethiopian Prime Minister Abiy Ahmed.

Mr. Abiy, 43, is Africa's youngest head of government.

Mr. Abiy has been praised for introducing a series of reforms.

He came into office in April 2018 after months of anti-government protests forced his predecessor to resign.

Mr. Abiy has introduced massive liberalizing reforms to Ethiopia, shaking up what was a tightly controlled nation.

He freed thousands of opposition activists from jail and allowed exiled dissidents to return home. He also allowed the media to operate freely and appointed women to prominent positions.

And in October last year, he was awarded the Nobel Peace Prize, the only head of state to win the prize since Mr. Trump was elected in 2016.

Why did he win the Nobel Peace Prize?

The Norwegian Nobel Committee said Mr. Abiy was honored for his "decisive initiative to resolve the border conflict with neighboring Eritrea."

The two countries fought a bitter border war from 1998 to 2000, which killed tens of thousands of people. Although a ceasefire was signed in 2000, the neighbors technically remained at war until July 2018, when Mr. Abiy and Eritrea's President, Isaias Afwerki signed a peace deal. So, for two decades, the long border was closed, dividing families and making trade impossible.

The Nobel Committee said it hoped the peace agreement would help to bring about positive change to the citizens of Ethiopia and Eritrea.

Since the peace deal with Eritrea, Mr. Abiy was also involved in peace processes in other African countries, the committee said.

Did Trump help broker peace between Ethiopia and Eritrea? Not really. The US influence in the peace talks was minimal. The United Arab Emirates which has a lot of influence in the Horn of Africa, was key in helping to bring the two parties together, says the BBC's former Ethiopia correspondent, Emmanuel Igunza.

Saudi Arabia also played a key role in helping end the dispute.

Media caption: Near Zalambessa relatives who had not seen each other for more than two decades hugged and kissed.

The peace deal helped bring back Eritrea from the cold after sanctions were imposed in 2009.

The UN Security Council lifted the sanctions in November 2018, four months after the peace deal was signed.

Why did Trump make the comments at this time?

This is not clear, given that the Nobel Peace Prize was awarded on 11 October last year, and Mr. Abiy gave his acceptance speech in Oslo, Norway, on December 10.

Interestingly, Mr. Trump did not officially congratulate Mr. Abiy but his daughter, Ivanka Trump, who serves as his senior adviser, and the US Secretary of State Mike Pompeo did so.

However, Mr. Trump publicly said he deserved the Nobel Peace Prize for, among other things, his efforts to convince North Korea's leader Kim Jong-un to give up nuclear weapons.

MY PERSONAL OPINION ON
THIS SUBJECT IN 2020:

First, Mister Egocentric, normally the committee that governs decisions for Nobel prizes, does not award a Nobel Prize to a dictator, an impostor president who inherited a first impeachment, and a second impeachment, lost the Senate, lost the House, and a one-term president. Who was also the worst President of the United States, since George Washington, proof that you are not a good president, you did not pass the test for a second term, finally you all have the flaws in the world. See the list of monstrous flaws that are part of this monster DNA.

WE'RE WATCHING TRUMP'S 7TH BANKRUPTCY UNFOLD:

October 13, 2020

As a businessman, Donald Trump ran six businesses that declared bankruptcy because they couldn't pay their bills. As president running for a second term, Trump is repeating some of the mistakes he made as a businessman and risking the downfall of yet another venture: his own political operation.

In the 1980s, Trump was a swashbuckling real-estate investor who bet big on the rise of Atlantic City after New Jersey legalized gambling there. He acquired three casinos that by 1991 couldn't pay their debts. The Taj Mahal declared bankruptcy in 1991, the Trump Plaza and the Trump Castle in 1992.

Lenders restructured the debt rather than liquidate and Trump put his casino holdings into a new company that went bankrupt in 2004. The company that emerged from that restructuring declared bankruptcy in 2009. Trump's 6th bankruptcy was the Plaza Hotel, which he bought in 1988. It went bankrupt by 1992.

Trump's surprise victory in 2016 paralleled the arrival of the brash upstart in Atlantic City more than 30 years earlier. But in the fourth year of his presidency, the Trump operation is once again reeling. Voters give him poor marks for handling the coronavirus crisis, underscored by an outbreak at the White House that infected Trump himself. Democrat Joe Biden is beating Trump in most swing states and an Election Day blowout is possible. Trump has suggested that he won't leave office if he loses, threatening a constitutional crisis and his own political legacy.

The lessons of Trump's bankruptcies explain much of the Trump campaign's current tumult. Here are 5 similarities:

Supporters of President Donald Trump wave flags as the Presidential motorcade carrying Trump arrives at the Trump International Hotel on September 12, 2020 in Washington, DC.

Winning the 2016 election was the biggest deal of Trump's life, and he pursued it vigorously, with his "Make America Great Again" campaign that effectively targeted disaffected working-class voters who felt ripped off by corporate greed and offshoring. Trump's 2020 campaign is vapid by comparison. There's no unifying campaign slogan, no clear agenda for a second term, no tangible pitch to voters. Mostly, Trump just tries to bash

Biden and scare voters into thinking Democrats will let criminals roam freely and tax everybody into poverty. It's like Trump closed a megadeal in 2016 but can't get excited about negotiating an extension in 2020.

He ignores warnings and overshoots. Trump got into trouble in Atlantic City because he didn't know when to stop. Casinos were profitable where he bought his first two, the Plaza and the Castle. But as casinos proliferated in Atlantic City, the market got saturated and profit margins plunged. Some experts warned Trump was vastly overspending when he took on $820 million in debt to develop the Taj Mahal in the late 1980s.

But Trump brushed them off and relied on his own rosy assumptions. The casino had cash-flow problems from the beginning and declared bankruptcy in July 1991, just 16 months after its lavish opening.

THE FORMER TRUMP TAJ MAHAL IS SEEN IN ATLANTIC CITY, N.J MONDAY, JUNE 19TH 2017.

Unkept promises. While seeking a license for the Taj Mahal in 1988, Trump told gaming officials he could lock in financing at the lowest possible "prime" rate, which was around 9% at the time. That helped him get the license, even though some officials had doubts about Trump. But Trump ended up paying a 14% rate, which contributed to the casino's cash flow problems and its bankruptcy. Trump left hundreds of contractors unpaid as the casinos cratered, and some workers ultimately lost pensions.

As a candidate and then president, Trump promised to drain the swamp, release his tax returns, make Mexico pay for a border wall, revive the coal industry and vanquish the coronavirus by summer. Nope, nope, nope, nope and nope. As for a second term, Trump is promising 10 million new jobs, more tax cuts, a quick return to normal, and a redo on unfulfilled 2016 promises, such as a terrific new health care plan. Most politicians overpromise, but Trump does it on an almost outlandish scale.

He holds his partners hostage. Trump's lenders lost hundreds of millions of dollars on his bankruptcies and other underperforming businesses, but they've often written off the losses and extended Trump even more credit, because it's better than liquidation. Had his casinos stopped operating, it would have devastated the local economy. So, lenders and gaming officials found ways to keep Trump in business; while reducing the control he had over those businesses so he couldn't single-handedly get in over his head again.

Dozens of Republican senators and members of Congress are now tied to Trump in the political equivalent of a banking relationship. As Trump won control of the Republican Party, fellow Republicans lent him their support in an all-or-nothing bid for political dominance. When Trump was winning, so were they. But if Trump goes down, some of those will sink with him.

That could cost Republicans Senate elections in states such as Arizona, Colorado, Iowa, Maine and North Carolina and give Democrats control of the Senate. If Biden wins the White House as well, Democrats would control the legislative and executive branches in a withering wipeout for Trump and his GOP allies.

So, if Trump loses in 2020, and suffers the type of embarrassing setback he did with his casino or hotel failures, it certainly won't be the end of Donald Trump. In 2008, when Trump was struggling to sell condominiums in his new Chicago tower, he sued the lender, Deutsche Bank, to get out of some of the loan payments. The two parties settled after two years of legal wrangling, and in 2011 Deutsche Bank started lending Trump money again. Trump probably hopes 2020 voters are equally forgiving. We'll see.

Trump never put in place a coronavirus program.

CHAPTER EIGHTEEN

THE ABNORMAL PRESIDENCY:

One of the things Trump has forced presidential scholars to realize "is the extent to which shamelessness in a president is really empowering, Trump dramatically changed the presidency. Here's a list of the 20 most important norms he broke.

1. Personally, profiting from official business.
2. Not releasing tax returns.
3. Refusing oversight.
4. Interfering in department of justice investigations.
5. Abusing appointment power.
6. Insulting allies while cozying up to authoritarians.
7. Coarsening presidential discourse.
8. Politicizing the military.
9. Attacking Judges.
10. Politicizing diplomacy and foreign policy.
11. Undermining intelligence agencies.
12. Publicizing lists of potential Supreme Court picks.
13. Making far more false or misleading claims than any previous president.
14. Abusing the pardon power.
15. Using government resources for partisan ends.
16. Making racialized appeals and attacks.
17. Dividing the nation in times of crisis.
18. Contradicting scientists.
19. Derailing the tradition of presidential debates.
20. Undermining faith in the 2020 election results.

Trump has famously survived two impeachments, two divorces, six bankruptcies, twenty-six accusations of sexual misconduct, and an estimated four thousand lawsuits.

Few people have evaded consequences more cunningly.

That run of good luck may well end, perhaps brutal.

These lawyers are criminal liars.

A website designed to raise $2 million in defense funds for Kyle Rittenhouse, the Illinois teenager charged with killing two men and injuring a third during street protests in Kenosha, Wis., in August, has prompted concerns among experts who call it a dangerous step toward injecting brand marketing into criminal defense.

Rittenhouse is charged with first-degree intentional homicide and first-degree reckless homicide in the killings of two men, Anthony Huber and Joseph Rosenbaum, on August 25th following protests over the police shooting of Jacob Blake. He is also charged with attempted first-degree intentional homicide for allegedly shooting and injuring a third man, Gaige Grosskreutz, along with possession of a dangerous weapon while under the age of 18 and two counts of first-degree reckless endangerment.

How the lives of Kyle Rittenhouse and Joseph Rosenbaum clashed in a fatal shooting in Kenosha, Wis.

Since his arrest, Rittenhouse emerged as a folk hero for the far right. The Fightback Foundation raised $2 million in bail money that secured his freedom in late November. He is awaiting trial while living with his family in an undisclosed location in the Midwest. Far-right and gun rights groups including the National Association for Gun Rights and American Wolf 689 have raised money for living expenses.

John Pierce, a Los Angeles-based attorney for Rittenhouse, said the website is controlled by the teen's family and is not connected to any outside organization. Pierce started out on Rittenhouse's criminal defense team until he stepped down to focus on filing future civil defamation cases involving the family. He is not receiving payment from the funds the website generates, he said.

"We have to do anything and everything to ensure that he gets the best possible defense, and that is expensive," he said. "We need to rise as much as we can. So, we're taking any and all measures to raise money. Pierce SHAME ON YOU, you are a rat, and all rats deserve to d...

An 11-minute video documentary on the site uses video footage from that night to walk viewers through the shootings while portraying the victims as dangerous. It also poses questions about Rosenbaum's death, saying that "it remains unclear if all four of [his] wounds were caused by Rittenhouse."

Pierce defended the site, saying "the notion of a fair trial was blown out of the water" when celebrities and political figures used the case to portray Rittenhouse "as a mass murderer and white supremacist."

"A 17-year-old American citizen is being sacrificed by politicians," a narrator says at the conclusion of the video. "But it's not Kyle Rittenhouse they're after. Their endgame is to strip away the constitutional right of all citizens to defend our communities, our personal property, our lives and the lives of our loved ones. This is the moment when the home of the brave rise to defend the land of the free." As usual, who is responsible? The arms dealers and the NRA.

That language casts Rittenhouse as a relatable figure and "an honorable person who was forced to shoot people in a matter of self-defense," said Tim Calkins, a brand-marketing expert at Northwestern University's Kellogg School of Management. Oh yeah, you are an idiot, if Rittenhouse had stayed home watching the news on TV, he would not have needed to defend himself and kill 2 innocent people. Calkins! You are a bloody liar and a killer. The only thing that interests you is the dirty dollar signs.

My opinion in this case is simple; you kill someone, walking in the street, you deserve a life sentence in jail, period. What about you, the lawyers, with your behavior and vicious talk, you should be accused and charged for inciting others to walk the streets with heavy guns. And what about the deaths, they didn't deserve to die and this bloody National Association that raised money… you see, they are also inciting the killing. When will this country close this Pandora box?

A matter of self-defense? In this case, pure BULLSHIT! Nobody forced this killer to go out at night, and parade with his gun. If you watched the video, this guy was looking for prey.

What stupid nonsense! Since when do you have to save the reputation of a killer.

Shame on you!

DONALD TRUMP'S NIECE SAYS 'THIS CRUEL AND TRAITOROUS' PRESIDENT DESERVES TO BE PROSECUTED:

President Donald Trump's niece says her uncle is "criminal, cruel and traitorous" and belongs in prison after he leaves the White House.

Mary Trump, a psychologist, author and outspoken critic of her estranged relative, rejects the notion that putting a former president on trial would deepen the nation's political divisions.

"If anybody deserves to be prosecuted and tried, it's Donald," she added." Otherwise, we just leave ourselves open to somebody who, believe it or not, is even worse than he is."

Mary Trump, the daughter of the president's elder brother, Fred Jr., announced this week that she is writing a follow-up to this summer's scathing bestseller about her uncle, "Too Much and Never Enough, How My Family Created the World's Most Dangerous Man."

America is "looking down the barrel of an explosion of psychological disorders" from the "trauma of living in a country in which the pandemic didn't just strike, but was completely mishandled," Mary Trump told the AP.

With a doctorate in clinical psychology, she argues that the U.S. needs to reimagine how it deals with mental health and mental illness, treating them with the same vigor as physical illnesses.

Mary Trump's critical writings come amid legal fights with her family.

Her uncle, Robert Trump, sued to block "Too Much and Never Enough" from hitting store shelves, citing a family agreement not to publish stories about core family members without their approval, but a court rejected that.

In September, Mary Trump sued the president, Robert Trump and their sister Maryanne Trump Barry, a retired federal judge, alleging that they cheated her out of millions of dollars while squeezing her out of the family business. Robert Trump died in August and the lawsuit is pending.

When her book about the family was published in July, Trump tweeted that Mary Trump was "a seldom seen niece who knows little about me, says untruthful things about my wonderful parents (who couldn't stand her!) and me," and violated a non-disclosure agreement.

The announcement of Mary Trump's second book came as her uncle continued to falsely insist, he won reelection but that the vote was rigged in favor of Democratic rival Joe Biden. The president spent the better part of the last month complaining about the results, dispatching a band of lawyers led by former New York City Mayor Rudy Giuliani to mount futile legal challenges.

Mary Trump said the president's post-election behavior "makes perfect sense," given his personality, psychology, and lifelong disdain for losers.

Full Coverage: Mary Trump.

"This is somebody who's never won legitimately in his life," she said. "But he's never lost either. Because in his view, winning is so important and he always deserves to win that it's OK to lie, cheat and steal."

Mary Trump said the president inherited his acerbic behavior from his father, Fred Trump, a real estate developer who died in 1999. She called her grandfather "a horrible human being who just reveled in other people's humiliation."

"It's not simply that Donald is horrible and incompetent and cruel, it's that he's been allowed to be," she said. "Every transgression that's gone on unpunished has been an opportunity for him to push the envelope even further. That's partially why we're going to see him smashing as much stuff on his way out the door as he can."

Mary Trump acknowledges that she has seen the president only sporadically over the last 20 years — she wrote in "Too Much and Never Enough" that he invited her to a family dinner at the White House in 2017 — but, she argues, "he hasn't changed at all." "I'm essentially looking at the same person I knew when I was growing up," she said.

No ex-president has ever been arrested after leaving office, but Mary Trump argues that shielding powerful people from punishment has historically harmed the country. She used Confederate General Robert E. Lee's post-war absolution as an example.

"I think it would be a tragedy if Donald and everybody who's enabled him and committed crimes with him are not held accountable," Mary Trump said. "It would make it impossible for this country to recover in the long term.".

For Trump and his gang, it's OK to lie, cheat and steal."

OPINIONS:

December 11, 2020

The biggest mistake was actually made four years ago, which can be explained but not, as it turns out, justified. On the eve of Election 2016, someone wrote that we'd survive as a nation no matter who won, Donald

Trump or Hillary Clinton. I did not say we'd be fine. Mere survival seemed a fairly safe bet and, so, I gambled all my chips on our system of checks and balances.

I had become convinced six weeks before Election Day in 2016 that Trump was going to win. This insight was based upon my familiarity with his base, the folks Clinton fatefully called "deplorables." But I thought we'd get through it okay. That proved to be a mistake.

No one could have predicted the coronavirus pandemic, which has taken nearly 295,000 American lives so far. In retrospect, it's not surprising that Trump mishandled matters during the early stages of the virus when swift, decisive actions might have made a difference. We've come to expect not just worse from him but the worst.

Not much could be worse than hosting superspreader events and refusing to wear a mask or urging people to not fear the virus because, after all, he caught it and was treated by the best doctors in the world. It isn't much of a leap from that kind of behavior to 49 percent of Americans saying they would not get the coronavirus vaccine if it were available today.

Republicans continue to stall essential covid-19 relief funding, while the amicus-brief signatories apparently would rather cling to a possible Trump run in 2024 than act with character and courage. Worst of all, people whose minds have been warped by lies, conspiracy theories and disinformation would rather risk death and/or harm to others and themselves rather than wear a mask for a few more weeks.

For Pete's sake, people: What is wrong with you?

What's wrong is Trump, was Trump, forever-will-be Trump. His overthrow-campaign is almost certainly doomed because there simply is no evidence to support his claims of voter fraud. Facts still matter. But the mess he'll leave behind in less than 40 days won't be tidied up soon.

THE ELECTORAL COLLEGE VOTES ARE CAST. IT'S ALL OVER.

December 14, 2020.

Remember all those terrible things Donald Trump was going to do? On November 3rd, he was going to foment violence at the polls; he was going to get Russia and China to launch cyberattacks on his behalf; he was going to get rogue state legislators to sabotage the electoral college; he was going to take his voter fraud case all the way to the Supreme Court, and he was going to win.

And then he didn't. The 2020 election went smoothly. The results were clear and decisive. Trump cried fraud, as expected, and then lost nearly 60 court cases trying to prove it. Election officials did their jobs. States certified their results. And today, after six weeks of Trump's best efforts to sabotage democracy, the Electoral College is voting to confirm his defeat.

And yet so many of us still fear this person as if he was invincible. If he fires a Pentagon official, we worry he's "plotting a military coup." If he tweets angrily at an election bureaucrat, we worry he's overturning the election. Since his defeat, Trump's supporters have retreated into a world of denial and conspiracy theories.

Until the transition began, I myself worried that Trump would somehow get the Supreme Court to reverse the election for him. I never dreamed he'd bring a case so half-baked, and bungle it so badly, that the Supreme Court wouldn't even hear it. He'd been bluffing all along, he was never a powerful fascist who had bent the judiciary to his will. Even on the left, he had us all conned.

As we try to make sense of what happened these past four years, maybe it's more comforting to think of Trump as an evil wizard than as a pathetic faker with debatable mental health problems. Maybe it makes it less embarrassing that our country ever succumbed to him in the first place if that is so. But in the end, he appears to be exactly the same person who rode down that tacky golden escalator five years ago, shrill, ignorant, unprepared, and ridiculous. The fact that we elected this person president even once is a national humiliation.

On the other hand, it turns out America has more strength left in its institutions than we thought. Trump did everything he could to attack our democratic system, but the system held, in some cases, thanks to members of his own party. Brad Raffensperger, Georgia's Republican secretary of state, oversaw his state's election with honesty and integrity, despite receiving death threats from the right. Pennsylvania's Judge Matthew Brann, a Republican, delivered the most epic takedown of Rudy Giuliani's "not a fraud" fraud case. There are many others. They all deserve credit and commendation.

So maybe we're readier than we think for whatever Trump does next. He may try to start a TV network for his own propaganda — if he has time between the lawsuits he'll be fending off. And he seems likely to run for president again in 2024, which means he'll have four years to prepare. So, we'll see.

AFTER THE SUPREME COURT DISMISSES TEXAS CASE, TRUMP SAYS HIS EFFORTS TO CHALLENGE ELECTION RESULTS ARE 'NOT OVER':

DECEMBER 13, 2020

President Trump signaled that he will continue to challenge the results of the 2020 election even after the Electoral College meets Monday in most state capitols to cast votes solidifying Joe Biden's victory.

In a Fox News interview that aired Sunday morning, Trump repeated his false claims of election fraud and said his legal team will continue to pursue challenges, despite the Supreme Court's recent dismissal of a long-shot bid to overturn the results in four states that Biden won.

"No, it's not over," Trump told host Brian Kilmeade in the interview, which was taped Saturday at the Army-Navy game at the U.S. Military Academy. "We keep going, and we're going to continue to go forward. We have numerous local cases. We're, you know, in some of the states that got rigged and robbed from us. We won every one of them. We won Pennsylvania. We won Michigan. We won Georgia by a lot."

Trump lost those swing states and others to Biden, who won 306 electoral votes to Trump's 232.

The electors are expected to follow the vote of their state. After voting, they must sign six certificates, one of which is submitted to the president of the Senate, currently Vice President Pence. Both chambers of Congress, the House and the Senate, will meet in joint session on January 6th to officially count the votes.

Once the voting is complete, Biden is expected to deliver remarks Monday night in Wilmington, Del., on "the electoral college vote certification and the strength and resilience of our democracy," according to his transition team.

"I think the campaign is taking our arguments that we tried to get in front of the U.S. Supreme Court, they are now going to take those, I think, state by state," Texas Attorney General Ken Paxton (R), who spearheaded the lawsuit that was dismissed by the Supreme Court, said in an interview on "Sunday Morning Futures" on Fox. Paxton added that "they are legitimately good constitutional arguments that don't depend on actually proving every little instance of fraud."

Attorney General William P. Barr, who was appointed by Trump, said earlier this month that he has "not seen fraud on a scale that could have effected a different outcome in the election," undercutting Trump's claims of widespread and significant voting irregularities.

Some Republicans have worried that Trump's efforts to undermine the legitimacy of the presidential election could deter some GOP voters from going to the polls January 5th in Georgia, which is holding two Senate runoffs that could determine which party controls the upper chamber.

Sen. David Perdue (R-Ga.), who along with Sen. Kelly Loeffler (R-Ga.) who is running for reelection, urged Republicans to cast their ballot, even if they don't trust the system.

Perdue is facing Democrat Jon Ossoff, while Loeffler is running against the Rev. Raphael Warnock (D).

Rep. Cedric L. Richmond (D-La.), who will soon be joining the Biden administration as a senior adviser, on Sunday, played down the significance of Republicans' refusal to acknowledge Biden's win. In an interview on "Face the Nation," Richmond argued that "this is just a small portion of the Republican conference" that is hesitant to publicly recognize Biden's victory "because they are scared of [Trump's] Twitter power and other things."

"They recognize Joe Biden's victory," Richmond said. "All of America recognizes Joe Biden's victory. I talk to Republican members of Congress all the time, and they say one thing privately; they say another thing publicly."

November 30, 2020

President Trump did something this weekend that would have been unimaginable two years ago: he attacked Georgia Gov. Brian Kemp (R) as being soft on voter fraud.

Yes, that Brian Kemp.

"The governor's done nothing," Trump complained Sunday on Fox News Channel. "He's done absolutely nothing. I'm ashamed that I endorsed him."

Trump then tweeted about Kemp on Monday morning, calling him the "hapless Governor of Georgia" and urging him to overrule Georgia Secretary of State Brad Raffensperger (R).

From the start of his tenure as secretary of state until his election as governor, Kemp purged about 1.4 million voters from Georgia's rolls, with Democratic opponent Stacey Abrams long questioning his legitimacy because of it. After he won the 2018 race for governor, the newly Democratic-controlled

U.S. House sent letters to him and his successor, Raffensperger, saying they were investigating the situation.

As with Kemp, when Raffensperger was first running for secretary of state, voter fraud was a key focus of the GOP primary and beyond. At the time, Raffensperger repeatedly said his goal was "to make sure only Americans vote in our elections."

In April, with mail ballots expanding amid the coronavirus outbreak — in a move somewhat similar to Kemp's a decade prior — Raffensperger launched a task force to root out potential fraud. The state Democratic Party at the time called it "state-sponsored voter intimidation."

"At the end of the day, the voter was responsible, and the voters knew what they were doing," Raffensperger said. "A double voter knows exactly what they are doing, diluting the votes of each and every voter that follows the law."

Many Republicans have been pretty quiet about Trump's allegations. But perhaps the bigger point is that others who have shown a real desire to focus on alleged fraud have been unwilling to go along with the charade. And they've been doing it undoubtedly knowing full well that these Trump nasty-grams awaited them.

TO THE TRUMP SUPPORTER:

December 28, 2020

What is wrong with you people! It's over, do you understand? It's over, over and over!

These people are living in a fantasy world. There is something wrong with these people, mostly the supporters. They should be making an appointment with their doctors in order to get scanned, just to make sure they don't have a tumor in their brains.

Trump never put in place a coronavirus program.

CHAPTER NINETEEN

....

HERE ARE 76 OF DONALD TRUMP'S
MANY CAMPAIGNS PROMISE:

Jan. 22, 2016

These are the main ones, but there was a grand total of 282 campaign promises according to the Washington post, in November 2016.

Most presidential candidates are careful to not promise too much on the campaign trail. That's not at all the case for Republican front-runner Donald Trump. Listed below are 76 things that Trump said he would do if elected or predicted would occur as a result of his election. If he were to win the White House, Trump promised to:

1. Build a wall along the southern US border taller than the arenas where Trump holds his rallies, taller than any ladder and one foot taller than the Great Wall of China. This "artistically beautiful" wall will be constructed out of hardened concrete, rebar and steel, and it will be "the greatest wall that you've ever seen" -- so great that the nation will likely one day name it "The Trump Wall."

2. Make Mexico pay for the wall. If Mexico refuses, then the United States will impound all remittance payments taken from the wages of illegal immigrants, cut foreign aid, institute tariffs, cancel visas for Mexican business leaders and diplomats, and increase fees for visas, border-crossing cards and port use.

3. "If I become president, we're all going to be saying 'Merry Christmas' again."

4. Get rid of Common Core because it's "a disaster" and a "very bad thing." Trump says he wants to give local school districts more control and might even eliminate the Department of Education.

5. The Environmental Protection Agency might also disappear.

6. Get rid of Obamacare and replace it with something "terrific" that is "so much better, so much better, so much better."

7. Knock down the regulatory walls between states for health insurance, making plans available nationally instead of regionally.

8. Rebuild the country's aging infrastructure -- especially bridges and airports that look like they belong in a third-world country -- for one-third of what the United States is currently paying for such projects.

9. Save Medicare, Medicaid and Social Security without cutting benefits.

10. Defund Planned Parenthood.

11. "I will take care of women, and I have great respect for women. I do cherish women, and I will take care of women."

12. Frequently use the term "radical Islamic terrorism."

13. Temporarily ban most foreign Muslims from entering the United States "until our country's representatives can figure out what is going on." Trump would allow exceptions for dignitaries, business people, athletes and others who have "proven" themselves.

14. Bar Syrian refugees from entering the country and kick out any who are already living here. Trump says wealthy Persian Gulf nations like Saudi Arabia should pay to set up a heavily guarded "safe zone" in Syria.

15. Heavily surveil mosques in the United States. Trump said he's open to the idea of closing some mosques.

16. Create a database of Syrian refugees. Trump hasn't ruled out creating a database of Muslims in the country.

17. Never take a vacation while serving as president.

18. Prosecute Hillary Clinton for her use of a private e-mail server while serving as secretary of state.

19. Make medical marijuana widely available to patients, and allow states to decide if they want to fully legalize pot or not.

20. Stop spending money on space exploration until the United States can fix its potholes. Encourage private space-exploration companies to expand.

21. Pick Supreme Court justices who are "really great legal scholars."

22. Ensure that Iowa continues to host the nation's first presidential nominating contest.

23. Strengthen the military so that it's "so big and so strong and so great" that "nobody's going to mess with it.

24. Be unpredictable. "No one is going to touch us, because I'm so unpredictable."

25. Allow Russia to deal with the Islamic State in Syria and/or work with Russian President Vladimir Putin to wipe out shared enemies.

26. "Bomb the s--- out of ISIS." Also bomb oil fields controlled by the Islamic State, then seize the oil and give the profits to military veterans who were wounded while fighting.

27. Target and kill the relatives of terrorists.

28. Shut down parts of the Internet so that Islamic State terrorists cannot use it to recruit American children.

29. Bring back waterboarding, which the Obama administration considers torture. Trump said he was willing to use interrogation techniques that go even further than waterboarding. Even if such tactics don't work, "they deserve it anyway, for what they're doing."

30. Leave troops in Afghanistan because it's such "a mess." Protect Israel. And increase U.S. military presence in the East and South China Seas.

31. Find an "out" clause in the Iran deal and then "totally" renegotiate the whole thing.

32. "I promise I will never be in a bicycle race. That I can tell you." (This promise is connected to criticism of Secretary of State John F. Kerry, who was injured while riding a bicycle amid the Iran negotiations.)

33. Refuse to call Iran's leader by his preferred title. "I guarantee you that I will never be calling him the Supreme Leader... I'll say, 'Hey baby, how ya doing?' I will never call him the Supreme Leader."

34. Negotiate the release of all U.S. prisoners held in Iran before taking office. (Five hostages were recently released, including Washington Post reporter Jason Rezaian; Trump has taken some credit for this.)

35. Oppose the killing of journalists: "I hate some of these people, but I would never kill them."

36. Find great generals -- like the next Gen. Patton or Gen. MacArthur -- and not allow them to go onto television news shows to explain their military strategy: "I don't want my generals being interviewed; I want my generals kicking a--." Trump likes generals who are rough, foul-mouthed and beloved by their troops.

37. Drop that "dirty, rotten traitor" Bowe Bergdahl out of an airplane into desolate Afghanistan without a parachute.

38. Fire "the corrupt and incompetent" leaders of the U.S. Department of Veterans Affairs and dramatically reform the agency.

39. Invest more heavily in programs that help military veterans transition back to civilian life, including job training and placement services. Also increase funding for the treatment of post-traumatic stress disorder, traumatic brain injuries and mental health issues.

40. Bring back jobs from China -- and Mexico, Japan and elsewhere.

41. "I will be the greatest jobs president that God ever created." Trump says cities like Reno, Nev., will "be a big fat beautiful beneficiary" of these new jobs.

42. Students at Wofford College in South Carolina, where Trump attended a town hall meeting, will all have jobs at graduation.

43. Aggressively challenge China's power in the world by declaring the country a currency manipulator, adopting a "zero tolerance policy on intellectual property theft and forced technology transfer" and cracking down on China's "lax labor and environmental standards."

44. Rather than throw the Chinese president a state dinner, buy him "a McDonald's hamburger and say we've got to get down to work."

45. Replace "free trade" with "fair trade." Gather together the "smartest negotiators in the world," assign them each a country and renegotiate all foreign trade deals.

46. Put billionaire hedge fund manager Carl Icahn in charge of trade negotiations with China and Japan, and pick an ambassador to Japan who is "a killer," unlike the current ambassador, Caroline Kennedy.

47. Tell Ford Motor Co.'s president that unless he cancels plans to build a massive plant in Mexico, the company will face a 35 percent tax on cars imported back into the United States. Trump is confident he can get this done before taking office. (Last year he incorrectly said this had already happened.)

48. Force Nabisco to once again make Oreos in the United States. And bully Apple into making its "damn computers" and other products here.

49. Impose new taxes on many imports into the country. Numbers thrown around have included 32 percent, 34 percent and 35 percent.

50. Grow the nation's economy by at least 6 percent.

51. Reduce the $18 trillion national debt by "vigorously eliminating waste, fraud and abuse in the federal government, ending redundant government programs and growing the economy to increase tax revenues."

52. Cut the budget by 20 percent by simply renegotiating.

53. Get rid of the Dodd-Frank Wall Street Reform and Consumer Protection Act.

54. Simplify the U.S. tax code and reduce the number of tax brackets from seven to four. The highest earners would pay a 25 percent tax. The corporate tax rate would fall to 15 percent. Eliminate the "marriage penalty" for taxpayers and get rid of the alternate minimum tax.

55. No longer charge income tax to single individuals earning less than $25,000 per year or couples earning less than $50,000. These people will, however, be required to file a one-page form with the Internal Revenue Service that states: "I win."

56. Ensure that Americans can still afford to golf.

57. Allow corporations a one-time window to transfer money being held overseas, charging a much-reduced 10 percent tax.

58. Get rid of most corporate tax loopholes or incentives, but continue to allow taxpayers to deduct mortgage interest and charitable donations from their taxes.

59. On his first day in office, Trump would get rid of gun-free zones at military bases and in schools.

60. Use "common sense" to fix the mental health system and prevent mass shootings. Find ways to arm more of the "good guys" like him who can take out the "sickos." Get rid of bans on certain types of guns and magazines so that "good, honest people" can own the guns of their choice.

61. Impose a minimum sentence of five years in federal prison for any violent felon who commits a crime using a gun, with no chance for parole or early release.

62. Fix the background check system used when purchasing guns to ensure states are properly uploading criminal and health records.

63. Allow concealed-carry permits to be recognized in all 50 states.

64. Sign an executive order calling for the death penalty for anyone found guilty of killing a police officer.

65. Provide more funding for police training.

66. And provide more funding for drug treatment, especially for heroin addicts.
67. On the first day in office, terminate President Obama's executive orders related to immigration. This includes getting rid of "sanctuary cities" that Trump says have become refuges for criminals.
68. Deport the almost 11 million immigrants illegally living in the United States.
69. Triple the number of U.S. Immigration and Customs Enforcement officers.
70. Continue to allow lowly paid foreign workers to come to the United States on temporary works visas because Trump says they are the only ones who want to pick grapes.
71. End birthright citizenship.
72. Say things that are politically incorrect, because the country does not have time to waste with political correctness.
73. Republican Presidential candidate Donald Trump said, "We can't worry about being politically correct," in remarks to a Police Association.

    Make America great again -- and strong again, as it has become too weak.
74. Be a cheerleader for America and bring the country's spirit back. "Take the brand of the United States and make it great again."
75. Bring back the American Dream.
76. Start winning again. "We're going to win so much -- win after win after win -- that you're going to be begging me: 'Please, Mr. President, let us lose once or twice. We can't stand it anymore.' And I'm going to say: 'No way. We're going to keep winning. We're never going to lose. We're never, ever going to lose.'"

Trump never put in place a coronavirus program.

CHAPTER TWENTY

CORONAVIRUS: FRANCE'S FIRST KNOWN CASE IN EUROPE WAS IN DECEMBER: 2019

But the virus covid-19, first case was in Wuhan China, November 17,2019.

Arrived in France almost a month earlier than previously thought, a patient treated in a hospital near Paris on December 27, 2019 for suspected pneumonia, actually had the coronavirus, his doctor said.

This means the virus may have arrived in Europe almost a month earlier than previously thought.

Dr. Yves Cohen said that a swab taken at the time was recently tested, and came back positive for Covid-19.

The patient, who has since recovered, said he had no idea where he caught the virus as he had not travelled abroad.

THE COVID-19 FAILURES BY DONALD TRUMP:

It's an oversimplification to state that President Trump is responsible for more than 300,000 deaths. We should have been one of the developed world's best performers, instead of being among the worst. Much of the difference between how the United States should have fared and how it actually did can be chalked up to the ways that Trump bungled the pandemic; denying the seriousness of covid-19 and spreading misinformation about treatments; turning minor precautions such as masks into political litmus tests; ignoring his own scientists. But this president, instead, concentrated on organizing rallies in order to preserve his presidency and also, played golf.

Man in France may be the country's earliest COVID-19 case

May 7 2020

French man discovers he may be country's 1st COVID-19 case

PARIS -- For Amirouche Hammar, it started with a phone call from a doctor at his local hospital in a Paris suburb. "When he told me the news that I was positive with COVID-19, frankly it shocked me a little," Hammar told ABC News. The 43-year-old had found out ten days ago that he was infected with the virus back in December, over a month before the first cases were recorded in Europe.

TRUMP IS HIDING FROM THE COUNTRY WHILE IT'S ON FIRE:

Both the President and Bob Woodward knew this for months and kept it from the public.

Woodward knew the truth behind the administration's deadly bungling— and worse—he saved it for his book, which will be released to wild acclaim and huge profits after nearly 200,000 Americans died.

Another day, another book, another reason to believe that the American republic was not served well by the election of a vulgar talking yam. First came John Bolton. Then came presidential niece Mary Trump, measuring her uncle for a straitjacket. Then came Michael Cohen, who cops to shaking down Jerry Falwell for a valuable endorsement. And now come Bob Woodward one of the stone heads on journalism's Easter Island, marking the president as a liar on, among other things, the topic of the pandemic.

"This will be the biggest national security threat you face in your presidency," national security adviser Robert O'Brien told Trump, according to a new book by Washington Post associate editor Bob Woodward. "This is going to be the roughest thing you face. Matthew Pottinger, the deputy national security adviser, agreed. He told the president that after reaching contacts in China, it was evident that the world faced a health emergency on par with the flu pandemic of 1918, which killed an estimated 50 million people worldwide.

Ten days later, Trump called Woodward and revealed that he thought the situation was far direr than what he had been saying publicly. "You just breathe the air and that's how it's passed," Trump said in a February 7th call. "And so that's a very tricky one. That's a very delicate one. It's also more deadly than even your strenuous flu...This is deadly stuff," the president repeated for emphasis.

Trump admitted to Woodward on March 19th that he deliberately minimized the danger. "I always wanted to play it down," the president said.

Let us be clear. Both of these men knew before anyone else that the president was lying in public about the most serious public health crisis in a century. Both of these men knew before anyone else how serious that threat was, and how deadly the disease could be. Both of these men knew before anyone else that a potential disaster was not only possible, but increasingly likely. Both of these men knew!

The President knew and lied because he wanted to get re-elected. Woodward knew and kept it to himself because he had a book to sell. Who's worse? Far too measured a choice for this reporter, but, as someone who in his own small way practices the same craft as Bob Woodward, I have to wonder how Woodward could watch the president lie for six months as the body count rocketed skyward without his conscience tearing out his heart.

The book is based in part on eighteen on-the-record interviews Woodward conducted with the president between December and July.

The interviews with the president were conducted on the record. As early as January, Woodward could have broken a huge story quoting the President himself about how the President was lying to the public and risking public health. Maybe it would have forced a change of policy that would have saved lives. Worse—he saved it for his book, which will be released to wild acclaim and huge profits after nearly 200,000 Americans died because neither Donald Trump nor Bob Woodward wanted to risk anything substantial to keep the country informed.

For reasons of their own—venal, selfish, inexcusable reasons, all of them—both Donald Trump and Bob Woodward shirked the duties of their respective occupations and, eventually, hundreds of thousands of Americans may be dead in part because they did, the shame of this should be everlasting. Bob Woodward's nonfeasance in the face of this disaster should stand with Walter Duranty's covering for Stalin in the matter of the Ukrainian famine as eternal embarrassments to journalism and to simple humanity.

Shame on you, Mister Monster

TRUMP THE SPECIALIST IN
HOUSEHOLD DISINFECTANT:

After Donald Trump's ridiculous and dangerous suggestion in April 2019 that household disinfectants injected into people's bodies, should do the job. Even a child of 8 years old would not say such of thing, but remember that he said he knew everything, and he doesn't trust the scientists.

Trump, as a person and politician, is riddled with flaws. But he also has an ignominious superpower: He is completely unencumbered by the truth, the need to tell it or accept it. He will do and say anything that he believes will profit him. Furthermore, he has no great guiding principles. He is not bound by ethics or morals. This guy has no Boundary.

When the "Access Hollywood" tapes, on which Trump bragged about groping, also said to: grab them by the pussy, they like that, and sexually assaulting women, came out, Republicans were worried. They began to openly reject him. Some called for him to drop out of the race.

"But the image of Republicans running for the exits, a month before a presidential election, is as extraordinary as a party's nominee using vulgar, violent language that seems to reduce an entire gender to sexual anatomy. And this time, no amount of spin seems sufficient to control the damage Trump has wrought."

No one is as shameless a showman as Trump is. He was in survival mode. Nothing was too far; nothing was too crass.

At the debate, Trump dismissed his comments as locker room talk and denied that he had ever done the things he himself boasted about doing on the tape. As Trump said on the debate stage: "Nobody has more respect for women than I do."

Don't fall prey to false hope that defeating Trump will be easy, that his horrifically incompetent response to the coronavirus has doomed him. It hasn't. Trump will fight with everything he has to the bitter end to stay in power. He will never admit any fault. He will lie and lie and lie and lie some more. And the people who support him will stick with him every step of the way.

Be prepared for Trump to do anything and everything to win reelection in November. A man who can dismiss a recording of his own voice bragging about assaulting women is capable of anything.

As you will see later, at the end of December 2020, and the beginning of

January 2021. Trump and his traitors will, undermine our democracy, and attempt a "coup d'état". <u>Shame on them. Remember their faces.</u>

THE 6-YEAR-OLD TRUMP BRAIN: APRIL 24 2020

Trump said on Thursday that scientists should explore whether inserting ultraviolet light or disinfectant into the bodies of people infected with the coronavirus might help them clear the disease.

"Is there a way we can do something like that by injection, inside, or almost a cleaning?" Trump asked. "It would be interesting to check that."

"I do think that disinfectant on the hands could have a very good effect,"

Trump stood in the White House briefing room and suggested that injecting disinfectant into the body could possibly cure the virus

After this insane and dangerous remark, states saw a spike in poison control calls including using bleach on food products, applying household cleaning and disinfectant products to skin and inhaling or ingesting cleaners and disinfectants."

Trump pushed the use of hydroxychloroquine, without sufficient scientific backing, he doesn't trust the scientists.

IT IS WHAT IT IS: TRUMP CONTINUES TO DISMISS SEVERITY OF THE VIRUS AS OUTBREAK WORSENS:

Washington, dc - July 16 2020:

President Trump continued to propagate his long-held belief that the coronavirus pandemic is overhyped, incorrectly asserting that the U.S. has the lowest mortality rate of any country and that most non-fatal cases are harmless.

KEY FACTS

"It is what it is. Take a look at Europe," Trump said concerning the fact that the U.S. is seeing nearly 1,000 coronavirus deaths a day, despite saying he takes the virus "very seriously."

Trump also dismissed the country's 75,000 daily cases, asserting "many of those cases heal automatically."

"Trump also stood by what he said in January that the virus would "disappear," telling Wallace, "I'll be right eventually," and claiming, "I've been right probably more than anybody else Ah Ah.

Trump incorrectly claimed that the U.S. had "one of the lowest, maybe the lowest mortality rate anywhere in the world," citing a chart that omitted many countries with lower mortality rates, including Russia.

Trump also reiterated his opposition to a mask mandate, saying he wants Americans to "have a certain freedom," adding that "masks cause problems too."

NEWS PEG

Trump's abstinence towards stricter measures to mitigate the spread of violence may be causing his woes in the election. The Fox News poll, which put former Vice President Joe Biden up 8 points over Trump, had Trump's approval on the virus at 43%, compared to 56% disapproval. Asked who they would trust to do a better job on coronavirus, 51% of voters said Biden while just 34% said Trump.

Yes "have a certain freedom," That's what he previously said. Maybe we should say a number of deaths instead.

June 25 2020

The coronavirus pandemic is still raging in this country. In fact, in more than 20 states, the number of cases is rising. More than 120,000 Americans have died from the virus. This country has a quarter of all the cases in the world even though it makes up only 4% of the world population.

Things are so bad here that the European Union, which has lowered its rate, is considering banning U.S. citizens when it reopens its borders.

This situation is abysmal, and it would not have been so bad if President Donald Trump had not intentionally neglected his duty to protect American citizens.

From the beginning, Trump used every opportunity to downplay the virus, claiming in February, "Looks like by April, you know, in theory, when it gets a little warmer, it miraculously goes away." Well, we're now in June, summer. It's not just warm, it's hot. And the cases in the hottest states — those in the South and Southwest — are surging.

Trump has consistently been resistant to testing, falsely claiming that an increase in testing is somehow linked to an increase in cases. But in fact, the more you test, the more you are able to control the virus by identifying, isolating and treating the infected, thereby reducing the spread of the virus.

But Trump believes that to reveal the true extent of the virus's presence in this country would make him look bad. So, more people get sick and more people die.

He said in May: "When you test, you have a case. When you test, you find something wrong with people. If we didn't do any testing, we would have very few cases. They don't want to write that. It's common sense. We test much more."

What Trump is truly saying here is, let people get sick without proper surveillance. He is saying, let them suffer out of sight. He is saying, some will die, but so what.

At his rally in Tulsa, Oklahoma, Trump took a step deeper into the darkness, saying: "When you do testing to that extent you're going to find more people, you're going to find cases. So, I said to my people, 'Slow the testing down, please.' They test and they test. We got tests for people who don't know what's going on."

If there actually was a slowdown, it allowed the virus to spread and more people to get sick and die.

Trump stood in the White House briefing room and suggested that injecting disinfectant into the body could possibly cure the virus, known officially as SARS-CoV-2. After this insane and dangerous remark, states saw a spike in poison control calls. A survey for the Centers for Disease Control and Prevention found that a third of Americans were "engaged in non-recommended high-risk practices with the intent of preventing SARS-CoV-2 transmission, including using bleach on food products, applying household cleaning and disinfectant products to skin and inhaling or ingesting cleaners and disinfectants."

Trump pushed the use of hydroxychloroquine, without sufficient scientific backing, to prevent transmission of the virus or to treat infection, even saying that he took a dose of it himself. The Food and Drug Administration approved an emergency use of the drug for COVID-19. The federal government began to stockpile it. States requested doses from the federal stockpile.

During the height of the crisis, some states experienced a shortage of ventilators to treat gravely ill patients. Trump claimed that the Obama administration had left no ventilators in the national stockpile, that there were "empty cupboards." In truth, his own administration confirmed a few days ago that 16,660 ventilators were available for use when Trump took office and in March, the Trump administration outrageously distributed only 10,760 of them as of Tuesday.

Trump even mocked the wearing of masks, which experts say is a proven way to reduce virus transmission.

Now Trump is having another mask-optional rally with yelling people sitting and standing close together, a blatant violation of social distancing rules.

It seems that in every possible way, Trump has willfully and arrogantly put more Americans at risk of getting sick and dying, and the results have been inevitable: More Americans got sick and died.

At this point, how can we not label Trump a killer of American citizens by negligence, ignorance and incompetence?

Now on Christmas day 2020, 6 months later, you have 330,000 deaths in the USA. So, like some sources said in the past, 89% of those people could have been saved.

Trump never put in place a coronavirus program

CHAPTER TWENTY ONE

....

TRUMP IS LEADING OUR COUNTRY
TO DESTRUCTION:

We are experiencing "Groundhog Day" in America — but the result isn't sweet and funny as in the 1993 Bill Murray film. It's sick and psychopathic.

We have long had mass shootings in the United States because of the ready availability of guns. All the way back to 1966 when a former Marine and student mounted the clock tower at the University of Texas in Austin and killed 14 people with a rifle.

Americans were horrified, and rightly so; but things have gotten a whole lot worse since then. The 1966 attack is now tied for 11th place in the list of mass shootings here. Eight of the 10 worst modern mass shootings occurred in the past decade, and Saturday's attack at a Walmart in El Paso, which killed 20 people, is now the eighth worst in U.S. history.

The deadliest mass shooting — which left 58 people dead in Las Vegas — came less than two years ago. The second deadliest — 50 dead at a nightclub in Orlando — just three years ago.

This trend of mass shootings has intersected with another trend: the rise of white-supremacist ideology. Nine people shot to death in an African-American church in Charleston, S.C., in 2015. One killed with a car and 19 injured at a white supremacist rally in Charlottesville, in 2017.

Eleven shots to death in a Pittsburgh synagogue in 2018, and two more killed that year at a yoga studio in Tallahassee, Fla. One killed and three wounded in a synagogue in Poway, Calif., this year. Three killed just last week at a garlic festival in Gilroy, Calif. (although there is dispute over whether that shooting was motivated by white supremacist ideology).

In El Paso, a city with an 80 percent Hispanic population, the suspect is believed to have released a manifesto online in which he announced: "This attack is a response to the Hispanic invasion of Texas."

Let me help you out, Mr. President. I suggest that, until we figure out what the hell is going on, you institute a total and complete shutdown of your inciting, racist rhetoric. I also suggest that, until we figure out what the hell is going on, you call for a total and complete shutdown of sales of assault weapons such as the one used by the El Paso killer and for a total and complete regulation of the sale of handguns in America.

That's what you need to do, Mr. President, if you care at all about the well-being of the people of America. Yet you continue to spew hatred. On the very morning of the El Paso attack, you twice retweeted the notorious British hate-monger Katie Hopkins, spewing venom against Muslims. Last month, you told congresswomen of color to "go back" to where they came from. And in May, at a rally in Florida, you demanded, "How do you stop these people?" meaning undocumented immigrants. Someone shouted, "Shoot them." Instead of chastising this hate-monger, you chuckled and said, to loud cheers, "Only in the Panhandle can you get away with that stuff."

Whether you know it or not, Mr. President, you are recklessly enflaming the sickos of America. The very last line of the manifesto attributed to the alleged El Paso gunman could have come straight out of one of your speeches: "I am honored to head the fight to reclaim my country from destruction."

You also refuse, Mr. President, to address the easy availability of weapons of war in America. Assault rifles are the preferred weapons of mass shooters, and yet you refuse to ask Congress to ban their sale — or, even better, to buy back all of the existing assault weapons, as was done in Australia in 1996 after the worst mass shooting in that country's history. Australia hasn't seen such a massacre since. The United States, by contrast, mass shootings just this has had 249 years.

TRUMP CARES MORE ABOUT THE STOCK MARKET THAN HUMANS:

March 23 2020

Until Monday morning, President Trump's most horrifying utterance with regards to the coronavirus was his sarcastic reaction to news that Sen. Mitt Romney (R-Utah), whose wife has multiple sclerosis and therefore is in the high-risk category for infection, was self-isolating due to potential exposure to the coronavirus. "Gee, that's too bad," Trump snaked about his political rival. As bad as that was — mocking the possible life-threatening illness of others — he managed to top that with a truly horrifying tweet:

Donald J. Trump March 23 2020

The cure — social distancing — has been imposed to save thousands of lives. But in Trump's mind, the resulting economic slowdown and bear market from those measures are worse than a potentially catastrophic death toll. That's the only reasonable interpretation for his outburst, which coincides with the reporting from the New York Times that, "at the White House, in recent days, there has been a growing sentiment that medical experts were allowed to set policy that has hurt the economy, and there has been a push to find ways to let people start returning to work."

For Trump and many in his party, what matters most is money. ("Some Republican lawmakers also pleaded with the White House to find ways to restart the economy, as financial markets continue to slide and job losses for April could be in the millions.") To them, letting medical experts set policy to combat a pandemic is a serious error. "Worse" than the deaths of thousands of Americans, in the minds of the narcissistic president, is the chance that his reelection could be impaired by bad economic numbers. Does it dawn on him that thousands of dead Americans might reflect poorly on him as well?

Here we see the gap between Trump's pecuniary and political interests (which he thinks depend entirely on the stock market) and the experts trying to get us to do things that would prevent greater loss of life. Attacking political rivals and congratulating himself on his response (and forcing recitals of praise from advisers) — tells us that even a pandemic, in his mind, is all about him.

CORONAVIRUS: THE FIRST THREE MONTHS AS IT HAPPENED:

March 28 2020

President Trump and others have repeatedly downplayed the threat of covid-19 by comparing its lethality to seasonal influenza, which claims tens of thousands of lives in the United States every year. But covid-19 may be many more times as lethal for an infected person than the seasonal flu.

Nearly 400,000 Americans have now died from covid-19. It took 12 weeks for the death toll to rise from 200,000 to 300,000. The death toll leaped from 300,000 to almost 400,000 in less than five weeks.

It took just over a month for the U.S. coronavirus death toll to climb from 300,000 to nearly 400,000

This is the quickest pace of 100,000 deaths since the pandemic began.

Source: Post reporting and Johns Hopkins University

Nearly 400,000 Americans have now died from covid-19. It took 12 weeks for the death toll to rise from 200,000 to 300,000. The death toll leaped from 300,000 to almost 400,000 in less than five weeks.

It took just over a month for the U.S. coronavirus death toll to climb from 300,000 to nearly 400,000

This is the quickest pace of 100,000 deaths since the pandemic began.

Source: Post reporting and Johns Hopkins University

Trump never put in place a coronavirus program.

CHAPTER TWENTY TWO

....

DONALD TRUMP'S PRESIDENCY: A SHOCKING LIST OF THINGS HE'S DONE:

OCTOBER 6 -2020

Did not get Mexico or Congress to pay for the border wall. Taunted North Korea. Met privately with Russian president. Did not release tax returns.

He is responsible for a lot of madness and destruction during his Presidency. I have, below, highlighted the most important.

White House: he did not convince his wife to move into the White House bedroom. He maintained ownership of his companies: he doubled membership fees for his Mar-a-Lago beach resort. He warned the inauguration crowd of foreign attempts to "ravage" the United States. He told his first lie in office, describing the modestly sized inauguration crowd as the largest in history when he saw pictures of his predecessor's larger crowd; he urged his press secretary to repeat the crowd description as history's largest; an "alternative fact", he did not release tax returns.

On January 20, 2017, on inauguration day, Trump said he was going to "drain the swamp". We'll see... And he was the subject of an historic event on the day following the inauguration. With the largest protests in the nation's history organized against him by members of the female sex about which he had previously advised grabbing them "by the pussy".

He signed an order on January 25, 2017 to build a wall between Mexico and the United States that he claimed Mexico would pay for; he learned that the Mexican president cancelled his meeting with him and would not pay for the wall. He spoke on the phone on January 28, 2017 with the prime minister of the U.S. ally, Malcolm Turnbull from Australia and hung up on him. He also spoke on January 28, 2017 on the phone with the president of

the U.S. adversary, Vladimir Putin from Russia. He signed an order banning
refugees on grounds of security on January 27, 2017. He signed an order
banning travelers from seven Muslim-majority countries also on grounds of
security on January 2017, and he fired the acting attorney general, Sally Yates
on January 30, 2017.

He heard a Black reporter, April Ryan, on February 16, 2017 ask if he
would meet with a Congressional Black Caucus and asked her, "You want to
set up the meeting? Are they friends of yours?" He declared free press "the
enemy of the American people."

On February 10, 2017 he greeted the Japanese Prime Minister Shinzo
Abe and shook hands for 19 seconds. He tweeted that he would bring the
border-wall price "WAY DOWN." And, finally, he did not get Mexico to pay
anything for the wall.

On June 7, 2017 he told the FBI director: James Comey "I hope you can
let this go." about the investigation into a national security adviser lying about
his communication with the Russian ambassador. He held a rally; he attacked
"dishonest media." He gave a speech and threatened to "do something" about
the media. He blocked press members from press briefings and skipped press
dinners.

Trump tweeted on March 4, 2017 that his predecessor Barack Obama
tapped his phone. He attacked a judge for "unprecedented overreach" for
blocking travel ban. He heard GOP congressman call on him to release tax
returns and he did not release said tax returns.

He used the State Department website to advertise his Mar-a-Lago resort.
He allowed [pats her lower hips with both hands] his daughter to meet with
the president of China when he heard that her company had won trademarks
from the government of China; he heard public outrage, allowed his daughter
to sit in on a meeting with the German Chancellor.

He tweeted that the media should not investigate his campaign's links
with Russia but should investigate is predecessor tapping his phone. He
tweeted that North Korea was "looking for trouble"; he also tweeted that his
relationship with Russia "will work out fine."

On April 15, 2017 he heard tens of thousands of protesters demand
that he releases his tax returns but he did not release them. His wife had to
prompt him to put his hand over his heart during the national anthem at an
Easter event on April 17, 2017. He heard a German minister say "the mix
of politics with family and business reminds us of nepotism." On March
2, 2017 he called the president of the Philippines, congratulated him on

his policy of shooting drug suspects on sight in the streets, and praised an "unbelievable job".

Trump did not get money from Congress for the border wall. He did make plans with the Russian leader for a meeting. On July 16, 2018 he tweeted that his predecessor's health-care act was a "lie" and "dead." He fired the FBI director. James Comey on July 1, 2018. He saw a report stating that he asked an independent FBI director to pledge him loyalty. He tweeted on May 2017, when he fired the FBI director: "better hope there are no 'tapes' of our conversations!" He heard reports that state that he asked fired FBI director to drop the investigation. He called the fired FBI director "a real nut job." He heard that Saudi Arabia and United Arab Emirates pledged $100 million to a fund backed by "she's hot, right?" daughter.

On August 3, 2018 he had his hand swatted by his wife on the tarmac. On May 26, 2017 he shoved Prime Minister of Montenegro out of the way during a photo op thus obtaining better position. On May 27, 2017 he learned that the FBI was scrutinizing his son-in-law for proposing a secret communications channel with Russia. Called the leaks "troubling".

On July 7, 2017 he met Russian president Putin at G20, in Hamburg Germany. His wife Melania tried to break it up, failed and he then met the Russian president secretly. On July 24, 2017 he heard that his son-in-law Jared Kushner denied that he had colluded with Russia. He tweeted that the attorney general is "beleaguered," and should investigate election rival's relationship with Russia.

On August 13, 2017 he learned about the woman murdered in Charlottesville, Va., amid marches by racists masquerading as golf caddies with tiki torches yelling about blood and soil; he condemned violence "on many sides, on many sides," and praised "very fine people on both sides." He retweeted a cartoon of a train killing a journalist. He received thanks from the former leader of the Ku Klux Klan David Duke August 15, 2017 and received accolades from the chief strategist, and former executive chairman of a racist news site On August 25, 2017 he pardoned a racist sheriff, Joe Arpaio.

It was heard that the media reported that the Trump Organization contacted Kremlin about a Moscow deal during the election; it was also heard that the campaign manager's lawyer was subpoenaed by the special counsel investigation. On November 26, 2016 we heard: "is it wrong to be more sexually attracted to your own daughter than your wife?" and his daughter complained about liberal critics' "unrealistic expectations." On September 18, 2018 he shook his wife, Melania's hand, told her to "go sit down," and pushed her off stage. On December 5, 2019 he called the North Korean dictator Kim Jung Un, "rocket man". On September 22, 2017 he called a kneeling NFL player a "son of a bitch," as he requested team owners to remove the player from field after calling the president a "moron".

On September 29, 2017 he heard the Puerto Rican mayor Carmen Yulin beg for hurricane assistance; and he attacked the mayor. He said that a hurricane is not a "real catastrophe". He threw paper towels at hurricane victims and informed hurricane victims, "You've thrown our budget a little out of whack."

He did not release his tax returns and appointed gold-level Trump Hotel member ambassador to Canada. He requested that the secretary of state compare IQ scores with him.

On October 17, 2017 he told a widow of Sgt. La David Johnson that her dead soldier husband "knew what he signed up for." What a disgraceful and stupid answer, from a president who didn't serve our country. On October 8, 2017 he tweeted about the Republican chairman of Senate foreign relations committee Bob Corker saying that he "didn't have the guts" to run for re-election,

On November 22, 2019 he requested that a judge give someone the death penalty. On November 5, 2017 he told Japan's prime minister that he would allow Japan's economy to come second after America's. On November 8, 2017 he told North Korea, "Do not try us." On July 20, 2017 he shook hands with the Russian president, Vladimir Putin, at dinner but not for 19 seconds.

On February 26, 2019 we learned about 20 women who accused him of groping and a congressional probe into more than one dozen sexual harassment and assault allegations was requested. When he saw photos of himself with the new accuser, he claimed they had never met.

On January 8, 2018 he assured the public that he is "a very stable genius". On January 8, 2018 he even mouthed wrong words to the national anthem at a football game in Atlanta.

On January 11, 2018 Trump posed query regarding the American policy of accepting immigration from "shit-hole countries." Then clarified, "I am not a racist." On January 12, 2018 we heard reports that his lawyer bribed a porn star Stormy Daniels with hush money after he slept with her and he described her as "she's actually always been very voluptuous". On January 23, 2018 we heard that wife would not attend Davos.

On February 6, 2018 he gave a speech in Cincinnati; he noted the lack of clapping and accused non-clappers of being "treasonous." He attacked the FBI, the DOJ, and the NFL. He also advocated for shutdown of the government he leads; he had his lawyer claim that he, the lawyer, not the president, paid the president's porn star girlfriend with own money, just because; he sent his "Did she look a little more stacked?" daughter to the winter Olympics. On February 21, 2018 he required a memo to appear empathic toward shooting victims; he proposed giving school teacher's guns; he advocated for the importance of strong mental health.

On February 3, 2018, Trump congratulated the Chinese president for eliminating term limits and announced "maybe we'll give that a shot someday." On December 12, 2017 he reiterated the claim that he "never met" a sexual assault accuser. On July 15, 2020 he reiterated the call for an investigation into his predecessor. He said that the deputy who did not shoot the gunman in Portland "certainly did a poor job."

On May 8, 2018 he learned that the porn star's lawyer said that a Russian oligarch put $500,000 into the president's lawyer's account. On May 16, 2018 he called undocumented immigrants "animals." He also called the FBI investigation a "witch hunt." He issued unprejudiced legal opinion, "I have the absolute right to pardon myself." On June 7, 2018 he opted not to prepare for his meeting with the North Korean dictator and he noted that when the North Korean dictator speaks, "his people sit up at attention." So, he said, "I want my people to do the same."

On June 20, 2018 he denied policies separating families at the border; and he stated, "You have to take the children away."

On June 7, 2018 he met U.S. allies, called the prime-minister Justin Trudeau of neighbor and ally Canada "meek," also "very dishonest and weak." On July 13, 2018 he kept the Queen of England waiting, did not bow, and said they had great "chemistry".

On July 24, 2018 he tweeted, "no president has been tougher on Russia than me." He also tweeted about the media "hating the fact that I'll probably have a good relationship with Putin." He finally tweeted that the DOJ and the FBI investigations are "a witch hunt, rigged, and a scam!"

On August 1, 2018 he tweeted about a request to attorney general Jeff Sessions to stop investigating his campaign, called the investigation a "TOTAL HOAX." Said his son's campaign behavior was "totally legal." And told critics to "be cool."

August 10, 2018, he tweeted about the attack on kneeling Black NFL player. On June 25, 2018 he called a critical Black congresswoman, Maxime Waters, an "extraordinarily low IQ person", and critical former Black staff woman "a dog", and critical Black interviewer "stupid". On April 26, 2018 he tweeted thanks to supportive Black rap artist Kanye West. On August 11, 2018 Trump welcomed a supportive white biker gang to his golf club, complimented on the "beautiful bikes," and mocked journalists for getting wet in the rain. On August 9, 2018 he supported the firing of Peter Strzok, an FBI agent who had criticized him. On August 15, 2018 he revoked security clearance of the former CIA director, John Brennan, who had criticized him.

On August 21, 2018 he was informed that his former lawyer pleaded guilty to paying hush money to a porn star on his behalf. On November 21, 2017 he announced that a White House lawyer Roy Moore was leaving after being accused of sexual assault. On October 6, 2018 Brett Cavanaugh, the assailant was sworn in as Supreme Court justice. He also said that he had successfully made America great again. On June 10, 2018 he tweeted about the attack on Canada and he did not get Mexico to pay for the wall.

On August 10, 2018 he tweeted an attack on the NFL. On September 12, 2018 he complained that the Puerto Rico storm response was under-appreciated and called the storm death toll a Democrat hoax. On March 25, 2019 he announced, "No collusion!" And he announced, "I don't have an attorney general." He also announced that the FBI is a "cancer in our country." On February 15, 2019 he then tweeted this query, "I want to know, where the money for border security and the WALL in this ridiculous spending bill?" But he did not get Mexico to pay for the wall.

He declared that sexual assault accusation against him to possibly be greatest injustice suffered by any candidate of any kind in all of history. On September 25, 2018 he was laughed at during a UN speech, claimed he was in on the joke. On October 2, 2018 he held a rally, laughed at sexual assault accuser and he apologized to Supreme Court nominee, Brett Kavanaugh, "on behalf of our nation." On October 9, 2018 he saw the U.S. ambassador to the UN Niki-Haley leave.

He did not get Mexico to pay for the wall and lost his midterms but he boasted of a "big victory." On November 7, 2018 he saw a White House reporter, Jim Acosta, have his microphone wrestled away by a staffer and had the White House revoke said reporter's credentials. He pretended not to know an appointee he had met more than one dozen times. On November 9, 2018 he accused the French president, Emmanuel Macron, of insulting him, On November 19, 2018 he criticized a general, William H. McRaven, who led the Osama bin Laden raid, and expressed anger with California foresters as he suggested raking to prevent fires. On November 20, 2018 he defended a

Saudi prince for the murder of journalist, Jamal Khashoggi. In other words, he gave his approval, between dictators "everything is fine Madame la Marquise".

On March 27, 2020 he tweeted about the attack on General Motors and also on the attack on his former lawyer. On November 30, 2018 he announced business dealings during campaign were "very legal," "very cool." He did not release his tax returns. He did not get Congress to pay for the wall. On February 27, 2019 he heard his former lawyer say he directed him to pay hush money to a porn star and called his former lawyer "a rat."

On January 10, 2019 he declared that he never said Mexico would pay for the wall and he asked the Democrats to pay for it. On January 9, 2019 he walked out of meetings and he did not get Democrats to pay for the wall.

On February 17, 2017 he called a highly regarded newspaper the "true enemy of the people." On August 23, 2017 he asked a Black actor, "What about MAGA?" He then accused said Black actor of racism. He did not release his tax returns. On February 25, 2019 he was accused of sexual assault by a former campaign staffer, Alva Johnson. On February 20, 2019 he was called "racist," "con man," "cheat" by his ex-lawyer. On February 20, 2019 he was told about the claim that U.S. adversary, North Korea, did not kill a U.S. citizen and pronounced the dictator innocent. He gave speeches, hugged the U.S. flag, and called a special investigation "bull-shit". On August 21, 2018 he expressed sympathy for a former campaign chairman, Paul Manafort, who was found guilty.

He was the subject of a House committee request for tax returns and did not release the tax returns. On June 13, 2019 he declared the mayor of London, Sadiq Kan, a "stone cold loser". On May 20, 2019 he said Iran he would "end" it in a fight. On July 1, 2019 he met the North Korean dictator, Kim Jong UN and shook hands. On May 9, 2019 he held a rally, suggested conditions under which migrants could be shot. On. June 24, 2019 he was accused of sexual assault again, said this one "not my type."

On July 22, 2019 he tweeted skepticism regarding whether four Black congresswomen "are capable of loving our country," and requested they "go back" to the countries they came from, while ignoring the fact that the three were born in the United States.

On July 29, 2019 he declared a major American city a "disgusting, rat- and rodent-infested mess". On September 3, 2019 he skipped comforting storm victims and played golf. On September 5, 2019 he took the initiative to issue weather warning of the storm for Alabama and disputed the National Weather Service correction.

On September 24, 2019 he learned about the impeachment inquiry launched against him for secretly coercing U.S. ally, Ukraine, to investigate the son of his future election rival and tweeted "Witch hunt garbage." On October 29, 2019 he was booed by baseball fans chanting "Lock him up!" On December 18, 2019 he became the third president in American history to be impeached.

On September 10, 2020 he tweeted that the deadly global pandemic was "very much under control," like the flu. Publicly, he said that the pandemic was the Democrats "new hoax." Publicly he said that he always knew that the pandemic was a pandemic, "I've felt it was a pandemic long before it was called a pandemic." On March 9, 2020 he announced, "I'll be shaking hands with people" and he blamed his predecessor's rule for lack of tests. On July 23, 2020, he blamed Mexico border for the spread of the virus.

On July 7, 2020 he described the deadly global pandemic as very mild, and 99 per cent of cases "totally harmless." On April 24, 2020 he mused whether injecting or ingesting cleaning products could cure the virus; as he denied responsibility for subsequent abuses of cleaning products.

On April 14, 2020 he corrected the widespread misapprehension among legal communities of democrat checks on power, explaining, "When somebody is president of the United States, the authority is total." On April 2, 2020 he heard that his son-in-law, Jared Kushner, was looking forward to the U.S. overcoming the pandemic, saying the U.S. would be "really rocking again" in a few months; On May 13, 2020 he heard his son-in-law warning that the U.S. could not overcome the pandemic and might have to postpone the election in several months.

On October 2, 2020 he did not wear masks but did take the drug. On May 24, 2020 he suggested that the Speaker of the House was a boozer and called his former election rival a "skank."

On June 3, 2020 he called Black protesters "thugs," threatened the "vicious dogs," with "ominous weapons." On May 30, 2020 he had the protesters attacked with tear gas for being in the street he wanted to cross for Bible photo op. On August 10, 2020 he had an aide explore adding his face to Mount Rushmore.

On August 20, 2020 he learned that "Sloppy Steve Bannon" his former chief strategist had been charged with defrauding donors to supposedly pay for the wall. On May 8, 2019 he learned about "failing," "fake" media revealed his tax returns, which said he owes hundreds of millions of dollars in loans, gave hundreds of thousands of dollars in consulting fees to his daughter you can call her 'a piece of ass. On November 20, 2020 Trump daughter, didn't pay taxes, basically at all. On October 2, 2020 he caught the deadly virus. He didn't get Mexico to pay for the wall. <u>He didn't release his tax returns.</u> Trump never put in place a coronavirus program.

CHAPTER TWENTY THREE

....

TRUMP'S LAST-DITCH EFFORT TO STEAL THE ELECTION IS THE BIGGEST FARCE OF ALL:

December 10, 2020

On December 9, 2020 Trump said, "We will be intervening in the Texas (plus many other states') case. This is the big one. Our Country needs a victory!" tweeted the soon-to-be-ex-president of the United States. A filing at the Supreme Court soon followed.

President Trump needs an intervention these days all right — but not of the kind he was talking about. And it's he who desperately needs a victory, not the country.

That's because Trump and his allies lost just about every lawsuit, they filed to try to keep him in office. By one Democrat election lawyer's count, they have just one win and 55 losses to show for their efforts (a ratio that would be even more lopsided if he had counted multiple losses in each case). Adding insult to injury, the Trumpistas' solitary victory was a piddling, technical one that affected just a tiny number of ballots, nowhere nears enough to change the result. Sad!

Trump and his litigation boosters lost every which way, and everywhere. In state courts and federal courts. In trial courts and appellate courts, intermediate and supreme. Before Democrat judges and Republican ones. In Pennsylvania, Georgia, Michigan, Wisconsin, Arizona and Nevada — every state that could possibly matter, on substantive grounds and procedural ones, on the facts, and on the law.

They've already lost a case in the U.S. Supreme Court — and are about to lose there again very, very soon.

Their problem is that they have nothing to sue about, and never did.

The words of a Trump-appointed member of the federal appeals court in Philadelphia pretty much sum things up: "Calling an election unfair does not make it so.

And time's up. All the contested states have certified their Biden-Harris slates of electors before the deadline set by federal law. That means that the certifications "shall be conclusive, and shall govern in the counting of the electoral votes." The electors will meet and vote in their respective states on Monday. The result will be Biden 306, Trump 232. A landslide, according to Trump.

It's the big one, all right, the biggest farce of all. It's a case the state of Texas filed on Monday, directly in the Supreme Court, against Pennsylvania, Georgia, Michigan and Wisconsin. In a move that says more about the legal judgment (poor) and the moral fiber (absent) of their attorneys general than it does about the merits of the case, 17 states have now filed a brief in support of Texas, along with Trump. More than half the House Republicans — 106 — also joined the follies.

Filed by Texas's ethically challenged attorney general, Ken Paxton, the case is legally preposterous. By Texas's own admission, it's "challenging" the other states' "management of the 2020 election." No constitutional provision, no statute and no principle of law give one state the standing to challenge another state's handling of an election. In our system, Texas isn't the boss of Pennsylvania. Allowing such suits would invite a multistate free-for-all every time a presidential election is held.

Greg Sargent: How Mitch McConnell might quietly make it easier to cripple Biden.

What of the Texas lawsuit's merits? It has none.

Texas' proposed complaint even has a claim that, given Trump's middle-of-election-night lead in the defendant states, there was less than a "one in a quadrillion" chance that Biden should have won. Do they really think the justices of the Supreme Court are that stupid?

And what relief does the Texas suit seek? For the court to declare that the 62 electoral votes of Pennsylvania, Georgia, Michigan and Wisconsin "cannot be counted." That's a quote.

That any member of any bar, let alone a member of the Supreme Court bar, could file such flimsy tripe in any court, let alone the Supreme Court, is an embarrassment to the legal profession. For public officials such as Paxton and his fellow Republican attorneys general to call for the wholesale disenfranchisement of the people of four states is an affront to the rule of law, an insult to an independent judiciary and a contempt of democracy.

The big fraud of 2020 didn't take place in any voting booth, drop box or tabulation center. It happened after the election, at the presidential lectern, at news conferences and in legal briefs orchestrated to support the fiction that Donald Trump won. History will record that the scam didn't succeed.

FRAUDULENT FUNDRAISING:

Lately Trump amassed over $ 200 million, supposedly to fund his rallies. Really? I knew most of the supporters were stupid and naive, but not at this level, so I will repeat: you really are fish, hungry to bite this hook. Wake up! With this money he will do the same as with the money he has stolen from you all his life, and especially to pay his personal debts after January 2021.

THE DICTATORS:

March- 2021

Here is a description of the dictator Trump's attraction towards his fellows, and some general information.

There is a proverb that says: follow the footsteps of money. What must be remembered is that during the murder of journalist JAMAL KHASHOGGI on the order of Prince MOHAMMED BIN SALMAN, Mr. Trump approved this murder. So, it is easy to understand this behavior on the part of the President of U.S.A since this President and his family owed millions of dollars to this "nice" dictator. Another proverb: tell me who your friends are and I will tell you who you are.

Next November 3rd, if Donald J Trump is not re-elected in the months that follow, he will face a lot of bankruptcies. He is not what they say, he is not a billionaire.

So let go a step further with the story that Trump is a billionaire, and one of the greatest builders in the world. Sources say that this is just a show and a lot of bragging on his part. Remember the Trump Plaza, the Taj Mahal Casino in Atlantic City (which he obtained in 1990), and the following year he went bankrupt. Plus, he has the guts to say that he is a successful businessman. It's ridiculously crazy, zany, and absurd. It's all just a show!

In a few months we will be able to see the real face of this clown. Every time he opens his mouth to move his jaws, he never makes sure that the switch of his neurons is in the ON position.

Finally, for "Mr. Hoax" and his family, it will soon be the descent into hell, and maybe also the bottom of the barrel. If he is not re-elected on November 3rd, then will come the accusations, and the charges as well as the disclosure of his tax returns that the Manhattan district Attorney requests, and all that this involves.

The second most dangerous person in the White House is William. He is a liar and a hypocritical traitor. His attorney's license should be removed for life. He is also a traitor working for Trump, not for the American people, and getting paid with the US $ taxpayer's money.

The third most dangerous person in the white house, is Mitch. This person is in collusion with one of the directors of the famous NRA organization. . There is a lot of money flowing from this organization, and from someone at the White House.

And another traitor is his personal lawyer, Rudy whose salary is paid with taxpayer's money.

There is a proverb that says follow the footsteps of money.

All these people are responsible for thousands of deaths every year in the United States. There are no such killings elsewhere in the world to avoid all this you will have to dismantle this Pandora's box.

So, these people and the president, with his behavior, have their hands full of blood.

"Mr. Hoax", with his unhinged rhetoric and actions, also with a lack of transparency, no plan for the COVID 19 pandemic, the result will be catastrophic: up to two million deaths in 2023.

President Donald Trump is bypassing Congress to sell $8 billion worth of arms to Saudi Arabia by invoking a loophole in the Arms Export Control Act.

The loophole gave the State Department the authority to sell arms if an "emergency exists". The Trump administration has reportedly referenced the recent tensions with Iran to justify the sale.

Saudi Arabia is involved in a bloody war in Yemen against Iran-backed Houthi rebels. Thousands of civilians have been killed.

A US-made bomb was reportedly used in an August 2018 Saudi-led coalition airstrike in Yemen that hit a school bus and killed dozens — including children under age 10.

Democratic Sen. Chris Murphy, who's been among the most vocal critics of US support for the Saudi-led coalition in Yemen, said this sets a dangerous precedent for future presidents.

"If he does this, it allows every president to ... sell weapons to the Middle East without a check from Congress," Murphy said.

Never in the history of the United States of America has there been a quartet so in love: four dictators; one of which is an American president: Donald J Trump, he said I be a dictator for one day, oh ya, Kim Jong Un, Jamal Bin Salman, and Vladimir Putin.

After three meetings with the North Korean dictator, Trump repeated multiple times that he received rather curious messages: a declaration of love from the tenant of the White House, going so far as to say that the two men had fallen in love.

But after all these meeting for four years, and talks with dictator Kim, no tangible results, if we remember at his arrival at the white house, he said with his usual bragging that he will take care of Mr. Rocket man.

Concerning the relationship that Trump maintained, and still ongoing today, with Prince Jamal Bin Salman, it is very complex to understand. We must refer to the contract of 8 billion dollars to Saudi Arabia; this contract never received the approval of congress; Trump bypassed congress which thereby endangered the security of the nation.

And we must remember that this sale of weapons allowed this dictator to kill thousands of people including women, children, and old people in Yemen. So, Mr. Trump still has his hands stained with blood.

According to some sources, the prince was offered an unbeatable price and no other supplier could provide him with this type of weapons. Mr. Trump and his family would naturally receive a special interest loan, which will be due in the near future, and we're talking about hundreds of millions of dollars here, some say maybe close to a billion dollars.

As mentioned above with the assassination of journalist Jamal Khashoggi on October 2, 2018, Donald J. Trump gave his approval for this murder. I believe he had no choice to keep his mouth shut, because of the money he received from the prince. Once again Donald J. Trump has his hands stained with blood.

And the Prince knew ahead of time, that he could proceed with his project to kill the Washington Post reporter without having any response from the US government, this president has no empathy for anyone.

And as I have already said, this monster has no empathy for others except for himself.

As for the other dictator, Vladimir Putin, everyone knows that without Putin, "Mr. Hoax" would never have had the chance to reach the highest seat of this country, that's why I say this President is an impostor.

So, we can conclude here that, this President is an impostor, and that, during the meeting with Putin on July 16, 2018 in Helsinki, at the podium, Trump declared that he'd rather believe Putin than his own intelligence agents. To say such things, you have to be cynical and completely deranged.

So, poison is the weapon of choice for the dictator Putin. It's a regime that kills adversaries at home and abroad.

The next day the international press declared that Trump was on a honeymoon with this dictator.

How much money does Trump owe this killer, and to the other killers BSM.

This man is going to shred the constitution because his brain is sorely messing around. He is not able to run the country. He is deranged mentally. He never apologized or empathized with these thousands of deaths and more from COVID 19 to this day.

AMERICA! Wake-up before it's too late! Globally, we're watching you.

Some sources say that "Mr. Hoax" hired a friend of his named Joe Shapiro, to take exams so that he would have a better shot at transferring from college at FORHAM UNIVERSITY to the more prestigious, WARTTON SCHOOL at the UNIVERSITY of PENSYLVANIA; and, don't forget that he's one of the biggest cowards of the United States. In the fall of 1968, Trump received a timely diagnosis of bone spurs in his heels that led to his medical exemption from the military during Vietnam. How much money was in the bribe he gave to his doctor, <u>LARRY BRAUNSTEIN</u>, who practiced podiatry in Jamaica, Queens, He has the guts to say that soldiers are losers and suckers! Imagine in 2018 when he cancelled a visit to the US cemetery outside Paris, France; he said that it was "filled with losers" what a disgrace, this person is a master cheater.

Speaking of cheaters, we must remember that at the beginning of 2014 with the CNBC conducting an on-line poll to determine the most important influential business people for the next campaign, we will explain to you in detail further on, how Trump fraudulently interceded with the system to manage to be at the top of the candidates list. With this fraud, it unfortunately allowed him to become the Imposter President.

The second amendment guaranties all American citizens the right to bear arms. This stupid cowboy and archaic law enacted in 1689 was ratified for the last time on December 15, 1791. Nothing is going to change in this country, you will kill each other like you did in the civil war, oh yes! I know what you will answer, that this law is to protect us, what hypocrisy!

You know what? If someone enters a school and kill kids, or if someone comes to your house and shoots you down and you die, or kills you in the street, are the guns you bought at the store going to protect you? The answer is no. So, don't be stupid, you know very well that if you are dead, it is due to what it is. There is a weapon which was bought somewhere. On the other hand, if there are no stores to sell these guns, one thing for sure is you wouldn't be 6 feet underground, unless you are <u>ROBOCOP.</u>

I'm sure you will agree with me, about this. If not, then explain to me why our country is the worst on this planet regarding the number of deaths per year, example, in 2019, close to 40,000 gun-related deaths. Remember, only in 2019, under Donald Trump, there were 62 mass shootings. Here are few examples: LAS VEGAS, EL PASO, DAYTON, PITTSBURGH and so on.

And some say that by 2050 our country will have 300,000 gun-related deaths per year.

The master killer Trump is responsible for 89 % of the deaths that have resulted from the virus until now, and also 99 % of the massacres that took place across the country since he has been in power and this, because his behavior is erratic, and every time he opens his mouth, more lies and devil's gall that will set this country on fire soon. There is another proverb that says: play with fire and you will burn yourself.

In the animal world, predators kill for food but in the United States, American Homo sapiens kill for power, glory and money.

This week in a rally this President said that 85% of those wearing masks get covid-19… and his herd applauded. What a masquerade, where is the logic in all of this? His son <u>BARRON</u> got the virus and dozens of others also got the virus in the White House. The last one, <u>Chris Christie</u>, got the virus and he said that he was wrong to not wear a mask in the White House.

Today there are 4 demons on the planet. Which one of these demons will be responsible for the destruction of this planet? Now don't get me wrong, we are very close to this eventuality. I feel that the most fanatic and dangerous one among these 4 demons is DONALD J. TRUMP. Be careful FBI, keep your eyes and ears open on these last days which remain until November 3rd because, if this madman realizes that he is going to lose the election he could panic, and to distract the world he could make an irreparable gesture. Do not rely on the cowardly puppets of this caucus to confront the monster; most of them will defecate in their pants.

So, the Republicans are all afraid of the monster; they are all cowards. What are you waiting for? Enough is enough! Send this clown back to his palace, don't forget, is watching you. the world

Finally, in the last weeks of 2019, the BBC mentioned some very interesting news regarding this virus. A patient treated in a hospital near Paris, France on the 27th of December, had the corona virus. The patient must have been infected between the 14th and the 22nd of December. The patient's name is <u>Amirouche Hammar.</u> With the social media that the world has today you then have this President that says that, for 3 months, he doesn't know anything about it. His answer was: it's a hoax by the democrats. For 10 months he said this word more than a thousand times. This is the reason why, in my book, I gave him the name: Mr. Hoax.

For the sake of the United States and the whole world, I hope we will elect a new president in the person of Mr. Joe Biden.

NOTES:

I allowed myself this little note to relate an event that happened recently during a Trump rally that took place in Florida. A CNN reporter was interviewing people over 60 years old. I was stunned to hear the stupidities that these people answered to the questions asked by the reporter. He asked one of them if he was not afraid of dying being among this multitude of people without masks and who did not respect the two meters. Their answers were that they were immune like the clown who was on the microphone. One said, <u>"I am healthy and God will protect us"</u>, and another one said yesterday that, <u>"if I'm going to get sick and die, I guess it's my turn."</u> Ridiculous! No respect for those who died of the virus.

Why are there so many Trump supporters wanting to kill themselves? This president, with his super spreader events, thinks he is a SUPERMAN or JESUS CHRIST! What a masquerade! It doesn't make sense! By doing so, Mr. Hoax says it is Ok to die. For those of you who don't know JESUS CHRIST, he died 2020 years ago; even if he already said that he was the chosen one on the 24th of August 2019, if you believe he is what he says then you are all a bunch of nuts, naïve and ignorant.

Abraham Lincoln said if you think education is expensive, try ignorance. That says everything.

And we can say here that the future of this country is not out of the woods, this country will not be the same. In the coming days, the United States, with this pandemic, will be out of control and this, thanks to the SUPERSPREADER with his crazy rallies. And after 9 months, he does not have a plan to reduce the cases of this covid-19 virus.

If we listen to all the comments of these Republican supporters, there is only one thing to say: they are so ignorant and so naïve. These people live on another planet. Wake-up! We're in 2020. One last piece of news: October 16, 2020, former chief-of-staff, JOHN KELLY, told friends that TRUMP is the most stupid person he ever met, that says everything.

WILLIAM BARR'S BOMBSHELL ABOUT TRUMP IS MORE REVEALING THAN IT SEEMS:

Having gone to extraordinary lengths to help Donald Trump corrupt the presidency, William P. Barr is working overtime to launder his post-Trump reputation. But the former attorney general's latest cleanup exercise may end up showing that the stain of his corruption is even darker than we thought — in a way that soils other Republicans as well.

Barr has offered fresh details about Trump's effort to subvert the election to journalist Jonathan Karl. These are supposed to be exonerating. But they open up new lines of inquiry about the post-election conduct of Barr himself, and show that the machinations of Senate Minority Leader Mitch McConnell (R-Ky.) are more depraved than we knew.

Several weeks before, in early November, Barr had taken the extraordinary step of authorizing U.S. attorneys to open election fraud investigations. The move attracted scalding criticism — the department long refrained from such investigations until results were certified, to avoid this very sort of politicization.

Barr is now claiming he always knew the fraud claims were nonsense. As he told Karl, "My suspicion all the way was that they were ''all bullshit''

Yes, Barr ultimately did admit that there was not substantial election fraud, but he hedged, saying there wasn't enough to swing the outcome.

INSIDE THE EXTRAORDINARY EFFORT
TO SAVE TRUMP FROM COVID-19:

His illness was more severe than the White House acknowledged at the time. Advisers thought it would alter his response to the pandemic. They were wrong. Health and Human Services Secretary, Alex Azar's phone rang with an urgent request: could he help someone at the White House obtain an experimental coronavirus treatment, known as a monoclonal antibody?

If Azar could get the drug, what would the White House need to do to make that happen? Azar thought for a moment. It was October 1, 2020, and the drug was still in clinical trials. The Food and Drug Administration would have to make a "compassionate use" exception for its use since it was not yet available to the public. Only about 10 people so far had used it outside of those trials. Azar said of course he would help.

A short time later, FDA Commissioner, Stephen Hahn, received a request from a top White House official for a separate case, this time with even greater urgency: could he get the FDA to sign off on a compassionate-use authorization for a monoclonal antibody right away? There is a standard process that doctors use to apply to the FDA for unapproved drugs on behalf of patients dealing with life-threatening illnesses who have exhausted all other options, and agency scientists review it. The difference was that most people don't call the commissioner directly.

The White House wanted Hahn to say yes within hours. Hahn, who still did not know who the application was for, consulted career officials. The FDA needs to go by the book, the officials insisted. They kept pressing him to effectively cut corners. "No, we can't do that," Hahn told them several times. "We're talking about someone's life.

When Hahn later learned the effort was on behalf of the president, he was stunned. "For God's sake, he thought, it's the president who's sick, and you want us to bend the rules?" Trump was in the highest-risk category for severe disease from covid-19 — 74 years of age, he rarely exercised and was considered medically obese.

A five-day stretch in October 2020 — from the moment White House officials began an extraordinary effort to get Trump lifesaving drugs, to the day the president returned to the White House from the hospital — marked a dramatic turning point in the nation's flailing coronavirus response. Trump's brush with severe illness and the prospect of death caught the White House so unprepared that they had not even briefed Vice President Mike Pence's team on a plan to swear him in if Trump became incapacitated.

For months, the president had taunted and dodged the virus, flouting safety protocols by holding big rallies and packing the White House with guests not wearing masks. But just one month before the election, the virus that had already killed more than 200,000 Americans had sickened the most powerful person on the planet.

Trump's medical advisers hoped his bout with the coronavirus, which was far more serious than acknowledged at the time, would inspire him to take the virus seriously. Perhaps now, they thought, he would encourage Americans to wear masks and put his health and the medical official's front and center in the response. Instead, Trump emerged from the experience triumphant and ever more defiant. He urged people not to be afraid of the virus or let it dominate their lives, disregarding that he had had access to health care and treatments unavailable to other Americans.

TRUMP SUES NEW YORK TIMES AND NIECE MARY TRUMP OVER TAX RECORDS STORY:

September 22, 2021

Former president Donald Trump has sued his niece, Mary L. Trump, and the New York Times over the publication of a 2018 article detailing allegations that he "participated in dubious tax schemes ... including instances of outright fraud" that allowed him to receive over $413 million from his father, Fred Trump Sr., while significantly reducing taxes.

The suit, filed in a Dutchess County, N.Y. court on Tuesday, alleges that Mary Trump, the New York Times and at least three of its reporters "engaged in an insidious plot to obtain confidential and highly-sensitive records" about the former president's finances. According to the lawsuit, Donald Trump suffered at least $100 million in damages as a result of the alleged actions.

The New York Times and the three reporters named in the suit — David Barstow, Susanne Craig and Russ Buettner — won the 2019 Pulitzer Prize in Explanatory Reporting for their 18-month investigation that culminated in the article.

Trump asks judge to block release of tax returns, blasts Biden Justice Dept. for authorizing release

Donald Trump's suit alleges that the New York Times influenced Mary Trump to help them acquire confidential documents despite a settlement agreement that she had signed after a legal challenge to Fred Trump Sr.'s will. In her 2020 book "Too Much and Never Enough," Mary Trump detailed how she helped the reporters obtain Donald Trump's financial records.

At 3 a.m. one day in 2017, she took 19 boxes of documents from Farrell Fritz, the law firm that helped her challenge the estate of Fred Trump Sr., and handed them over to the journalists.

In 2020, Mary Trump also sued Donald Trump and two of the former president's siblings, saying that they defrauded her out of tens of millions of dollars decades ago by allegedly manipulating the value of properties and lying to her about the worth of her inheritance.

News of Donald Trump's lawsuit was first reported by the Daily Beast. Mary Trump told the news website that the legal action was motivated by "desperation". ... The walls are closing in and he is throwing anything against the wall that will stick. "As is always the case with Donald, he'll try and change the subject."

Trump never put in place a coronavirus program.

CHAPTER TWENTY FOUR

....

TRUMP IS INCITING CHAOS ON JANUARY 6, BOTH IN AND OUTSIDE THE CAPITOL

On January 6, the day Congress meets in a joint session to accept the results of the presidential election, should be a testament to America's enduring democracy. Yet it may become a demonstration of its poor health. President Trump, along with craven enablers such as Sen. Josh Hawley (R-Mo.), is seeking to upend what should be a solemn but largely perfunctory proceeding to ratify the victory of President-elect Joe Biden. The result could be a shameless show of support by numerous congressional Republicans for erasing the votes of millions of Americans — and, perhaps, mayhem incited by the president in the streets of D.C.

"Big protest in D.C. on January 6. Be there, will be wild!" Mr. Trump tweeted earlier this month in an appeal to his supporters to come to the capital to buttress his campaign to overturn the election results. He followed up Sunday, "See you in Washington, DC, on January 6. Don't miss it. Information to follow!" And again, on Wednesday, "JANUARY SIXTH, SEE YOU IN DC!"

That the president is actively seeking to incite street protests is a matter of more than a little concern to D.C. officials who — based on the behavior of some of Mr. Trump's supporters at two previous rallies — fear there could be violence. While daytime demonstrations were largely peaceful on November 14th and December 12th, destruction and bloodshed broke out when night came. During the December 12th event, four people were stabbed, and members of the Proud Boys — a far-right group linked to white supremacy and categorized by the FBI as an extremist organization — were seen roaming the streets and assaulting bystanders.

Nonetheless, Mr. Trump — who told the Proud Boys during the first presidential debate in September to "stand back and stand by" — issued his un-camouflaged summons to "Be there, will be wild!" So much for the law-and-order president. Just as hypocritical are the Republican members of Congress — the latest being Mr. Hawley — who plans to raise objections to the certification of electoral votes for Mr. Biden.

Republican congressional leaders have acknowledged that Mr. Trump's desperate efforts to stop Mr. Biden from being sworn in to office are bound to fail. We can only hope the damage from the chaos Mr. Trump is inciting doesn't extend to human lives.

WE JUST SAW AN ATTEMPTED COUP D'ÉTAT. TRUMP -- BLAME HIS REPUBLICAN ENABLERS:

January 6, 2021

Let's be clear: What happened Wednesday afternoon at the U.S. Capitol was an attempted coup d'état, egged on by a lawless president desperately trying to cling to power and encouraged by his cynical Republican enablers in Congress.

It was perhaps inevitable that President Trump's chaotic and incompetent tenure in office would end with riots and tear gas. Not since British Major Gen. Robert Ross set fire to the president's residence and the Capitol building in 1814 have, we seen such a scene at the hallowed citadel of our democracy, as an angry and disillusioned mob — whipped into frenzy by Trump himself — forced its way into the Capitol to disrupt the official certification of Trump's electoral defeat.

Images from this shameful day will endure forever: crowds storming the security barricades, overwhelming outnumbered and seemingly unprepared Capitol police, and breaking windows to pour into the seat of American power. Police officers inside the House of Representatives chamber, guns drawn and aimed at the main doors, where protesters threatened to force their way inside. A scarf-draped rioter sitting smugly in the chair where, an hour earlier, Vice President Pence had presided over the Senate.

THE PROUD BOYS OUTSIDE THE U.S. ON JANUARY 6TH:

With the Proud Boys outside the U.S. on January 6, the central act of our democracy — the peaceful and orderly transfer of power — was not allowed to take place. Blame the rioters themselves, who must take responsibility for their own actions. But blame Trump above all.

Trump told his MAGA legions that he didn't really lose the election, that in fact he could not possibly have lost, and that somehow, he would manage to remain their president for a second term. Then, it was going to be the certification of the vote totals — but all the states certified their results. Then it was going to be the courts that rode to the rescue — but courts, at every level, including the U.S. Supreme Court, tossed out his frivolous lawsuits like so much scrap paper.

Finally on January 6, Congress — or perhaps Pence, acting alone — would surely throw out the electoral votes from states Trump falsely claimed to have "won," thus giving him the glorious victory he deserved. He urged his followers to come to Washington to "Stop the Steal" — to keep Congress from doing its constitutional duty in counting the electoral votes. And Hawley, Cruz, Scalise and scores of other congressional Republicans went along with this ridiculous fairy tale so as not to anger the president or his supporters.

But then January 6 arrived. Pence issued a statement early in the day making it clear that he would obey the Constitution, not Trump's autocratic wishes. And the many thousands of Trump supporters who had gathered on the Ellipse to hear Trump give a long and angry rant, and who obeyed his order to march on the Capitol, became a guided missile aimed at the heart of U.S. democracy.

Biden gave a televised address calling for an end to the "insurrection" and the restoration of "decency, honor, respect, the rule of law." Trump posted a desultory video statement on social media urging rioters to "go home" but repeating his claims that the election was "stolen."

But somehow our damaged nation has to make it through those next two weeks. Police and the National Guard are more than capable of reestablishing order in the streets. The wounds Trump inflicted upon the nation, however, are ragged and deep. We will be paying for the mistake of electing this bitter, twisted man president for a long, long time.

THE PRESIDENT AS PARIAH: TRUMP FACES A TORRENT OF RETRIBUTION OVER HIS ROLE IN THE US CAPITOL SIEGE:

January 13, 2021

On January 11, 2021 He has been banned on social media, shunned by foreign leaders, impeached (again) in the House, threatened with censure by the Republicans, deserted by Cabinet members, turned on by Senate Majority Leader, Mitch McConnell, R-Ky. canceled by his hometown of New York City, dropped by the PGA golf tour and snubbed by New England Patriots Coach Bill Belichick.

The fallout on Trump for his role in riling up thousands of supporters in a speech leading to their deadly siege on the U.S. Capitol last week, has intensified quickly — leaving the world's most powerful leader as a pariah in many quarters, more isolated than ever.

Trump won 74 million votes in the November election — the second-most ever behind President-elect Joe Biden's 81 million — but Twitter, Facebook and YouTube have cut him off from easily reaching them in the real-time stream of explosive, demeaning and sometimes dangerous missives that have defined his presidency. Three banks, two real estate companies and the 2022 PGA Championship tournament have severed ties with the Trump Organization at a time when Trump and his family are facing mounting pressure from massive financial debts.

Leaders in tiny Luxembourg canceled meetings with Secretary of State, Mike Pompeo, and Belgian leaders condemned the attack on the Capitol, prompting the top U.S. diplomat to scrap a final foreign trip to Europe this week. And some Republicans — beyond Sen. Mitt Romney, R-Utah, the lone GOP lawmaker to buck Trump in January's impeachment trial — voiced support for the second impeachment effort from Democrats on Wednesday.

"There has never been a greater betrayal by a president," Rep. Liz Cheney, R-Wyo. the third-ranking House Republican, said in a statement ahead of the vote. House Minority Leader Kevin McCarthy, R-Calif., reportedly floated the idea of censuring Trump, though he opposed impeachment.

TRUMP IS ISOLATED AND ANGRY AT AIDES FOR FAILING TO DEFEND HIM AS HE IS IMPEACHED AGAIN:

January 13, 2021

When Donald Trump, on Wednesday, became the first president ever to be impeached twice, he did so as a leader increasingly isolated, sullen and vengeful.

With less than seven days remaining in his presidency, Trump's inner circle is shrinking; offices in his White House are emptying; and, the president is lashing out at some of those who remain. He is angry that his allies have not mounted a more forceful defense to his incitement of the mob that stormed the Capitol last week, advisers and associates said.

Though Trump has been exceptionally furious with Vice President Pence, his relationship with lawyer Rudolph W. Giuliani, one of his most steadfast defenders, is also fracturing, according to people with knowledge of the dynamics between the men.

Trump has instructed aides not to pay Giuliani's legal fees, two officials said, and has demanded that he personally approve any reimbursements for the expenses Giuliani incurred while traveling on the president's behalf to challenge election results in key states. They said Trump has privately expressed concern with some of Giuliani's moves and did not appreciate a demand from Giuliani for $20,000 a day in fees for his work attempting to overturn the election.

The House of Representatives voted on January 13 to impeach President Trump a second time after the deadly U.S. Capitol breach.

One of Trump's few confidants these days is Sen. Lindsey O. Graham (R-S.C.) who broke with the president last week over attempts to overturn the election only to be welcomed back into the president's good graces a couple of days later. Graham traveled to Texas on Tuesday in what was Trump's last scheduled presidential trip, spending hours with Trump aboard Air Force One talking about impeachment and planning how Trump should spend his final days in office.

What do you mean cheated? He is a master in cheating! Do you think he really knows how many thousands of people he has been cheating during his whole life! This is ridiculous! He cheated his family, cheated his staff, cheated his customers, and cheated his contractors! Cheated the government of the

United States, cheated the New York City, cheated his foundation, cheated all his mistresses, cheated all his wives, cheated his landlords, cheated the election results, cheated the election officials, and others, but, worst of all, he cheated the CNBC nomination on-line poll, for the 2016 election results, that why he's an impostor. Without this scheme, mounted from scratch by his fixer, this monster would never have been President of the United States of America.

Trump asked Sen. Graham to lobby fellow senators in order to acquit him in his eventual impeachment trial, which Graham did from Air Force One as he worked through a list of colleagues to phone. A few senators called Trump aboard the presidential aircraft on Tuesday to notify him of their intent to acquit. During the flight home, Graham said, he tried to calm Trump after Rep. Liz Cheney (Wyo.), the No. 3 House GOP leader, announced she would vote to impeach.

"I just told him, 'Listen, Mr. President, there are some people out there who were upset before and are upset now, but I assure you, most Republicans believe impeachment is bad for the country and not necessary and it would do damage to the institution of the presidency itself," Graham recalled.

On January 13, 2021 McConnell effectively guaranteed that outcome Wednesday, releasing a schedule after the House impeachment vote that would push a trial until after President-elect Joe Biden's inauguration.

Trump has been more concerned with other actions that could have serious consequences for his post-presidential life, according to people familiar with the president's concerns. The developments include Twitter and other social media companies suspending his accounts, the PGA of America cancelling a golf tournament at one of his properties, and Deutsche Bank announcing it would no longer finance his developments.

The White House released a video Wednesday evening featuring Trump seated behind the resolute desk in the oval Office pleading with supporters not to engage in further violence.

A senior administration official said Kushner, the president's daughter, Ivanka Trump, Deputy Chief-of-Staff, Dan Scavino, and Vice-president Pence persuaded Trump to film the video, telling him it could boost support among weak Republicans.

Usually we harvest what we sow, that's what my grandfather used to say, so what you have to do now is cry some kind of crocodile tears for having created chaos and violence for over 50 months! That is why this country now looks like a banana republic; but Mr. Biden will get our democracy back. I HOPE.

THESE ARE THE 10 REPUBLICANS WHO VOTED TO IMPEACH TRUMP:

January 14, 2021

Who are the 10?
Here they are in order of the most pro-Trump districts:

1. Rep. Liz Cheney, Wyoming's at-large district: Trump won Wyoming 70% to 27%, and she's the third-ranking leader in the House. Cheney was unequivocal in her statement, saying that Trump "summoned this mob, assembled the mob, and lit the flame of this attack." She called what Trump did the "greatest betrayal" of a U.S. president ever.

2. Rep. Tom Rice, South Carolina's 7th Congressional District: This is one that no one saw coming. The congressman, who has served since 2013, comes from a pretty pro-Trump district (Trump won it 59% to 40%), and there was no indication he would do so beforehand. Wednesday, Rice explained: "I have backed this President through thick and thin for four years. I campaigned for him and voted for him twice. But this utter failure is inexcusable."

3. Rep. Dan Newhouse, Washington's 4th: Trump won this central Washington state district by a handy margin, 58% to 40%. But for Newhouse, who has served since 2015 and has not been a prominent member, it was clear: "The mob was inflamed by the language and misinformation of the President of the United States. ... A vote against impeachment is a vote to validate unacceptable violence" and "to condone President Trump's inaction."

4. Rep. Adam Kinzinger, Illinois' 16th: Kinzinger's decision was probably the least surprising on this list. Despite coming from a district Trump won 57% to 41%, the Air Force veteran was outspoken recently against Trump's behavior. He said Trump "incited this insurrection" and "if these actions — the Article II branch inciting a deadly insurrection against the Article I branch — are not worthy of impeachment, then what is an impeachable offense?"

5. Rep. Anthony Gonzalez, Ohio's 16th: Gonzalez, a former NFL wide receiver, is in his second term in Congress. Trump won his district by 15 points, but Gonzalez was unequivocal: Trump, he said, "helped

organize and incite a mob that attacked the United States Congress in an attempt to prevent us from completing our solemn duties as prescribed by the Constitution." He added that during the attack, Trump "abandoned his post ... thus further endangering all present."

6. Rep. Fred Upton, Michigan's 6th: Upton has been in office since 1987. He comes from a district that is more moderate. Trump won it just 51% to 47%. Upton has a good relationship with the Democrats, including President-elect Joe Biden, and even has #WearYourMask in his Twitter bio. "But," he said, "it is time to say: enough is enough." He also cited Trump's efforts "to impede the peaceful transfer of power from one President to the next."

    Rep. Tim Ryan: Probe Underway on Whether Members Gave Capitol Tours to Rioters

7. Rep. Jaime Herrera Beutler, Washington's 3rd: Herrera Beutler was swept in with the Tea Party wave in 2010, but her district is a moderate one. Trump won it 51% to 47%. The now-mother of three and congresswoman from southwest Washington State declared on the House floor her vote in favor of impeachment: "I'm not choosing sides, I'm choosing truth."

8. Rep. Peter Meijer, Michigan's 3rd: Meijer is a freshman, who won his seat with 53% of the vote. Meijer, a Columbia University grad who served in Afghanistan, but, he said, Trump showed no "courage" and "betrayed millions with claims of a "stolen election." He added, "The one man who could have restored order, prevented the deaths of five Americans including a Capitol police officer, and avoided the desecration of our Capitol, shrank from leadership when our country needed it most."

9. Rep. John Katko, New York's 24th: Katko is a moderate from an evenly divided moderate district. A former federal prosecutor, he said of Trump: "It cannot be ignored that President Trump encouraged this insurrection." He also noted that, as the riot was happening, Trump "refused to call it off, putting countless lives in danger."

10. Rep. David Valadao, California's 21st: The Southern California congressman represents a majority-Latino district Biden won 54% to 44%. Valadao won election to this seat in 2012 before losing it in 2018 and winning it back in the fall. He's the rare case of a member of Congress who touts his willingness to work with the other party. Of his vote for impeachment, he said: "President Trump was, without

question, a driving force in the catastrophic events that took place on January 6." He added, "His inciting rhetoric was un-American, abhorrent, and absolutely an impeachable offense."

OPENING THE DOOR IN THE SENATE:

The 10 who voted with Democrats to impeach Trump could give a degree of cover and open the door a little wider for Republicans in the Senate to vote to convict Trump. Sen. Mitt Romney of Utah was the sole Republican senator to vote to convict Trump in 2020.

This time, there will be more. Some Republican senators called on Trump to resign, and even Senate Majority Leader Mitch McConnell said that he is undecided at this point. Like I said before, "I don't trust this TWO-FACED PERSON" he will never vote against TRUMP.

GOP Leader McCarthy: Trump 'Bears Responsibility' For the Violence, Won't Vote to Impeach. Another TWO-FACED PERSON who will never convict the king monster.

It's a long shot that Trump would ultimately be convicted, because 17 Republicans would need to join the Democrats to get the two-third majority needed for a conviction. But it's growing clearer that a majority in the Senate will vote to convict him, reflecting the number of Americans who are in favor of impeachment, displeased with the job Trump has done and voted for his opponent in the 2020 presidential election.

Trump never put in place a coronavirus program

CHAPTER TWENTY FIVE

FOR THOSE WHO LEFT TRUMP AFTER THE RIOT, CRITICS SAY IT'S TOO LITTLE — AND 4 YEARS, TOO LATE:

January 15, 2021

Sarah Matthews, a 25-year-old White House spokeswoman, said she watched the violent images unfolding at the Capitol last Wednesday with horror.

Before joining the Trump campaign, and later the White House, she had worked in Congress, and said that "seeing people I know, who were scared for their lives, just shook me to my core."

After President Trump sent out two halfhearted tweets calling on the angry mob, he had encouraged to remain peaceful, Matthews walked to the West Wing's lower press office where, in front of several colleagues, she appeared visibly shaken. Several hours later, Trump finally put out a video calling on his supporters to leave the Capitol and go home, but Matthews was disturbed by the president's ad-libbed remarks in which he called the protesters "very special" and said, "We love you."

"I knew I could no longer serve in the role effectively, and I couldn't walk into the building the following day and act like everything was fine, because it was indefensible," said Matthews, who sent out her resignation letter later that evening.

"My decision had nothing to do with distancing myself from this administration," said Matthews, who joined the White House last June.

The violent insurrection at the Capitol on January 6, incited by Trump just 14 days before the inauguration of President-elect Joe Biden, set off a dramatic wave of resignations and attempts at distancing — from Cabinet secretaries to former senior advisers to West Wing aides like Matthews. Transportation

Secretary, Elaine Chao, and Education Secretary, Betsy DeVos, resigned, as did deputy national security adviser, Matthew Pottinger, Melania Trump's Chief of Staff, Stephanie Grisham, and White House social secretary, Anna Cristina "Rickie" Niceta, among others.

Republicans suddenly distance themselves from Trump's false election claims

Republicans who had echoed President Trump's false election claims suddenly distanced themselves after a pro-Trump mob breached the U.S. Capitol on January 6.

Trump's presidency, after all, is littered with crises of conscience — his Muslim ban; his failure to condemn the white-supremacist violence in Charlottesville; his decision to separate undocumented immigrant children from their parents and put them in cages; and his tear-gassing of largely peaceful protesters in Lafayette Square, to name a few.

Then-White House press secretary, Stephanie Grisham, watches a press event in the Rose Garden at the White House on November 25, 2019.

An administration where former top economic adviser, Gary Cohn, voiced his "distress" to the Financial Times in the wake of Charlottesville, but only actually resigned after a dispute over tariffs, is hardly a bastion of courage and conviction, critics say.

It's easy to quit when everything is done, and the Pandora's Box is empty. Maybe you should look at yourself in the mirror, to see what you haven't been doing all this time. For years watching the train monster without saying anything. This demagogue said all kinds of offenses against his opponents and incited to violence every day. So, I say to you, without naming anybody, because the list is too large, all the staff who worked for this monster, including the Senators, the republicans, also FOX-NEWS, you are partly responsible for this mess. Moreover, you are complicit of 89% of the COVID-19 deaths. SHAME ON YOU!

MITCH MCCONNELL:

The ignorant, two-faced liar, and the top hypocrite, doesn't know his American history. Or pretends not to, in order to please his MOB BOSS.

I believe you should go back to school, March 23, 2021 on CNN, you said, and I quote "filibuster has no racial history" oh really. 1846, 1922, 1935, 1957, these dates don't mean few things to you, if not then it's time to go to a nursing home. I have a reminder for you; Lincoln said "If you think education is expensive, try ignorance". That's especially for you.

Trump's most enduring legacy could be the historic rise in the national debt:

January 14, 2021

One of President Donald Trump's lesser known but profoundly damaging legacies will be the explosive rise in the national debt that occurred on his watch.

It rose almost $7.8 trillion during his time in the White House — approaching World War II levels, relative to the size of the economy. This time around, it will be much harder to dig ourselves out.

The financial burden that he's inflicted on our government will wreak havoc for decades, saddling our kids and grandkids with debt.

Trump will have the worst job record in modern U.S. history. It's not just the pandemic.

The national debt rose by almost $7.8 trillion during Trump's time in office. That's nearly twice as much as what Americans owe on student loans, car loans, credit cards and every other type of debt other than mortgages, combined, according to data from the Federal Reserve Bank of New York. It amounts to about $23,500 in new federal debt for every person in the country.

The combination of Trump's 2017 tax cut and the lack of any serious spending restraint helped both the deficit and the debt soar. So, when the once-in-a-lifetime viral disaster slammed our country and we threw more than $3 trillion into covid-related stimulus, there was no longer any margin for error.

Falling deeper into the red is the opposite of what Trump, the self-styled "King of Debt," said would happen if he became president. In a March 31, 2016 interview with Bob Woodward and Robert Costa of The Washington Post, Trump said he could pay down the national debt, then about $19 trillion, "over a period of eight years" by renegotiating trade deals and spurring economic growth.

After he took office, Trump predicted that economic growth created by the 2017 tax cut, combined with the proceeds from the tariffs he imposed on a wide range of goods from numerous countries, would help eliminate the budget deficit and let the United States begin to pay down its debt. On July 27,

2018, he told Fox News's Sean Hannity, "We have $21 trillion in debt. When [the 2017 tax cut] really kicks in, we'll start paying off that debt like its water."

Meanwhile, Trump's claim that increased revenue from the tariffs would help eliminate increase deficits by about $1.9 trillion over 11 years. (Or at least reduce) our national debt hasn't panned out. In 2018, Trump's administration began hiking tariffs on aluminum, steel and many other products, launching what became a global trade war with China, the European Union and other countries.

The tariffs did bring in additional revenue. In the fiscal year 2019, they netted about $71 billion, up about $36 billion from President Barack Obama's last year in office. But although $36 billion is a lot of money, it's less than 1/750th of the national debt.

By early 2019, the national debt had climbed to $22 trillion. Trump's budget proposal for 2020 called it a "grave threat to our economic and societal prosperity".

FINALLY, THESE REPUBLICANS CAN STOMACH TRUMP NO MORE:

January 13, 2021

It may be too little too late, but in the end a few brave Republicans found their voices and spoke up to protect American democracy from President Trump's depredations.

Liz Cheney (Wyo.), the No. 3 Republican in the House and scion of a revered Republican family, changed the debate overnight when she said she would vote to impeach the man who "lit the flame" of last week's deadly attack on Congress. "There has never been a greater betrayal by a President of the United States of his office and his oath to the Constitution," she said.

Lesser-known but no less brave was Rep. Dan Newhouse (R-Wash.), who, at 1:42 p.m. Wednesday, stood on the floor and announced: "There is no excuse for President Trump's actions. With a heavy heart and clear resolve, I will vote yes on these articles of impeachment."

Less than five minutes later, another Republican from Washington, Rep. Jaime Herrera Beutler, rose to declare that she, too, would vote to impeach. "I'm not afraid of losing my job, but I am afraid that my country will fail," she said.

Now, our nation's capital is under siege by the MAGA mob. Approximately 2,000 National Guard troops bivouacked in the halls of Congress before Wednesday's impeachment debate, the first such deployment since the Civil War and part of a force of 20,000 coming to defend the capital from attack by pro-Trump rioters.

Rep. Tom Cole (Okla.) kicked off the impeachment debate for Republicans by asking "for God's blessing and protection . . . for all who come to this chamber."

Rep. Seth Moulton (D-Mass.), a veteran, observed that "there are more troops right now in Washington, D.C., than in Afghanistan, and they are here to defend us against . . . the president of the United States and his mob." He urged Republicans to see the warrior's defending democracy and "take a tough vote."

In the end, 10 honorable House Republicans took that tough vote — even though it could cost them their jobs, and even though Senate Majority Leader Mitch McConnell (R-Ky.) let it be known, in the middle of the House debate, that he would block a Senate trial until at least January 19 — the day before Trump leaves office.

One after the other, several of the 139 House Republicans who last week voted to overturn the election results now justified votes against impeachment because "our country needs unity" (Rep. Debbie Lesko, Ariz.) and "our nation is still healing" (Rep. Guy Reschenthaler, Pa.). Several of those who last week engaged in a seditious act now cited Lincoln's second inaugural call to "bind up the nation's wounds." What a bunch of hypocrites, and puppet cowards! What have you done to heal your demagogue sick man? Where were you? Maybe on Fantasy Island? Shame on you!

"Unity, after they voted to overturn a free and fair election?" replied Rep. Jim McGovern (D-Mass.). He said that the Capitol attack "would never have happened if everybody had stood up in unity and called out the president when he was not telling the American people the truth."

Some always defended Trump's words inciting the Capitol insurrection, employing a web of false equivalences, whataboutisms and warnings that impeachment "will cause further unrest," as Ronny L. Jackson (R-Tex.), Trump-doctor-turned-congressman, put it. Rep. Matt Gaetz (Fla.) denounced the "unconstitutional" election. Qanon-admiring Rep. Lauren Boebert (R-Colo.) declared: "I call bull crap!" Jordan pushed an effort to strip Cheney of her leadership position.

Cole called Trump's words "inappropriate and reckless." Freshman Rep.

169

Nancy Mace (S.C.) said "I hold him accountable . . . for the attack on our Capitol." Rep. Tom McClintock (Calif.) said Trump "was wrong." Rep. Jodey Arrington (Tex.) said Trump used "poor judgment."

After such personal terror at Trump's hands, it's disturbing that only 10 Republicans found the courage to break with him. But at least a few survived the Trump era with their souls.

My opinion: Bravo for the 10 real patriots who decided to impeach the monster.

LIZ CHENEY SLAMS TRUMP'S ATTEMPT TO BRAND THE 2020 ELECTION 'THE BIG LIE':

May 3, 2021

Rep. Liz Cheney made clear Monday that she will continue to publicly denounce former president Donald Trump over his false claims that the 2020 election was stolen, imperiling her position in House Republican leadership as GOP members continue to rally around Trump.

Cheney quickly condemned Trump's comment as well as anyone who supports his statements about the election.

"The 2020 presidential election was not stolen" Cheney tweeted. "Anyone who claims it was is spreading THE BIG LIE, turning their back on the rule of law, and poisoning our democratic system."

Hours later, Trump released another statement, this time attacking Cheney by calling her a "big-shot warmonger" and claiming that people in Wyoming "never liked her much."

House Minority Leader Kevin McCarthy (R-Calif) and Rep. Liz Cheney (R-Wyo.) disagreed on February 24th on former president Donald Trump's role in the Republican Party. Cheney said that challenging Trump's false statements about the election is an issue of principle, but has she increasingly angered her GOP colleagues and faced renewed calls to step down from the No. 3 leadership post in the conference.

Cheney was one of 10 House Republicans to vote to impeach Trump in January on charges that he incited the January 6 storming of the U.S. Capitol with false claims of a stolen election. Some Republicans demanded she be stripped of her leadership post over that vote, but she beat back an initial challenge overwhelmingly, with 145 members of the conference supporting keeping her in the position. Only 61 voted to remove her during the closed-ballot vote.

"We can't whitewash what happened on January 6 or perpetuate Trump's big lie," she said while being interviewed at the conference by former House speaker Paul D. Ryan (R-Wis.), according to the network. "It is a threat to democracy. What he did on January 6 is a line that cannot be crossed."

McCarthy, who was one of the congressional Republicans who voted to contest the election results, said in January that Trump "bear's responsibility" for the attack, but he defended Trump's response in a recent "Fox News Sunday" interview. At the House Republicans' annual policy retreat last month, he also pointedly declined to say whether Cheney was still a "good fit" for the party's leadership team.

"We're different political parties. We're not sworn enemies. We're Americans," she said. Trump never put in place a coronavirus program.

CHAPTER TWENTY SIX

'TRUMP WAS COMORBIDITY':

May 6, 2021

Just published: The Premonition: A Pandemic Story by Michael Lewis.

New York Times: "We do not yet know how the movie ends."

But Lewis, whose book is among the first wave of narrative accounts of the pandemic, is more interested in how it began. Believed to be a rich country best prepared for a pandemic, we ended up with almost a fifth of the world's Covid-related deaths. Popular blame has centered, not undeservedly, on former President Donald Trump, who ignored his advisers' warnings, publicly downplayed Corvid's dangers in the hopes of preserving his re-election chances and left states to fend for themselves."

But Lewis has a different thesis. As one character puts it, 'Trump was comorbidity.

"But the rot ran deep through the American system of public health, and in particular the Centers for Disease Control and Prevention, once considered a crown jewel of the American government."

The mind is like a parachute, it is only useful if it is open. But trump, because he lives in another fantasy world, he cannot open his mind. Facebook's Oversight Board upholds ban on Trump. At least for now.

May 6, 2021

Donald Trump's ban from Facebook and Instagram has been upheld by Facebook's Oversight Board.

It has ordered Facebook to review the decision and "justify a proportionate response" that is applied to everyone, including ordinary users.

The former president was banned from both sites in January following the Capitol Hill riots.

The Oversight Board said the initial decision to permanently suspend Mr. Trump was "indeterminate and standardless", and that the correct response should be "consistent with the rules that are applied to other users of its platform".

At a press conference, co-chair Helle Thorning-Schmidt admitted: "We did not have an easy answer."

She added that she felt Facebook would "appreciate the decision".

"We are telling Facebook to go back and be more transparent about how it assesses these things. Treat all users the same and don't give arbitrary penalties."

In the meantime, Mr. Trump, who is also banned from Twitter, launched a new website on Tuesday to update supporters with his thoughts.

Following the ruling, Mr. Trump wrote that "what Facebook, Twitter, and Google have done is a total disgrace". Oh, oh, sorry YOU are the disgrace.

"Free speech has been taken away from the President of the United States because the radical left lunatics are afraid of the truth," he said, referring to himself as president.

But you don't know the meaning of this word "TRUTH" because you are the biggest liar in the world.

Republicans are undermining American democracy. Here's how it could backfire on them.

April 22, 2021

A Reuters/Ipsos poll conducted this month contained an ominous indicator of the state of U.S. democracy. According to the poll, 60 percent of Republican voters still believe the 2020 election was "stolen" from former president Donald Trump — and 55 percent of Republicans think the 2020 election was rife with voter fraud and other forms of election-rigging.

These authoritarian machinations are a serious threat to American democracy. But what Republican leaders may not realize is that their lies about the quality of U.S. elections pose a serious threat to their political chances in the 2022 midterms, too. Republicans seem not to care about the violent consequences of spreading lies about election fraud or torching faith in democratic institutions.

As political scientist Emily Beaulieu Bacchus of the University of

Kentucky has shown in her research, election boycotts in broken democracies frequently backfire, inadvertently giving more political power to their rivals. Because of the staying power of Trump's lies about election fraud within the Republican base, a split is likely to emerge in the GOP. Next year,

In Georgia's 2021 special election, a preview of this phenomenon already played out after Trump spread lies about his election defeat. Two unhinged Trump acolytes, Sidney Powell and L. Lin Wood, called for a boycott. Some in Georgia's Republican Party blamed that attempted boycott for the party's ensuing razor-thin losses, which handed control of the U.S. Senate to the Democrats. Imagine that replicated in all 50 states.

MCCONNELL FOCUSES '100 PERCENT' ON BLOCKING BIDEN — AND ZERO PERCENT ON AMERICA:

May 26, 2021

It has long been obvious that Mitch McConnell puts party before country, but this week he actually admitted it.

The Senate minority leader told Republican colleagues that they should oppose the creation of a January 6 commission, no matter how it is structured, because it "could hurt the party's midterm election message," as Politico's Burgess Everett reported.

And so, as early as Thursday, McConnell will use the filibuster to thwart a bipartisan effort to prevent further attacks on the U.S. government by domestic terrorists — because he thinks it's good politics for Republicans.

On May 6, 2021 McConnell, asked this month about the ouster of Rep. Liz Cheney (R-Wyo.) from GOP leadership, and whether he was concerned that many Republicans believe Donald Trump's election lie, replied, twice: "One hundred percent of my focus is on stopping this new administration." True to his word, McConnell has blocked everything — even if it means undercutting Republican negotiators.

TRUMP'S EVER-PRESENT — AND STILL GROWING — EXPLOITATION OF THE JUSTICE DEPARTMENT:

JUNE 11, 2021

It has been clear for a very long time that then-President Donald Trump sought to politicize and weaponize the Justice Department. This is a guy, after all, whose most popular rally cry during his campaign was "lock her up," about his opponent.

Even then-Attorney General, William P. Barr, a fan of a powerful chief executive if there ever was one, decided he needed to at least make a show of publicly telling Trump to knock it off.

He fired the man leading the Russia investigation involving himself, then-FBI Director, James B. Comey.

He tried to remove Comey's effective replacement, special counsel Robert S. Mueller III, according to the testimony of former White House counsel Donald McGahn.

He repeatedly pressured then-Attorney General, Jeff Sessions, to fire then-FBI Deputy Director Andrew McCabe. Sessions ultimately fired McCabe hours before McCabe was able to retire with full benefits.

He toyed with firing various other figures involved in or adjacent to the Russia probe, including Sessions (who ultimately resigned in the face of the pressure) and Deputy Attorney General, Rod J. Rosenstein.

He intermittently suggested that the DOJ should investigate Hillary Clinton again, not just for her private email server as secretary of state but also her campaign role in the Steele dossier and allegedly rigging the 2016 Democratic primary.

He repeatedly applied pressure on the DOJ to take it easy on his allies facing legal pressure, apparently ultimately succeeding in the cases of Michael Flynn and Roger Stone.

Even just this week, we got the latest evidence of Trump's ploys. While discussing Trump's efforts to get him to help in removing Mueller, McGahn talked about how frequently Trump wanted to have the "same conversation" over and over again.

THERE'S NO ESCAPE FROM HOLDING TRUMP ACCOUNTABLE:

June 12, 2021

The revelation that the Trump Justice Department secretly sought the phone records of two Democrat members of the House Intelligence Committee who were among President Donald Trump's sharpest critics (along with those of their aides and family members) was the shock that the system needed.

It underscored the tension between two essential goals for the Justice Department under Attorney General Merrick Garland: how to depoliticize a department that effectively became an arm of the White House under Trump without evading the imperative of requiring a lawless presidency to answer for its abuses.

But the disclosures about the previously secret Justice Department efforts under Attorneys General Jeff Sessions and William P. Barr to obtain the phone records of two California Democrats, Reps. Adam B. Schiff and Eric Swalwell, raised an uncomfortable but fundamental question: Does fighting against using the justice system for political purposes require a new administration to expose and, if appropriate, prosecute a previous administration for the very violation the responsible newcomers are trying to avoid?

In the meantime, Senate Majority Leader Charles E. Schumer (D-N.Y.) joined Judiciary Committee Chairman Richard J. Durbin (D-Ill.) in calling on Sessions and Barr to testify before Durbin's committee.

But as the flare-up over the investigation into Schiff and Swalwell made clear, the Biden administration may not have this luxury. Garland is right to do all he can to keep his department out of politics. Unfortunately, the nature of Trump's presidency will complicate any path back to the old ways and the old rules. It's Trump's poisoned chalice.

So, President Donald Trump's Oval Office meeting on Dec. 18, 2020, has always been particularly revolting to me. The day before, former national security adviser, Michael Flynn, appeared on the conservative cable network Newsmax to argue that Trump could deploy the military to rerun the 2020 presidential election. The next day, Trump had Flynn into the Oval Office to discuss the idea.

The revelations keep coming about Trump's subversion of his office and the Justice Department in a desperate and lawless attempt to retain power. We know that Trump contemplated having the federal government seize voting machines in key states. We know he pressured local election officials to "find" more votes and urged state legislators to overturn legitimate election results. We know he gathered protesters, and incited and sent them to the U.S. Capitol to threaten members of Congress if they did not overturn the election.

Now, from detailed reporting in The Post, we know that Trump — both directly and through proxies — pressured employees of the Justice Department to investigate a raft of bogus election fraud claims. He had a draft Supreme Court filing sent to the acting solicitor general that would have disputed the election results in six states.

It is astounding to see the chief-of-staff to the president, Mark Meadows, pressing a series of insane conspiracy theories with the Justice Department — including one alleging that the election had been stolen by military satellites controlled in Italy. The two chiefs-of-staff I worked for in the White House would have laughed at such garbage and resigned if ordered to spread it.

It is astounding that the then-head of the Civil Division at the Department of Justice, Jeffrey Bossert Clark, should be sympathetic to Trump's entirely baseless claim of fraud in the Georgia outcome, and internally advocate a theory justifying the appointment of alternate electors.

And despite all this, the vast majority of elected Republicans have chosen to stand with a president who would have conducted a coup if it had been within his power. Despite all this, 175 House Republicans, along with 35 GOP senators, voted against a commission to investigate the January 6 assault on the Capitol. Conservative media is in full, "big lie" swing, blaming liberal activists or the FBI for inciting Trump's violent crowd, or denying that the day was violent at all. Twenty-one House Republicans refused to support awarding the Congressional Gold Medal to the police officers who defended the Capitol on January 6— effectively siding with the forces of sedition. These 175 republicans and the 35 GOP senators are without a doubt all traitors.

THE 21 REPUBLICANS WHO VOTED AGAINST THE BILL ARE:

Lauren Boebert of Colorado. John Rose of Tennessee. Andy Harris of Maryland.

Omas Massie of Kentucky. Bob Good of Virginia. Louie Gohmert of Texas.

Barry Moore of Alabama, Ralph Norman of South Carolina. Chip Roy of Texas.

Matt Rosendale of Montana. Paul Gosar of Arizona. Scott Perry of Pennsylvania.

Marjorie Taylor Greene of Georgia. Andy Biggs of Arizona. Matt Gaetz of Florida.

Warren Davidson of Ohio. Greg Steube of Florida. Andrew Clyde of Georgia.

Jody Hice of Georgia. Mary Miller of Illinois. Michael Cloud of Texas.

It is clear what these Republicans are saying to Americans: Serving the country has ceased to interest them, and their deepest loyalty now belongs to power alone. It is also clear what they're saying to Trump: He has their full permission to assault, once again, the political system he tried and failed to destroy.

Trump never put in place a coronavirus program.

Chapter Twenty Seven

....

THE COMPANY ONCE CLOAKED TRUMP IN GILDED FAME. NOW IT FACES FELONIES, DEBT AND TOXIC BRANDING:

The Trump Organization, even if it avoids a conviction, is at its lowest point in decades

July 2, 2021

The full impact of the 10 felony counts on Trump's business brought against it by Manhattan District Attorney Cyrus R. Vance Jr. (D) — as well as 15 felony counts against his chief financial officer — remains to be seen. The company and CFO, Allen Weissenberg, pleaded not guilty to all the charges. Trump was not charged in the case. But we see later.

Trump will remain a wealthy man regardless of whether his company is convicted of any of the charges. But the indictment adds to a growing pile of uncertainties about his company that experts say makes its future less clear than at any time since Trump's much publicized collapse in Atlantic City and New York in the 1990s.

If convicted, the company could face hefty fines or other court-imposed penalties, according to legal experts. A felony conviction can complicate the company's efforts to secure bank loans or even municipal licenses to sell alcohol or get construction permits.

Prosecutors allege a 15-year tax fraud scheme as the Trump Organization and its CFO are arraigned on multiple felony counts

His two oldest children, Donald Trump Jr. and Ivanka Trump, have followed his path out of the business and into the political sphere. And some of his top properties have suffered severe drops in revenue, with more than $300 million in debt to refinance or pay off in the next few years.

D'Antonio and another Trump biographer, Gwenda Blair, both said the indictment of the Trump Organization comes during what appears to be the company's most difficult moment since Trump's financial crash in the early 1990s.

During that period, Trump found himself hundreds of millions of dollars in debt, and he lost control of prized assets — including an airline, a yacht and New York's Plaza Hotel. His business empire did not fully recover for a decade, until Trump gained television fame and made tens of millions as the star of NBC's "The Apprentice."

Barbara Res, a top construction executive at the Trump Organization from 1980 to 1998, said Trump was already facing a problem caused by his political career. His company is still built around the old gold-plated luxury brand, aimed at wealthy urban dwellers and tourists. But his political career alienated most of that demographic. Now, Res said, "Most of his [company's] brand talks to people who are not his supporters."

Res said she expects the indictment will further restrict Trump's ability to attract partners and lenders. "Why would you want to be associated with Trump if you didn't have to be?" Res said Thursday. "I think it will have a dramatic impact on the company."

That impact will almost certainly be more severe if the company or Weisselberg, or both, are convicted of the felonies Vance and New York Attorney General Letitia James (D) leveled in court Thursday.

Prosecutors charged the company with what they called a 15-year "scheme to defraud" the government of taxes through what they described as a wide-ranging effort to hide compensation provided to Weisselberg and other employees, including apartments, luxury cars, bonuses and private school tuition for employees' children. It's "fairly unusual" to prosecute this type of crime, said Columbia University law professor John Coffee Jr. But he said: "That's not a defense. Just because a prosecutor normally goes after other bigger crimes, that's not a defense."

"This may be just the beginning, to become applying strong pressure on Mr. Weisselberg to flip him," he said.

"I think of Weisselberg and Donald as brothers who were brought into the company at the same time. And one was the outside man and one was the inside man," D'Antonio said. He said Weisselberg's inside-man role was especially important because of the company's complex finances:

Daniel Goldman, a former assistant U.S. attorney and lead House impeachment lawyer in 2019, said that Trump's political framing of the charges is focused on business partners, lenders and others who impact the former president's bottom line.

"He is trying to take the attack in belittling these charges so they won't end their relationship with him," Goldman said. "He's basically trying to save his company."

Legally, Trump's tech lawsuit is a joke. But it raises a serious question:

July 8, 2021

Former president Donald Trump's lawsuits against Facebook, Twitter and YouTube have been rightly derided as wrong on the facts, preposterous on the law and doomed to be thrown out of court.

Facebook, Twitter and Alphabet (which owns Google and YouTube) barred Trump from their platforms after he incited violence on January 6. They are private companies, and they had every right to do so. They may (and most people would agree should) ban child pornography, racist appeals or, yes, calls to violence.

Trump's lawsuits purport to get around this little problem by claiming that Facebook, Twitter and YouTube are "state actors". Which is, as experts told The Post, a "crackpot theory" and a "complete misinterpretation" of the law?

I still think they have an obligation to do so at times. But they are not wrong to fear the cost of any apparent high-handedness. Trump has no legal case underneath all his lies and self-pity, though, he may have a point.

Trump's latest ridiculous lawsuit shows how small he has become

July 7, 2021

For someone who filed thousands of lawsuits during his career in business, former president Donald Trump has been rather quiet on the legal front since he left office — particularly if you don't count the criminal charges his business and associates are facing — with only a few minor suits filed here and there.

But that ended on Wednesday. Trump announced that he has filed suit against Facebook, Google, Twitter, and their CEOs, a class action that will at last seek justice for the people those companies have so grievously wronged, starting with Trump himself.

It sounds like something big: a former president, facing off against some of the biggest, most influential and most profitable tech companies in America. But, in fact, it's puny and pathetic.

Of course, this is only the latest in a long-running series of complaints from conservatives about social media companies, which gained urgency when Facebook and Twitter removed Trump's accounts after the 2020 election.

And what is this suit about? It's about money, of course. As soon as Trump announced the suit, fundraising texts were blasted out to his supporters.

"President Trump is filing a LAWSUIT against Facebook and Twitter for UNFAIR CENSORSHIP!" they read. "Please contribute IMMEDIATELY to INCREASE your impact by 500% and to get your name on the Donor List President Trump sees!"

Five dollars? Ten dollars? Whatever you can contribute to help Trump, get out that credit card and do it now.

This is a reminder of Trump's truest nature: a sad small-timer telling everyone how big he is.

For much of his career, there has been no scam too small for him to pull and no product too cheesy for him to hawk, whether it was steaks or ties or vodka or vitamins. That last one involved people sending in a urine test, after which they'd receive a package of vitamins supposedly tuned to their unique metabolism. You can guess how it ended.

If it could bring in a few bucks, he did it. And that's what he's still doing.

REMARKS:

Hello, you naïve, and ignorant enablers, if you don't know what to do, with your money send a few million to the RED CROSS.

Idiots are like red lights, you have them on every street corner, but the most dangerous idiot is in MAR- A- LAGO.

WHAT HAPPENED ON JANUARY 6TH WAS HORRIFYING

What happened on January 6th was horrifying: an attempted coup, inflamed by social media, incited by the defeated president and televised in real time. But what happened before January 6th, we are beginning to learn, was equally horrifying: a slow-motion attempted coup, plotted in secret at the pinnacle of government and foiled by the resistance of a few officials who would not accede to Donald Trump's deluded view of the election outcome.

That is the unnerving picture that is only beginning to fully emerge of what was happening behind the scenes as Trump, enraged by his loss, schemed to overturn clear election results with the connivance of, not only top White House aides, but also senior officials at the Justice Department who were maneuvering around their chain of command to bolster Trump's efforts.

We have known for months that Trump — heedless of constraints on hijacking Justice Department operations to his own political ends — pressed Justice Officials to intervene on his behalf. For example, he urged Rosen to appoint special counsels to investigate unfounded claims of voter fraud.

We knew that when Rosen balked, Trump entertained a plan to oust Rosen and replace him with Jeffrey Clark, the acting head of the civil division, who was more willing to push Trump's fanciful assertions of fraud.

We knew that Clark had drafted a letter to Georgia state legislators asserting that the department was investigating claims of fraud in the state.

Many have argued that President Donald Trump's efforts amounted to an attempted coup on January 6th.

The cockamamie letter itself recently emerged. Dated December 28, 2020, it stated that the department had "identified significant concerns that may have impacted the outcome of the election in multiple States, including the State of Georgia." This despite the conclusion by Attorney General William P. Barr, before he resigned that month, that the department's investigation had not uncovered "fraud on a scale that could have affected a different outcome in the election."

The Clark letter not only urged Georgia Gov. Brian Kemp (R) to call the legislature into special session to consider "this important and urgent matter" but also advised the legislature of its "implied authority under the Constitution of the United States to call itself into special session for the limited purpose of considering issues pertaining to the appointment of Presidential Electors." It

183

was to be signed by Rosen, acting deputy attorney general Richard Donoghue and Clark himself.

Clark had insisted that his dealings with the White House were "consistent with law" and that he had merely participated in "a candid discussion of options and pros and cons with the president."

Sen. Richard Blumenthal (D-Conn.) told CNN on Sunday that he was "struck by how close the country came to total catastrophe."

"What was going on in the Department of Justice was frightening," Senate Judiciary Committee Chairman Richard J. Durbin (D-Ill.) said on CNN's State of the Union. "I think it's a good thing for America that we had a person like Rosen in that position, who ... withstood the pressure."

Will that always be the case? Will the country be able to dodge future bullets, from Trump or his successors? I would like to think so. But if there is anything the past five years have shown, it is the disappointing fecklessness of too many of those in power in the face of the Trumpism onslaught.

4 FLAWS IN TRUMP'S FIGHT TO HANG ON TO HIS TAX RETURNS:

04-08-2021

On Friday, the Justice Department ordered the Internal Revenue Service to hand over former president Donald Trump's tax returns to Congress. On Monday, Ronald Fischetti, a lawyer for Trump, said Trump intends to fight the order.

"There is no evidence of any wrongdoing here and I object to the release of the returns not only on behalf of my client but on behalf of all future holders of the office of the president of the United States," Fischetti said in statement. He added that "this politicization and harassment of Mr. Trump is uncalled for and outrageous" and that he had "never seen anything like this." Mr. Fischetti, you are right, we have never seen a bigger crook president than this.

First, there is considerable evidence of wrongdoing. The Trump Organization — a closely held company run by Trump himself and his family members — was recently indicted on charges of tax fraud. Prosecutors described a 15-year tax avoidance scheme "constituting a systematic ongoing course of conduct with intent to defraud." The 15 counts included falsification of records.

February 27, 2019, Trump's former longtime personal lawyer, Michael Cohen, testified before Congress about crimes he said he had committed at Trump's behest. Those crimes included misusing charity funds, and bank and insurance fraud. Cohen testified that Trump inflated or deflated the value of properties depending upon his needs at a given moment. Cohen presented copies of Trump's bank and financial records to back up his claims.

"His biggest fear," Cohen said later in an interview, "is that he will end up with a massive tax bill, fraud penalties, fines, and possibly even tax fraud."

The records revealed struggling properties, outsized tax write-offs and a taxpayer in serious trouble with hundreds of millions of dollars in debt coming due.

In a 2016 presidential debate against his opponent Hillary Clinton, Trump bragged that not paying taxes made him "smart".

Second, contrary to Fischetti's implication, Congress had a legitimate legislative purpose for requesting the tax returns, perfectly valid under its oversight duties. The House Ways and Means Committee sought Trump's returns to determine whether the IRS was fully and appropriately auditing the president. Trump is on extremely weak footing here. Congress is permitted wide latitude to investigate the executive branch, which is key to our system of checks and balances. Moreover, Section 6103(f) of the Internal Revenue Code, 26 U.S.C. § 6103(f), requires, in mandatory terms, that the Treasury "shall furnish" the committee with "any" requested tax return information

The fourth hole is fairly obvious: How is making Trump's tax returns available to Congress "harassment" — unless Trump has much to hide? He was, after all, the first president to refuse to disclose his taxes. Richard M. Nixon voluntarily released his returns; Nixon subsequently released his tax returns for every year between 1969, when he entered office, and 1972.

Every president since Nixon voluntarily released his tax returns.

Perhaps someone should tell Fischetti that Hillary Clinton voluntarily made all of her tax records available. The Clintons complied with every request and in the end, no evidence was found that they had engaged in any financial wrongdoing.

Nixon and the Clintons voluntarily made their financial records public when they were questioned because innocent people are not afraid to testify or show such records. But Trump is not innocent.

Only innocent people are not afraid, to release their records, that doesn't apply to Trump, why? Because he is a crook.

Trump never put in place a coronavirus program.

CHAPTER TWENTY EIGHT

. . . .

GEN. MILLEY STRESS TEST:

18-09-2021

The final months of Donald Trump's presidency were a stress test for Gen. Mark A. Milley, chairman of the Joint Chiefs of Staff. He feared that Trump would use a violent crisis at home or abroad to draw the military into his machinations to retain power.

Milley was determined to prevent this politicization of the military, and the nation owes him a debt of thanks for his vigilance. He is our hero of the decade.

Milley came under fire in the run-up to the publication of "Peril," by Bob Woodward and Robert Costa of "The Post". The book provides new documentation on what has been whispered for months — that Milley reached out to foreign military leaders and U.S. politicians to counteract Trump's ability to use a violent crisis for political advantage.

Milley's detractors have focused on his October 30, 2020, and January 8 telephone calls to Gen. Li Zuocheng, his Chinese counterpart, to calm Chinese fears that Trump might take rash military action. This criticism is misplaced. Military-to-military contacts to "deconflict" crises are common and essential.

Milley's predecessor, Gen. Joseph F. Dunford Jr., recalled in an interview that, in 2018, he had contacted Gen. Valery Gerasimov, the Russian chief of military staff, to ease his fears of instability while Russia was hosting the World Cup soccer tournament that summer. Dunford said he encouraged NATO to call off a scheduled military exercise, just as Milley did in advising postponement of an Indo-Pacific Command exercise after the January 6 insurrection at the Capitol.

Avoiding unintended confrontations is part of the job for a chairman of the Joint Chiefs of Staff. And though the chairman isn't formally in the chain of command, Dunford and others say there was nothing improper in Milley's request that commanders keep him informed, as the president's chief military adviser, if Trump gave an order to use nuclear weapons or other military force.

The focus on Milley misses a larger point: he was just one of a half-dozen senior military and civilian officials who took similar unusual steps during the final months of Trump's administration to prevent what they feared might be a domestic or international catastrophe. This group — which quietly placed guardrails around the president's actions — included <u>Secretary of State Mike Pompeo, Attorney General William P. Barr, CIA Director Gina Haspel</u> and other senior officials, according to Woodward and Costa's book.

For Milley, the worries about Trump's manipulation of the military began in June 2020, when Trump wanted to invoke the Insurrection Act and deploy uniformed active-duty troops to quell violent protests that followed the murder of George Floyd. Milley told colleagues later that when Trump's adviser, Stephen Miller, demanded troops during an oval Office meeting on June 1, arguing that "the barbarians are at the gates", Milley cut him off, saying, "Shut the fuck up, Steve." <u>Trump backed down.</u>

Later that day, Milley made an error he still regrets. In his baggy camouflage uniform, he accompanied Trump and Defense Secretary Mark T. Esper across Lafayette Square to a photo-op in front of St. John's Church. <u>"I realized it was a mistake halfway across, but by then it was too late,"</u> he said later.

Milley worried after the election that Trump was trying to seize what he called the intelligence "power ministries" of government — the CIA, FBI and NSA. He refused to endorse a December plan to break up the National Security Agency from Cyber Command and install a Trump loyalist at the NSA. Meanwhile, Barr had rejected an effort to dump Christopher A. Wray as head of the FBI, Woodward and Costa write. And as I reported in April, Haspel said in December that she would quit if Trump fired her deputy and installed Trump zealot Kashyap <u>Patel.</u>

Woodward and Costa quote Milley's January 8 reassurance to House Speaker Nancy Pelosi (D-Calif.) that he would prevent any misuse of the military. She was concerned because Trump had fired Esper and installed as acting defense secretary an inexperienced Christopher C. Miller, along with a group of top aides headed by Patel as chief of staff.

Pelosi wasn't the only politician Milley contacted in the turbulent transition months. He told colleagues he spoke with Senate Republican and Democrat leaders Mitch McConnell and Charles E. Schumer, and Sens. Jim Inhofe (R-Okla.) and Jack Reed (D-R.I.), the two leaders of the Senate Armed Services Committee.

THE EASTMAN MEMO WAS ALARMING. LEGALLY SPEAKING, IT WAS ALSO NONSENSE:

The wild scenarios a Trump attorney dreamed up would never have worked out.

23-09-2021

After Joe Biden won the 2020 election, but before the results were certified, John Eastman, a former law professor at Chapman University's School of Law and an active member of the Federalist Society, outlined a six-step scheme to overturn the election and hand the presidency back to Donald Trump. Eastman's scheme, which was revealed this week, had no chance of succeeding — but the memo tells us much about Trump's intentions and state of mind on January 6th when a horde of his supporters stormed the Capitol to try to obstruct the constitutional process from confirming the election result.

Eastman detailed the plan for what would happen on January 6th, the day Congress would count electoral votes. Under this scheme, Vice President Mike Pence would begin counting electors from the states alphabetically, "without conceding" that he was following the procedure outlined in the Electoral Count Act. When reaching Arizona, Pence would announce that "he has multiple slates of electors and so is going to defer decision on that until finishing the other states."

Even if Pence had agreed to go along with this scheme — which he didn't — the plan would have gone off the rails right there because, in fact, no states put forward alternate slates of electors. The "alternate electors" were Trump allies claiming, without authority, to be electors. Members of Congress would have, therefore, objected immediately to Pence's false statement and his refusal to count certified electors. Chaos would have ensued.

Then, according to Eastman's memo, after counting each state and concluding with Wyoming, the last state in alphabetical order, Pence would announce that "because of the ongoing disputes in the seven States, there are no electors that can be deemed validly appointed in those States." Pence would then announce that Trump had won the majority of valid votes, whereupon he "gavels President Trump as reelected".

Eastman anticipated that there would be objections after Pence announced Trump's reelection. One possibility his memo envisioned was that Democrats would insist on following the Electoral Count Act, which requires disputes to be resolved separately by each house of Congress.

But in reality, this wouldn't have happened. The "disputes" had been manufactured and, as numerous courts held, were not based on the law or facts. And Pence didn't have the authority to do anything other than to count the electoral votes.

While Eastman's scheme would not have succeeded in keeping Trump in power, it could have given further credence to his lie that the election had been stolen from him, thus stoking more unrest and resentment among his supporters.

Trump introduced Eastman at a rally near the White House as "one of the most brilliant lawyers in the country." Trump also appeared to refer to the scheme outlined in Eastman's memo (which was, of course, not yet available to the public) when he told the assembled crowd on January 6th that Eastman "looked at this and said, 'What an absolute disgrace that this can be happening to our Constitution.' And then he looked at Mike Pence, 'and I hope Mike is going to do the right thing. I hope so. I hope so. Because if Mike Pence does the right thing, we win."

The memo also makes clear exactly why Trump turned the crowd that day against Pence. At about noon on January 6th, Trump told rallygoers that if Pence didn't "come through," it would be a "sad day for our country". The mob got the message. Several hours later, the Trump supporters roamed the Capitol calling out for Pence to be hanged.

THE ARIZONA 'AUDIT' JUST DESTROYED A BIG GOP LIE — IN MORE WAYS THAN ONE:

24-09-2021

The news that the sham Arizona "audit" has "confirmed" President Biden's victory is being widely cast as a huge setback for purveyors of former president Donald Trump's "big lie" about the 2020 election.

That's because it's already clear that some Republicans will not use the audit news to affirm that confidence in our election system has been restored. Instead, they'll use it to continue undermining that confidence, for the express purpose of justifying further anti-democratic tactics.

After nearly six months and almost $6 million — most of it given by groups that cast doubt on the election results — the draft report shows that the review concluded that 45,469 more ballots were cast for Biden in Maricopa County than for Trump, widening Biden's margin by 360 more votes than certified results.

A spokesman for the audit, Randy Pullen, told an Arizona news outlet that it found there wasn't "massive fraud."

THE NEW YORK TIMES ADDS THIS:

Among other alleged discrepancies, the reports claimed that some ballots were cast by people who had moved before the election, that election-related computer files were missing and that some computer images of ballots were missing.

So, we can see what's really happening here. Yes, the audit isn't declaring outright that the election's outcome was indeed fraudulent. But it is declaring there are still many reasons to doubt that outcome, that election officials who actually operated in good faith are covering this up, and that the right response is more voting restrictions.

Which blows up another GOP big lie: the notion that such audits are merely about "restoring confidence" in our elections and in "election integrity"?

But, now that this audit "confirmed" Biden's win, it is still telling us that we should doubt our electoral outcomes, and that more voting restrictions are necessary to allay those doubts.

The conclusion to this ugly saga did backfire, in that it blew up efforts to sustain the big lie about 2020. But the real story here is that it blows up the big lie that Republicans investigating "election fraud" are merely trying to restore confidence in our elections, when in fact they continue to try to undermine it. And that story isn't going away.

REPUBLICANS ARE FEELING LIBERATED
— TO SET THE COUNTRY ON FIRE:

Today 29-09-2021

When Joe Biden ran for president in 2020, he predicted that once Donald Trump was turned out of office, the Republican Party would become more reasonable. Republicans would have an "epiphany," he said, even asserting that the GOP Senate would become "mildly cooperative."

It's unclear whether Biden genuinely believed that or simply found it useful to be seen expressing a hope for bipartisanship. But the common response at the time was that he was being naive. The GOP would not change.

Eliot Ness, the Incorruptible, was not naive like Joe Biden and the Democrats, to bring down the Mafioso, Al Capone. Here, it's the opposite, we have a Republican two-faced Mitch McConnell, and his gang, who is doing everything in his power to discredit Joe Biden as well as his budgets.

Yet, today, we can see that Republicans have reacted conversely. They've gotten more radical, more determined to create destruction and division, more willing to set the country aflame if they think the conflagration will burn their opponents.

Their entire party seems determined to make sure that a pandemic that has killed nearly 700,000 Americans will go on as long as possible.

In 2017, it was a scandal when then-President Donald Trump said there were "very fine people on both sides" of the Charlottesville rally where neo-Nazis chanted "You will not replace us!" But in 2021, "Great Replacement" theory — which posits a conspiracy to replace White people with dark-skinned immigrants — has become standard conservative rhetoric.

Let there be no misunderstanding: The Great Replacement is an idea created by white supremacists and promoted for years by white supremacists. Today you can hear it invoked on Fox News.

It is simply mind-boggling that in the past few months, the idea and the slogan have become just one more thing Republicans say. Tucker Carlson the modern Nazi is compared to propaganda minister Joseph Goebbels in the 1930-1945 Hitler government. He uses his nightly cable news program to explicitly endorse it: "This policy is called 'the great replacement,' the replacement of legacy Americans with more obedient people from far-away countries," Carlson has said.

AS A STUNNING NEW REPORT REVEALS TRUMP'S THREAT TO DEMOCRACY, REPUBLICANS SHRUG: 10-21-2021

As you probably learned in high school, John Adams insisted that a republic had to be "a government of laws, and not of men." But as a new Senate report on President Donald Trump's efforts to enlist the Department of Justice in his attempt to overturn the 2020 election shows, the law by itself was not sufficient to prevent the coup Trump wanted to carry out.

The law was an impediment, to be sure. But what we learn from the new report is this: Trump did successfully install some people within the government willing to betray their country and everything it is built on, but ultimately failed because he didn't have enough of them and ran out of time.

The report contains new details based on interviews with former Justice Department officials who witnessed the coup attempt. It tells how Trump allies like Rep. Scott Perry (R-Pa.) and Pennsylvania State Sen. Doug Mastriano were in regular contact with Trump in the days after the election and made their own attempts to pressure department officials.

But most shocking is the story of Jeffrey Clark, the acting head of the department's civil division. Despite having no authority over election law, he held meetings and conversations with the president about the election behind the back of Acting attorney general Jeffrey Rosen at the end of December and the beginning of January.

Things intensified when Clark presented Rosen and his deputy, Richard Donoghue, with a letter that he wanted them to sign, urging state legislatures to hold special sessions for the purpose of replacing legally appointed slates of electors with new slates, with the clear implication that Trump would then be declared the winner.

When Rosen was appalled and disgusted by Clark's letter, Clark's response was basically extortion. He told Rosen that Trump had suggested to him that Trump could fire Rosen and install Clark in his place. Clark said that if Rosen signed the letter, he would turn down Trump's offer and Rosen could keep his job.

It all came to a head at an extraordinary White House meeting on January 3rd, with all the major players in attendance. "One thing we know is you, Rosen, aren't going to do anything to overturn the election," Trump said, according to Rosen's testimony. The question being discussed was whether Trump would fire Rosen and replace him with Clark, who would then begin pressuring state legislatures to overturn their election results. Here's what happened next:

At some point during the meeting, Donoghue ... made it clear that all of the Assistant Attorneys General would resign if Trump replaced Rosen with Clark. Donoghue added that the mass resignations likely would not end there, and that U.S. Attorneys and other DOJ officials might also resign in masse.

Not only that, White House counsel Pat Cipollone and his deputy said that they, too, would resign. Cipollone called Clark's letter to legislatures a "murder-suicide pact". Trump backed down. when confronted with the possibility of mass resignations that would eclipse the Saturday Night Massacre? "President Trump listened

The people who do the most damage to our country and democracy aren't necessarily brilliant supervillains.

Sometimes calamity occurs because a bunch of scoundrels and fools are presented with an opportunity to do their worst. And in this case, those scoundrels and fools were stopped only because some other people managed to find an ounce or two of courage.

Which makes you wonder what will protect us if Trump, or someone like him, becomes president again?

Trump never put in place a coronavirus program.

CHAPTER TWENTY NINE

....

THE WORST PRESIDENT IN HISTORY:

President Donald Trump has long exulted in superlatives. The first. The best. The most. The greatest. "No president has ever done what I've done," he boasts. "No president has ever even come close," he says. But as his four years in office draw to an end, there's only one title to which he can lay claim: Donald Trump is the worst president America has ever had.

In December 2019, he became the third president to be impeached. Last week, Trump entered a category all its own, becoming the first president to be impeached twice.

It is helpful to think of the responsibilities of a president in terms of the two elements of the oath of office set forth in the Constitution. Firstly, presidents swear to "faithfully execute the Office of the President of the United States." This is a pledge to properly perform the three jobs the presidency combines into one: head of state, head of government, and commander in chief. Secondly, they promise to "preserve, protect and defend the Constitution of the United States."

Trump was a serial violator of his oath—as evidenced by his continual use of his office for personal financial gain—but focusing on three crucial ways in which he betrayed it helps clarify his singular historical status. First, he failed to put the national-security interests of the United States ahead of his own political needs. Second, in the face of a devastating pandemic, he was grossly derelict, unable or unwilling to marshal the requisite resources to save lives while actively encouraging public behavior to spread the disease. And third, held to account by voters for his failures, he refused to concede defeat and instead instigated an insurrection, stirring a mob that stormed the Capitol.

And remember this:

AN OPEN LETTER WRITTEN BY A FLORIDA JUDGE ON CANADA / UNITED STATES RELATIONS:

September 21, to 2018

Robert Meadows (Circuit Court Judge, Florida) wrote:
Here is awareness from an American on the growing trade war with the United States and Canada. "Have you ever stopped to consider how lucky we Americans are?"

To have the neighbors that we have? Look in a world where some people have been stuck.

Sharing a border over the past half-century:

South Korea / North Korea -China / Russia.

Greece / Turkey - Iran / Iraq - Israel / Palestine - India / Pakistán.

We have Canada! Canada, about as nice a neighbor as you could hope for.

Despite "American exceptionalism and TRUMP songs on:

"America first. Instead, America alone, Canadians smile, does their business and goes about their business."

They are on average more educated, have a higher standard of living, free health care, and almost no gun problems. They treat immigrants with respect and have taken over 35,000 Syrians in the past two years. They are with us in NATO, they fought, on our side in WWI and WWII, the Korean War, the Gulf War, the Bosnian War, Afghanistan, the Kosovo War, the Vietnam War, and came to our defense after September 11th. They were regular consumers of American imports, reliable exporters of metals and petroleum products. They are the largest importer of American products from 37 states, and a partner of NASA in our space missions. After September 11th, to help us, many American planes were diverted to Newfoundland, an island province off the east coast of Canada, where Americans remained free with these Canadians for two weeks, and were treated like royalty. In return for their hospitality, the TRUMP administration imposed a 20% tariff on products from Newfoundland's only paper mill, threatening its survival.

And what do Canadians expect from us in return? Be respected for who and what they are: Canadians! That's what I call a very good neighbor.

But TRUMP, the King of Chaos, couldn't leave them alone on the basis of his illusions of perpetual victimization. He declared economic war on

Canada. And he did so, on the basis that Canada posed a risk to the national security of the United States!

For no good reason other than the little voices in his head telling him that it was a 'war' he could win, so why not do it? Again, we are talking about Canada, our closest ally, friend and neighbor. On behalf of an embarrassed nation, I apologize to the Canadian people for this stupid and utterly unnecessary animosity. Please keep the doors open, for we, the progressive American people, stand by your side and, Joe Biden will prove it!

THE DANGEROUS PSYCHOLOGY OF DONALD TRUMP:

November 1st 2020

Politicians who live in an angry narcissistic fog pose a clear threat to democracy and peace, and Donald Trump is a classic illustration of what this means in practice. But it isn't a simple issue of psychology.

For most of us, 'inner demons' such as our impulses towards predation, dominance and vengeance coexist with 'better angels' like compassion, fairness, self-control and reason. When social, material and cultural conditions favor our better qualities, violence remains low, but if conditions reward our inner demons, violence increases.

ideas to explore the dark nature of Trump's disordered mind, arguing that the real 'clash' are capable of empathy and reason, and a highly influential minority who suffer from dangerous disorders of character and personality.

This minority - made up of psychopaths, sociopaths and those with narcissistic personality disorder and paranoid personality disorder - are essentially devoid of conscience. Unfortunately, in a psychologically ignorant society, their dreams have a good chance of becoming reality for them and a nightmare for others."

Someone with Trump's disordered psychology is in control of America's nuclear arsenal. This piece was written when Trump announced his intention to withdraw from the Iran nuclear deal and threatened North Korea with "fire and fury like the world has never seen."

By examining the alarming summit in Helsinki in which he sided with Vladimir Putin, and against his own intelligence agencies, on the issue of Russia's interference in the 2016 US presidential election. In the context of a well-established pattern of attacks on democratic allies and praise for authoritarian leaders, this piece focused on Trump's paranoia in an effort to explain why it is entirely logical for him to seek alliances with authoritarian leaders.

Individuals with acute paranoia, which is a feature of pathological narcissism, are characterized by a worldview that sees other people as inherently untrustworthy and out to harm them at every turn. Paranoid leaders therefore recoil from alliances with democratic allies because they believe that such alliances are treacherous, and that only strong nations standing alone can survive. This is a conviction that's shared by other strongman leaders like Putin.

By this time, Trump was regularly being portrayed in the media as a narcissist, including in books like "Fire and Fury" by Michael Wolff which heightened concerns about Trump's mental fitness for office. What this word actually means by exploring the psychoanalytic understanding of narcissistic personality disorder.

People like Trump with narcissistic personality disorder are driven to live out their lives by damaging others and pursuing their grandiose destructive dreams.

"Disordered Minds: How Dangerous Personalities Are Destroying Democracy," which examines some of the 20th century's most appalling atrocities including the Holocaust, Stalin's Gulag, Mao's Great Famine, and Pol Pot's Killing Fields in Cambodia. In fomenting such horrors.

TRUMP IS TERRIFIED ABOUT GOING TO PRISON AFTER LOSING THE ELECTION:

The president is said to be not only worried about "existing investigations" but new federal probes into matters we don't even know about yet.

In September 2019, Donald Trump's lawyers debuted a bold new legal argument. Attempting to quash a subpoena from the Manhattan District Attorney's office, which had requested eight years of tax returns to determine if the Trump Organization has falsified business records relating to payouts made to a porn star and a Playboy model, the president's attorneys insisted that such a request was unconstitutional because the founding fathers believed sitting presidents should not be subject to the criminal process, which would "distract the president" from his duties. Pressed by a judge on this argument,

197

and the hypothetical Trump busted out during the 2016 election—that he could "stand in the middle of Fifth Avenue and shoot somebody" and not "lose any voters"—attorney William Consovoy insisted that yes, that kind of thing would fall under this concept of "presidential immunity," i.e., Trump could put a bullet in a random pedestrian and avoid prosecution until moving out of the White House.

Trump's lackeys, which include the Attorney General of the United States, have done their part to shield him from situations wherein he could be convicted of a variety of crimes, getting him through almost an entire term without an embarrassing situation wherein a sitting president is, say, found guilty of falsifying business records regarding a hush money payment he made to an adult-film star.

Unfortunately for Trump, if he loses the 2020 election, he'll no longer be able to use the staff of the Justice Department as his personal lawyers.

In unguarded moments, Mr. Trump has for weeks told advisers that he expects to face intensifying scrutiny from prosecutors if he loses. He is concerned not only about existing investigations in New York, but the potential for new federal probes as well, according to people who have spoken with him.

PRESIDENT TRUMP LOST HIS BID FOR RE-ELECTION:

November 7, 2020

But he and many of his most fervent supporters have refused to accept it. Trump's allegations and the hostility of his rhetoric — and his singular power to persuade and galvanize his followers — generated extraordinary pressure on state and local election officials to embrace his fraud allegations and take steps to block certification of the results.

"It was like a rumor Whack-A-Mole," said Georgia Secretary of State Brad Raffensperger. Despite being a Republican who voted for Trump, Raffensperger said he refused repeated attempts by Trump allies to get him to cross ethical lines. "I don't think I had a choice. My job is to follow the law. We're not going to get pushed off the needle on doing that. Integrity still matters."

All the while, Trump largely abdicated the responsibilities of the job he was fighting so hard to keep, chief among them managing the coronavirus pandemic as the numbers of infections and deaths soared across the country.

President Trump lost his bid for re-election, but he and many of his most fervent supporters have refused to accept it.

In the days after the election, as Trump scrambled for an escape hatch from reality, the president largely ignored his campaign staff and the professional lawyers who had guided him through the Russia investigation and the impeachment trial, as well as the army of attorneys who stood ready to file legitimate court challenges.

Instead, Trump empowered loyalists who were willing to tell him what he wanted to hear — that he would have won in a landslide had the election not been rigged and stolen — and then to sacrifice their reputations by waging a campaign in courtrooms and in the media to convince the public of that delusion.

The effort culminated November. 19th when lawyers Rudolph W. Giuliani, Jenna Ellis and Sidney Powell spoke on the president's behalf at the headquarters of the Republican National Committee to allege a far-reaching and coordinated plot to steal the election for Biden. They argued that Democratic leaders rigged the vote in a number of majority-Black cities, and that voting machines were tampered with by communist forces in Venezuela at the direction of Hugo Chávez, the Venezuelan leader who died seven years ago.

THE PRESIDENT AND HIS PARTY HAVE
GONE TO WAR AGAINST AMERICA:

December 10, 2020

Can call them reckless in their eagerness it's becoming hard to find the right words to describe what Republicans have become at this moment in history.

We can call them heartless in their willingness to deprive Americans of aid in such a desperate time. We can call them unhinged in their embrace of deranged conspiracy theories.

But now the Republican Party is quite literally becoming the enemy of America.

Consider the lawsuit filed by Texas Attorney General Ken Paxton asking the Supreme Court to essentially nullify the entire 2020 presidential election so it can be handed to President Trump, a suit about which Trump himself says, "This is the big one." It might have been just one more ridiculous publicity stunt by one of the many corrupt fools the GOP has managed to elect recently, but now, Republican attorneys general from 17 other states have filed a brief in support of the suit.

The suit claims that election results in Georgia, Michigan, Pennsylvania and Wisconsin should be thrown out and the decision left to Republican-controlled legislatures in those states, presumably so they could simply appoint pro-Trump electors and make him the winner.

Greg Sargent: Giuliani's vile admission perfectly captures the ugliness of the Trump era.

The entire premise of the suit is farcical. Republicans have not found evidence of fraud beyond ludicrous innuendo on the order of, "An election official gave one of our poll watchers a dirty look!" and the idea that one state could demand that the Supreme Court overturn the election results of another is absurd.

But that's just the beginning. The suit includes an "expert" statistical analysis purporting to show that there was "less than one in a quadrillion statistical improbability of Mr. Biden winning the popular vote" in the four states.

But the fact that Paxton is quite obviously an idiot doesn't for a moment mitigate the horror of what's happening here. This abomination of a lawsuit has the backing of the president, Republican state officials across the country, the conservative media and many Republicans in Congress, with some actively supporting it and others inviting Trump and his confederates to keep up the fight. We can contemplate their motivations — fear of their unhinged and potentially violent base is the primary one — but at the moment it doesn't really matter. What matters is that the Republican Party has all but declared war on the entire system of American democracy.

So, Republicans faced a choice. They could have supported Trump's impeachment over this repugnant abuse of his office. They could have condemned what he did, but concluded that it didn't rise to a level requiring removal. Or they could defend and endorse Trump's appalling behavior.

With just a few exceptions, they chose the last course. Having already decided that it was just fine that Russia helped Trump get elected in the first place, they planted their flag on the idea that presidents should be able to use the power of the United States for their own personal political gain. Trump forced them to choose between him and their country, and they chose him.

Now they're doing it again. But this time it's even worse. Trump has enlisted the Republican Party in a sweeping attack on America itself — our entire system of government and elections, and the very idea that the people get to choose their leaders. And with just a few exceptions, the GOP has joined in that attack.

None of us knows for sure what the future of the Republican Party looks like. Perhaps it will reform itself. But in its present, it is nothing less than a cancer on our democracy. I'd say that every Republican should be ashamed, were it not so abundantly clear that almost none of them have any shame at all, because they are traitors.

ANTHONY SCARAMUCCI:

Anthony Scaramucci to CNN in December 2020 said, how you could have placed in the White House a man who speaks the language of an 8-year-old child, this man has no shame and no antipathy and I believe, when it was created, there is a gene that was forgotten.

At the INTERVIEW he calls the US President "very crazy low life, full-blown racist, son of a bitch" manically, narcissistic, and" off his rocker".

He said something should be done, the 25th amendment as to be modified in order avoid a repeat of having another president like this fool.

Trump never put in place a coronavirus program.

CHAPTER THIRTY

....

THE 10 WORST THINGS TRUMP DID IN 2020.

December 29, 2020

This week, we offer the annual lists of the 10 best and 10 worst things President Trump did this year. Since 2020 was such a horrible year, we'll start with the worst things first:

10. He pardoned war criminals. Trump showed a flagrant disregard of the rule of law by pardoning Blackwater contractors who massacred unarmed Iraqi civilians, including innocent women and children.

9. He vetoed the bipartisan National Defense Authorization Act. Trump vetoed $741 billion in military spending and a 3 percent pay raise for our troops over an unrelated issue, and put Republicans who voted for it in the difficult position of having to choose whether to flip-flop or override his veto.

8. He ordered the drawdown of nearly all U.S. forces in Afghanistan and Iraq. Trump was apparently talked out of a complete withdrawal, but reducing to 2,500 troops in each country makes no strategic sense. Despite an ongoing terrorist threat, we will have fewer troops in Afghanistan or Iraq than we do in Spain.

7. He put millions in limbo by threatening to veto coronavirus relief. After Democrats refused multiple GOP offers since July, Congress finally approved an aid package just as much pandemic relief was expiring. But Trump refused to sign the bill for almost a week, forcing millions of Americans to spend Christmas wondering whether they would be left to fend for themselves during the worst of the pandemic.

6. He failed to ban travel from Europe in January. Trump announced a travel ban on January 31 on non-U.S. residents who had recently been in mainland China, saving countless lives. But he did not shut down travel from

Europe until March 11th almost six weeks later, because of objections from his economic advisers.

5. His jarring fights with reporters during coronavirus briefings alienated rather than united us. Trump proudly compared his press briefings to a Mike Tyson boxing match, but frightened Americans didn't want a boxing match; they wanted information and reassurance. In mid-March, 50.6 percent approved of Trump's handling of the pandemic, but by April, he lost the American people and never recovered.

4. His reluctance to embrace masks cost lives. His refusal to require masks at his Tulsa rally, the maskless superspreader event at the White House to announce Amy Coney Barrett's Supreme Court nomination, and the scene of him dramatically removing his mask on the White House balcony after returning from Walter Reed all became symbols of his Covid response failures.

3. He is failing to distribute more than half the available doses of vaccine. His administration is undermining the success of Operation Warp Speed by distributing only about 18 million doses this year when about 40 million will be available, leaving about 22 million Americans without any immunity during the deadliest period since the pandemic began.

2. He lost a winnable election and then refused to accept the results, or his own responsibility for losing. Trump lost because he alienated millions who approved of his policies but were tired of chaos. His mocking of Joe Biden's cognitive struggles offended seniors, and their support for Trump declined by five points in Arizona and 11 points in Georgia compared with 2016. And after winning suburban voters by two points in 2016, he lost them by 10 this year. He discussed imposing martial law at an oval Office meeting. The suggestion by Michael Flynn that Trump declares martial law and uses the military to re-run the election in swing states is insane.

Finally, one of the worst things Trump did is not on the list because the results are not yet in: He has barely lifted a finger in Georgia to save Republican control of the Senate. He is so focused on overturning the presidential election that he could very well hand Democrats control of the Senate on Jan. 5, and with it, unchecked power to reverse his achievements and enact a radical agenda. If that happens, Trump will leave the White House in infamy.

OPINIONS JAN-2021

Terrorist domestic chief Donald J Trump, and his 139 GOP.

Is the biggest loser in America history, he never read a book of his life, never writing the only thing he knows well, is tweeting, it's easier, is a coward and lazy person. But finely one thing he preferred with a big smile, when he put a signature on a document, which is wider than the document itself, a stupid and incomprehensible name, but one thing for sure every time he does that, it looks like a big show "APPRENTICE".

Jim is a traitor, hypocrite, he should resign. What kind of hypocrite he is, talking of healing, really, after 4 years, you didn't do anything to stop your monster, and instead you have fraudulently allowed not charging your Mob Boss, by lying under oath, with the first impeachment, you should ask yourself why another impeachment, you like this sentence, right "here we are again". Also, you should ask yourself why this country is so divided. Look yourself in a mirror each morning, if you have one.

Lind is a two-sided face Hypocrite; one day yes next day no. the same guy who said to throw out the Georgia legally ballots, the same guy who said in October 7, 2015 and I "quote" This guy kills the GOP party, and of course I'm talking about Trump the Monster.

Clay a stupid ignorant contradicted the results of his own party.

Milk the "big mouth" complicit in the COVID19 lies from the beginning, and encourage his Mob Boss.

January 6, 2021 Trump said, I will follow you to the Capitol, he repeats these words 4 times, but you know what he did instead, the coward hid himself in his bunker.

Let's be clear: What happened Wednesday afternoon at the U.S. Capitol was an attempted coup d'état, egged on by a lawless president desperately trying to cling to power and encouraged by his cynical Republican enablers in Congress.

Barry Moore (R) Alabama, in the "House debating article on impeachment" on January 13-2021 he said, and I quote, "for whatever reason Trump was impeached" I wonder if this Puppet knows on what planet he has lived on lately. Where were you? -- if we speak about Hypocrites, you won the jackpot, and by the way, you are a traitor of the worst kind, like your Mob Boss, a pariah, "Persona non grata."

The worst traitor list = Trump, Cru, Giu, Mea, McCar, Haw, Gra, Hig,

Mo, Gre, Eas Jord complicit in the Capitol riots on the January 6, 2021. All these people should be condemned and sent to jail for inciting insurrection at the Capitol.

I hope we remember those names (12) and others who tried to overturn the election results.

The VP was a stone statue when the journalist asked him if the President was responsible for the attack on the Sanctuary of our democracy. This guy is a coward, could you believe that a few hours before, this VP was to be hanged by Mob Boss rioters' orders, and he still respects this I. Hole. In my opinion, you are a yes man all the way, you are a disgusting person and shame on you. Is it this legacy that you want to leave to your children? History will remember you.

The American usually tends to forget, especially those who are hypocritical.

There are two types of dishonest people in the Republican Party.

The Gamers =McDonnell. Barr, Giuliani, Powell.

The Brakers =Cruz, Hawley, Meadows, Graham, McCarthy, Higgins, Moore, Greene, Jordan. (See below the definition of these people).

Being a person who acts in contradiction to his stated beliefs or feelings: being a hypocrite.

Finally, when we look at the results of the first weeks of 2021, we can say that 99% of republicans are all hypocrites and liars, and what does swear on the bible mean for republicans today? Nothing, it's only masquerade and pure comedy, you are making fun of all the American people, shame on you!

HOW DO WE HOLD THE TRAITORS TO DEMOCRACY ACCOUNTABLE:

December 14, 2020

Former New Jersey governor Chris Christie, a well-known Trump ally, and Sen. Bill Cassidy (R-La.), at least had the decency during their Sunday show appearances to recognize that Joe Biden won the presidential election and to deplore the Texas lawsuit seeking to overthrow our democracy.

Cassidy acknowledged on CNN's "State of the Union" that Biden "is the president-elect. He has 270 electoral-college votes. We're the law-and-order party. We are a nation with a constitution. We're a nation of laws and courts that interpret those laws." He added: "And this is how it breaks out, and the courts have ruled, President Biden's going to be our next president."

CNN's Jake Tapper wrapped up his show with some typically insightful remarks. "President Trump did us a favor by exposing these elected officials," Tapper said of the Republican officeholders who brought or signed onto the Texas lawsuit seeking to throw out other states' votes. "They are by definition people who signed on to a desperate desire to subvert the will of the American people, to disenfranchise voters in Georgia, Pennsylvania, Wisconsin and Michigan based on lies and conspiracy theories, putting an immoral and corrupt power grab above democracy." Tapper observed that "now we know clearly how much these individuals care about facts or truth, how much they care about democracy, or the principles that make this country great, which is to say not at all."

Nevertheless, before swearing in the new House members, Speaker Nancy Pelosi (D-Calif.) should repeat her own recent remarks. "The 126 Republican Members that signed onto this lawsuit brought dishonor to the House," she said in a statement last week. "Instead of upholding their oath to support and defend the Constitution, they chose to subvert the Constitution and undermine public trust in our sacred democratic institutions." She should remind lawmakers that their oath means something and that upon taking it, they should renounce their prior actions and fully acknowledge the election outcome.

And should they run again, their opponents should remind voters how these people betrayed U.S. democracy.

The degree to which the Republican Party embraced an attempted coup is both chilling and unsurprising given the GOP's descent into authoritarianism. It should prompt some soul-searching by Republicans who did not join the coup. Is this a party I should be associated with? Is this a party that can be trusted with power? If the answer to either question is no, they should form a new party whose only requirement is loyalty to the Constitution. Sadly, most of their fellow Republicans would be barred under that standard.

The word 'Oath' means something? Really? Are you crazy? These GOP don't know that word because their DNA is programmed to betrayed U.S. democracy.

THE SUPREME COURT REJECTS TEXAS BID TO UPEND ELECTION RESULTS:

The U.S. Supreme Court, on December 11ᵗʰ, rejected a long-shot lawsuit filed by Texas and backed by President Trump seeking to throw out voting results in four states. But this is not a matter of all's well that ends well. What was alarming about the Texas effort — what Pennsylvania Attorney General Josh Shapiro aptly described as "this seditious abuse of the judicial process" — was that it gained the support of so many others. Seventeen of 26 Republican state attorneys general. Nearly two-thirds of the House Republicans, some 106 on Thursday, with 20 more jumping on the bandwagon Friday, including the minority leader, Kevin McCarthy (Calif.).

So, history will record, but let me make it easier for the historians and, perhaps, impose a smidgen of accountability in the present.

REPUBLICANS FACED A SIMPLE CHOICE: FOR OR AGAINST DEMOCRACY:

December 12, 2020

House republicans faced what amounts to a choice between standing for or against democracy: whether to sign on to Texas Attorney General Ken Paxton's delusional lawsuit to overturn the presidential election. A large majority of them failed the test. More House Republicans, including Minority Leader Kevin McCarthy (R-Calif.), on Friday signed an amicus brief supporting Mr. Paxton, just hours before the Supreme Court unceremoniously rejected the suit. This is a disheartening signal about what these members of Congress might do on January 6 when at least some Republicans probably will object to the counting of President-elect Joe Biden's electoral votes.

Mr. McCarthy and the other extremists and toadies who have signed their names to President Trump's antidemocratic plot may think their complicity is costless, because the Supreme Court was bound to reject the Paxton lawsuit, as it did on Friday, and there are enough Democrats on Capitol Hill to foil any GOP mischief during the electoral vote counting. They are wrong. Their recklessness raises the once-unthinkable possibility that a Congress controlled by one party might one day flip a presidential election to its candidate in defiance of the voters' will, citing claims of mass fraud just as bogus as the ones Republicans have hyped up this year.

Some Republicans described the Paxton lawsuit honestly, including two senior Texas lawmakers. "I frankly struggle to understand the legal theory of it," said Sen. John Cornyn. "I'm not convinced." "I'm not supporting it," said Rep. Kay Granger. "It's a distraction."

Meanwhile, Gov. Gary R. Herbert (R-Utah) and incoming governor Spencer Cox, also a Republican, criticized Utah's attorney general for bringing their state into the Paxton lawsuit. And Sen. Mitt Romney (R-Utah) called it "madness" to propose that lawmakers should select the next president, which is the goal of the Paxton lawsuit and of the Republicans who intend to disrupt the January 6th electoral vote counting. "The idea of supplanting the vote of the people with partisan legislators, is, is so completely out of our national character that it's simply mad," Mr. Romney said. "Of course, the president has the right to challenge results in court, to have recounts. But this effort to subvert the vote of the people is dangerous and destructive of the cause of democracy."

THERE IS NO MIDDLE GROUND BETWEEN FACT AND FICTION ON THE ELECTION RESULTS:

December 20, 2020

As president Trump continues to lie about last month's election, national Republican leaders are trying to stake out what they imagine as a middle ground. While Joe Biden is the president-elect; the 2020 election was marred by substantial fraud and election irregularities. In fact, this is also a lie, and their dishonesty damages U.S. democracy.

At a Wednesday Senate Homeland Security and Governmental Affairs Committee hearing, Chairman Ron Johnson (R-Wis.) declared that it is "not sustainable" for a large proportion of Americans to believe the election results are illegitimate. He then set about encouraging this false belief by dignifying debunked attacks on the vote's integrity.

Former Trump election security Chief Christopher Krebs told the panel that the election was highly secure and that attacks on local voting officials were deeply unfair. Yet Mr. Johnson trotted out Trump lawyers who alleged massive numbers of illegal votes and blamed losses in court on negligent judges refusing to look at their so-called evidence.

Sen. Ran-Pau (R-Ky.) declared that "the fraud happened." Other GOP senators emphasized that their constituents thought the vote was rigged. The overall message, about perhaps the cleanest presidential election ever run in the United States.

And the Russia investigation was based on fact. Russia tried to aid Mr. Trump, the Trump campaign welcomed the help, and Trump allies had strong connections to the Kremlin, whereas claims about Mr. Biden's illegitimacy are based in partisan fantasies that have serially failed when scrutinized, in court and elsewhere.

Republicans are inaugurating a new, dangerous era in which political parties may refuse to acknowledge election results merely because they dislike the choices voters made. The damage is twofold: dignifying fake claims of widespread election irregularities shreds confidence in democracy, destabilizing the nation's politics and encouraging potentially violent resistance to duly elected leaders.

There is no middle ground between truth and lies. Republicans are promoting a dangerous fiction, which they will then rely on to make it even harder for Americans to vote

REMARKS: JANUARY 28, 2021

Trump did the unthinkable: a military coup on Jan 6, 2021. He tried to overturn the 2020 election; he also tried to sabotage the Electoral College. And democracy, if this isn't conspiracy then what does it take?

Now he's gone, but it's not over yet. This Traitorous Dictator, with his GOP puppets, you will see what he has in store for us in a few weeks and months. Because, we Americans, tend to forget very quickly and also are we used to hypocrisy and we are naïve.

Remember the members of the GOP; most of them are two-faced. They are also 360 degrees; one day what they say is an A, the next day is B. We have seen this lately with the vote on the second impeachment. The worst is yet to come, wake-up people, because this monster will bring hell to a second civil war.

Trump never put in place a coronavirus program.

CHAPTER THIRTY ONE

....

EXCLUSIVE: TRUMP'S 3,500 LAWSUITS UNPRECEDENTED FOR A PRESIDENTIAL NOMINEE: JAN-01-2016

As we speak today January- 01 -2021, let go back exactly 4 years ago January-01-2017, with a report from USA TODAY, regarding how this demagogue Donald J Trump came to the highest seat of the United States, by cheating, multiple lies, and more other flaws.

To my opinion is a crook, traitor, impostor, and the biggest racist in USA. Moreover, with is enablers this madman who behave like this, with big lies, which are now embedded in the Republican Party forever, we are not out of the wood yet.

With the latest behavior, of some GOP leaders like McC, McC, Cr-, Jac, and others.

Unfortunately, in the future the republicans can't not come to power legitimately, but they will try again fraudulently.

Donald Trump is a fighter, famous for legal skirmishes over everything from his golf courses to his tax bills to Trump University. But until now, it hasn't been clear precisely how litigious he is and what that might portend for a Trump presidency.

An exclusive USA TODAY analysis of legal filings across the United States finds that the presumptive Republican presidential nominee and his businesses have been involved in at least 3,500 legal actions in federal and state courts during the past three decades. They range from skirmishes with casino patrons to million-dollar real estate suits to personal defamation lawsuits.

The sheer volume of lawsuits is unprecedented for a presidential nominee. No candidate of a major party has had anything approaching the number of Trump's courtroom entanglements.

Just since he announced his candidacy a year ago, at least 70 new cases have been filed, about evenly divided between lawsuits filed by him and his companies and those filed against them. And the records review found at least 50 civil lawsuits remain open even as he moves toward claiming the nomination at the Republican National Convention in Cleveland in seven weeks. On Tuesday, court documents were released in one of the most dramatic current cases, filed in California by former students accusing Trump University of fraudulent and misleading behavior.

He sometimes refuses to pay real estate brokers, lawyers and other vendors.

As USA TODAY previously reported, he also uses the legal system to haggle over his property tax bills. His companies have been involved in more than 100 tax disputes, and the New York State Department of Finance has obtained liens on Trump properties for unpaid tax bills at least three dozen times.

Exclusive: More than 100 lawsuits, disputes, tied to Trump and his companies

And despite his boasts on the campaign trail that he "never" settles lawsuits, for fear of encouraging more, he and his businesses have settled with plaintiffs in at least 100 cases reviewed by USA TODAY. Most involve people who say they were physically injured at Trump properties, with settlements that range as high as hundreds of thousands of dollars.

The USA TODAY analysis included an examination of legal actions for and against Trump and the more than 500 businesses he lists on the personal financial disclosure he filed with the Federal Election Commission. USA TODAY also reviewed five depositions in which Trump sat for 22 hours of sworn testimony. This report is based on those legal filings as well as interviews with dozens of his legal adversaries.

A handful of the ongoing cases involve local or state government entities, with the possibility of personal legal disputes between the president of the United States and other branches of government if Trump is elected. For instance, the Trump team has filed a lawsuit seeking a state ethics investigation of the New York attorney general. The suit was filed in response to an ongoing fraud investigation into Trump University by the attorney general, an elected state official.

ALL 10 LIVING EX-DEFENSE SECRETARIES: THE ELECTION IS OVER. TRYING TO USE THE MILITARY TO DISPUTE THE RESULT WOULD BE DANGEROUS:

January 3, 2021

Efforts to involve the U.S. armed forces in resolving election disputes would take us into dangerous, unlawful and unconstitutional territory," write the 10 former defense secretaries: Ashton Carter, Dick Cheney, William Cohen, Mark Esper, Robert Gates, Chuck Hagel, James Mattis, Leon Panetta, William Perry and Donald Rumsfeld. "Civilian and military officials who direct or carry out such measures would be accountable, including potentially facing criminal penalties, for the grave consequences of their actions on our republic.

THE PRO-TRUMP MEDIA WORLD PEDDLED THE LIES THAT FUELED THE CAPITOL MOB. FOX NEWS LED THE WAY:

Jan. 7, 2021

"Fair and balanced" was the original Fox News lie, one of the rotten planks that built the foundation for Wednesday's democratic disaster.

Over decades, with that false promise accepted as gospel by millions of devotees, Fox News radicalized a nation and spawned more extreme successors such as Newsmax and One America News.

Day after day, hour after hour, Fox gave its viewers something that looked like news or commentary but far too often lacked sufficient adherence to a necessary ingredient: truth.

Birtherism. The caravan invasion. Covid denialism. Rampant election fraud. All of these found a comfortable home at Fox.

The mob that stormed and desecrated the Capitol on Wednesday could not have existed in a country that hadn't been radicalized by the likes of Sea-Han, Tuc- Car and Lau- Ing, and swayed by biased news coverage.

Since this is an especially good day for calling out the names of those to blame, here are a few more from the leadership of F- News: <u>Rup- Mur</u>. Lac- Mur. <u>Suz-Scot</u>

'What have they wrought? People like Jul Thompson, a right-wing activist who boarded one of the two buses from Western New York to Washington this week, then bragged to the hometown Buffalo News about being "absolutely justified" in egging on those who scaled a Capitol wall to penetrate the complex.

After all, she claimed, there had been rampant fraud, a stolen election and corrupt courts! "We would like all the courts to see the evidence of massive fraud and election interference... If they saw the evidence, they would have no choice but to rule for Trump." That all these allegations have been considered and rejected by the courts and roundly debunked didn't seem to enter her mind. What really? <u>They don't have brains, it's gelatin.</u>

Is Fox the only culprit? Of course not. Social media — the president's corrosive Twitter feed and the conspiracy-coddling hotbed of Parler — have played their necessary role.

THE RIOT HAPPENED BECAUSE THE SENATE ACQUITTED TRUMP:

Jan. 8, 2021

There was a terrible paradox in the images of Republican members of Congress driven into safe rooms by insurrectionists whom President Trump had whipped into frenzy. As a lawyer for the Democratic House managers at Trump's impeachment and trial

These same lawmakers refused to hold him accountable, knowingly unleashing the storm that swept over them, their Democratic colleagues and the nation on Wednesday. Impeachment manager Jerrold Nadler (D-N.Y.), the House Judiciary Committee chairman, had warned them: "President Trump has made clear in word and deed that he will persist in such conduct if he is not removed from power. He poses a continuing threat to our nation, to the integrity of our elections and to our democratic order. He must not remain in power one moment longer."

This last week's events — and indeed all the president's abuses during this election cycle and the last year — are a consequence of their refusal to convict him in his impeachment trial. With the sole exception of Sen. Mitt Romney

(Utah), not a single Republican in the Senate or the House would recognize the threat then. On the contrary. Sen. Susan Collins (Maine) went so far as to say: "I believe that the president has learned from this case." Mrs. Collins you are a naïve person, how old are you? The president has been impeached. That's a pretty big lesson. Stupid, naïve, liar, hypocrite, a bunch of cowards, goodbye democracy.

Yes, Trump did learn a lesson: <u>He learned that he can abuse his power and obstruct the investigation of that abuse, and get away unscathed to commit more high crimes and misdemeanors.</u> Abuse and obstruction were, of course, the two high crimes for which we prosecuted Trump in the Ukraine matter. The first article of impeachment laid out the abuse. It consisted of his pressure campaign on Ukraine to attack his most-feared opponent in the presidential race, Joe Biden, including the infamous July 2019 call to President Volodymyr Zelensky: "I would like you to do us a favor though."

Trump followed an identical pattern in his post-election assault on American democracy, culminating in another plea to another elected official to try to undermine Biden yet again. On Jan. 2, he called Georgia Secretary of State Brad Raffensperger and tried to use the power of the presidency to pressure the secretary to "find 11,780 votes" and to "get this thing straightened out fast." The president of the United States also suggested that not doing so would be "a criminal offense" and a "big risk to you" and "to your lawyer", you see again, cheating, threatening, lying, and abusing his power.

Moreover, it is a federal statutory felony if "a person" in any election for Federal office, knowingly and willfully attempts to deprive or defraud the residents of a State of a fair and impartially conducted election process, by the tabulation of ballots that are known by the person to be materially false, fictitious, or fraudulent under the laws of the State in which the election is held." This statute makes it clear that any Trump-sponsored search-and-rescue party for nonexistent votes — for example, 11,780 votes in Georgia — could constitute a crime in and of itself.

When the call failed, with Raffensperger rebuffing him, Trump turned to his last refuge and his latest high crime and misdemeanor: inciting his mob. They were his hardest-core supporters, urged by his Twitter feed to come to Washington. He urged them, "Be there, will be wild!" And when they gathered, he exhorted them to march on the Capitol and said, "If you don't fight like hell you're not going to have a country anymore."

Every Republican member of Congress who failed to impeach, convict and remove him bears some responsibility for what happened next. True, there are gradations of responsibility. But a handful of senators led by Sens. Ted (R-Tex.) and Josh Ha (R-Mo.), all of whom had voted to acquit on impeachment, doubled down. They picked up his false claims and drove them forward, joining about 140 of their peers in the House in announcing plans to object, baselessly, to the electoral slates from up to six states, all of which Biden won.

Nothing would have horrified the framers of the Constitution more than a president inciting an attack against his own Congress. It was a paradigmatic abuse of power, and with it — inevitably — came the obstruction of the truth. "We love you", even in the face of their violence.

And that shows the power and relevance of the institution. If, as it appears, there will be no invocation of the 25th Amendment to remove the danger of Trump in these waning days of his presidency, Congress is well advised to take a hard look at the remedy we tried. If it is tried again, and it fails again, will that make Trump's behavior any worse? And while we were not successful in convincing McConnell or almost any of his colleagues of the virtue of our first effort, perhaps they have learned a lesson from the last year, even if the president has not.

UPDATE: MARCH 5, 2021:

As I mentioned, earlier in this book, that one the most dangerous GOP member, was Mitch McConnell, and we have proof here as of March 5, 2021, that he is the person who should be charged and brought to jail, and that without delay. By his behavior over the past 50 months this person acts as if he were the right hand of a king.

His title the Majority leader is a joke, firstly he is mainly responsible for not having acted as a leader to lead his colleagues in the famous first impeachment, to indict this madman, and again the same thing in the second impeachment, he has forgot his title of leader at home, if he had done his job in both cases, we would not be in this situation today.

With this mad, mad demagogue walking around and inciting people to violence, and it's not over, he will commit other crimes in the days to come, and we must not forget that there are other perpetrators, of troubles to be eliminated, the most important such as CR, HA, Mc, GR, JAC, MEA, JOR, EAS and others, as well as the main F- NEWS liars who incite people to violence, and potentially ended up with another civil war in this country. Shame on you! You are two-faced.

WHAT TRUMP SAID BEFORE HIS SUPPORTERS STORMED THE CAPITOL, ANNOTATED:

January 12, 2021

Democrats are on the verge of impeaching President Trump again. On Monday, they introduced a single article of impeachment alleging that Trump incited the violent attempted insurrection at the U.S. Capitol last week.

Trump's speech included no overt calls for his supporters to actually enter the Capitol or resort to violent means. But it included plenty of allusions to the idea that Congress accepting Joe Biden's victory — an all-but-assured outcome at the time — was a result that simply couldn't be countenanced and must be stopped. He urged his supporters to "fight" and "fight like hell" and lamented that they didn't do so as hard as Democrats.

Trump's speech begins with a suggestion that his supporters -- whose numbers he vastly overstates as being in the hundreds of thousands -- are "not going to take it any longer." The speech ahead will be littered with references to the idea that his movement is in a desperate moment.

Go ahead; turn your cameras, please. Would you show they came from all over the world actually, but they came from all over our country? I just really want to see what they do. I just want to see how they cover it. I've never seen anything like it, but it would be really great if we could be covered fairly by the media. The media is the biggest problem we have as far as I'm concerned, single biggest problem.

(APPLAUSE)

The fake news and the big tech, big tech, is now coming into their own. We beat them four years ago, we surprised them. We took him by surprise and this year they rigged an election, they rigged it like they have never rigged an election before, and by the way, last night, they didn't do a bad job either, if you notice. I am honest, and I just again, I want to thank you.

All of us here today do not want to see our election victory stolen by bold and radical left Democrats, which is what they are doing, and stolen by the fake news media. That is what they have done and what they are doing. We will never concede. It doesn't happen. You don't concede when there's theft involved.[2]

Trump spoke less than two hours before Congress would begin making his loss official but he assured the crowd that he will "never concede." What's notable here is that he lumps in his supporters in that posture, also saying, "We will never give up."

(APPLAUSE)

Our country has had enough. We will not take it anymore, and that is what this is all about.

(APPLAUSE)

"Stop the Steal" is a group that organized this rally and others like it across the country. One of its organizers is Ali Alexander, a conspiracy theorist who has inhabited the fringes of the conservative movement. The name, as with much of Trump's rhetoric, references the idea that the election is being deliberately stolen rather than that there are simply doubts about its legitimacy.

(APPLAUSE)

Today I will lay out just some of the evidence proving that we won this election and we won it by a landslide. This was not a close election. You know I say sometimes jokingly, but there's no joke about it. I have been in two elections. I won them both and the second one I won much bigger than the first, okay?

(APPLAUSE)

Almost 75 million people voted for our campaign, the most of any incumbent president by far in the history of our country; 12 million more than four years ago.

(APPLAUSE)

They know that we were going to do well and we were going to win. What I was told, if I went from 63 million, which we had four years ago, to 66 million, there was no chance of losing. Well, we didn't go to 66, we went to 75 million, and they say we lost. We didn't lose. And by the way, does anybody believe that Joe had 80 million votes? Does anybody believe that?

(BOOING)

He had 80 million computer votes. It's a disgrace. There's never been anything like that. You can take Third World countries, just take a look, take Third World countries, their elections are more honest than what we have been going through in this country. It's a disgrace.

(APPLAUSE)

Not going to let it happen.

Fight for Trump. Fight for Trump. CROWD: Fight for Trump. Fight for Trump. Fight for Trump. Fight for Trump.

TRUMP: Thank you.

CROWD: Fight for Trump.

TRUMP: And I would love to have, if those tens of thousands of people would be allowed, the military, the Secret Service and we want to thank you — and the police and law enforcement — great, you're doing a great job.

And Rudy, you did a great job. (APPLAUSE) He's got guts. You know what? He's got guts, unlike a lot of people in the Republican Party, he's got guts, he fights, and he fights. And I will tell you thank you very much, John [Eastman], fantastic job. I watched — that's a tough act to follow those two. John is one of the most brilliant lawyers in the country and he looked at this, and he said what an absolute disgrace that this could be happening to our Constitution, and he looked at Mike Pence, and I hope Mike is going to do the right thing. I hope so. I hope so because if Mike Pence does the right thing, we win the election.

(APPLAUSE)

And I actually, I just spoke to Mike. I said, Mike, that doesn't take courage, what takes courage is to do nothing. That takes courage, and then we are stuck with a president who lost the election by a lot, and we have to live with that for four more years.

Many of you have traveled from all across the nation to be here, and I want to thank you for the extraordinary love. That is what it is; there's never been a movement like this ever, ever for the extraordinary love for this amazing country.

Trump never put in place a coronavirus program

CHAPTER THIRTY TWO

CAPITOL SIEGE WAS PLANNED ONLINE. TRUMP SUPPORTERS NOW PLANNING THE NEXT ONE:

Jan. 9, 2021

The planning for Wednesday's assault on the U.S. Capitol happened largely in plain view, with chatters in far-right forums explicitly discussing how to storm the building, handcuff lawmakers with zip ties and disrupt the certification of Joe Biden's election – in what they portrayed as responding to orders from President Donald Trump.

This went far beyond the widely reported, angry talk about thronging Washington that day. Trump supporters exchanged detailed tactical advice about what to bring and what to do once they assembled at the Capitol to conduct "citizens' arrests" of members of Congress. One poster said, "[expletive] zip ties. I'm bringing rope!"

"Given the very clear and explicit warning signs – with Trump supporters expressing prior intent to "storm and occupy Congress" and use "handcuffs and zip ties," clear plans being laid out on public forums, and the recent precedent of the plot to storm the Michigan Capitol building while Congress was in session – it is truly mind-boggling that the police were not better-prepared," said Rita Katz, executive director of site Intelligence Group, which was among the research groups that detailed what was coming in the weeks before the Capitol was attacked.

The desire to prevent a repeat of Wednesday's attack helped drive Twitter's decision to suspend Trump's account after years in which years he challenged their policies against hate speech and inciting violence. But Twitter said it was particularly concerned about contributing to a possible "secondary attack" on the U.S. Capitol and state government facilities next weekend.

'WE'RE GOING TO HANG YOU UNTIL YOU DIE': NEW HAMPSHIRE MAN ARRESTED FOR ALLEGEDLY THREATENING 6 MEMBERS OF CONGRESS:

JAN 12, 2021

A New Hampshire man has been arrested after he allegedly left threatening voicemails last month with six members of Congress, telling them to support President Donald Trump or risk being killed, according to the Department of Justice, in the latest instance of violence being threatened 33-year-old Ryder Vinegar, of Amherst, New Hampshire, was arrested on Monday in connection with the threats. He left voicemails for six members of Congress between December 16th and December 17th, according to the DOJ, threatening to hang them if they didn't "get behind Donald Trump".

Winegar was arrested in Boston and is scheduled to make an appearance before a magistrate judge on Tuesday afternoon.

"I got some advice for you. Here's the advice, Donald Trump is your president. If you don't get behind him, we're going to hang you until you die," Winegar allegedly said on one of the messages.

The FBI has launched a widespread investigation into a "seditious conspiracy" related to the Capitol insurrection, officials announced at a news conference Tuesday, as concern grows about legitimate threats to public officials ahead of the Jan. 20 inauguration. On Tuesday, authorities arrested 45-year-old Chicago-area resident Louis Capriotti for an alleged threat similar to the ones for which Winegar was arrested. According to the Department of Justice, Capriotti left a voicemail for a U.S. House member on Dec. 29 saying that he and others are planning to "surround the motherfucking White House and we will kill any motherfucking Democrat that steps on the motherfucking lawn," on Inauguration Day,

TRUMP FACES MOUNTING DEMANDS TO LEAVE OFFICE OR FACE IMPEACHMENT FOR INCITING CAPITOL MOB ATTACK:

Jan. 8, 2021

President Trump faces mounting pressure for his immediate ouster after he incited Wednesday's violent siege at the Capitol — an increasingly louder drumbeat chastising his actions that threatens not only to prematurely end his waning tenure but to put him in legal jeopardy once he leaves office.

In Congress, a growing cadre of House Democrats is pushing to before he is scheduled to leave office on January 20th. They are preparing to rapidly impeach Trump a second time introduce articles charging him with inciting an insurrection and having "gravely endangered the security of the United States" and its institutions.

In public, Trump has come as close as he is likely to get to admitting he lost the election, acknowledging that there will be a transfer of power and confirming Friday that he will not attend President-elect Joe Biden's inauguration, as you can see that he is a coward again. Trump has been told by attorneys that he could face legal jeopardy for inciting a mob; he has responded that it was never his intent to do so, according to a separate close adviser.

Meanwhile, Senate Republicans who declined an opportunity to evict Trump from office last year are rapidly turning against him — pledging to entertain whatever impeachment charges the House may send and, in the case of one prominent senator, demanding his immediate resignation.

"I want him out. He has caused enough damage," Sen. Lisa Murkowski (R-Alaska) said in an interview with the Anchorage Daily News published Friday. "He's either been golfing or he's been inside the Oval Office fuming and throwing every single person who has been loyal and faithful to him under the bus, starting with the vice president."

In a letter to Democratic lawmakers, Pelosi described speaking to the Joint Chiefs chairman, Gen. Mark A. Milley, "to discuss available precautions for preventing an unstable president from initiating military hostilities or accessing the launch codes and ordering a nuclear strike." She further described Trump as "unhinged" and said lawmakers "must do everything that we can" to protect the nation from him.

In a statement Friday evening, Pelosi reiterated that she and other House

Democrats hope Trump will resign. But if he doesn't, the House will move forward with legislation drafted by Rep. Jamie Raskin (D-Md.) that will create a commission on presidential disabilities to prepare for action under the 25th Amendment, as well as a motion for impeachment.

Trump's storm the Capitol in the worst breach of its security since the War of 1812. The worse losers and cowards, we ever saw, he can't attend the inauguration. Bravo Mr. Impostor, you win the jackpot. You are a disgrace for democracy! Oh, I'm sorry; you don't know the meaning of this word.

Lawmakers, politicians call for removal, impeachment of Trump

TRUMP'S FUTURE LOOKS ROTTEN:

January 14, 2021

President Trump faces a horrid future. He is the first U.S. president in history to be impeached twice; he lost the popular vote twice; he lost both the House and Senate for his party; and more than 383,000 Americans died from covid-19 on his watch. He has clearly sewn up the title of "worst president ever." If found guilty by a soon-to-be Democrat-controlled Senate, he will be unable to run for office again and may lose his post-presidential benefits (e.g., salary, travel allowance). But that is far from his biggest worry.

Trump may be sued civilly or charged criminally for tax avoidance or other financial crimes that state prosecutors in New York are investigating. Depending on the charges, he could face significant fines or even imprisonment. (Trump has maintained that he has done nothing improper.)

Speaking of finances, Trump reportedly has more than $400 million in loans coming due. However, his banks are cutting ties. Deutsche Bank, which holds about $340 million of the debt, and Signature Bank, do not want to do business with him. He might need help from his overseas authoritarian friends.

Trump may also face a federal criminal investigation for seeking to change election results in Georgia during two phone calls with state election officials — one of which was recorded. In addition to potential federal crimes for election offenses, prosecutors will need to look at whether his vague threat of criminal liability in his call with Georgia Secretary of State, Brad Raffensperger, qualified as extortion.

That was all before we got to his January 6 activities. Federal investigators and the U.S. attorney for Washington, D.C., as well as senior Justice Department officials will need to determine whether there is a basis to charge Trump with incitement to riot or conspiracy to commit sedition.

Beyond criminal liability, Trump could surely be sued by the relatives of those killed or injured during the siege, or to cover the costs incurred to repair the damage. He cannot be sued for "official conduct," but leading a riot to overturn an election will be difficult to slot into the category of "official duties," to put it mildly.

Even on the slim chance that Trump is never charged with any crime and manages to escape all civil liability, he will be deeply in debt (his original debt plus any costs to defend himself in court). He will also be a social and business pariah, banned from social media and unwelcome in most democratic countries. It is not clear how many people are going to pay to belong to a seditionist's Mar-a-Lago Club or stay at any of his properties.

Trump has famously survived two impeachments, two divorces, six bankruptcies, twenty-six accusations of sexual misconduct, and an estimated four thousand lawsuits. Few people have evaded consequences more cunningly. That run of good luck may well end, perhaps brutally.

IF REPUBLICANS CAN'T CAST TRUMP OFF, THEIR WOUNDS — AND THE COUNTRY'S — WILL ONLY GET DEEPER:

January 14, 2021

Watching Wednesday's impeachment proceedings in the House of Representatives, it struck me that neither left nor right seems to fully grasp our predicament.

Try assuming, instead, that they will be a political force to be reckoned with — and negotiated with — for the rest of everyone's life.

This was beyond a fantasy. To circle back to our earlier metaphor: Republicans who humored Trump's seditious lies as he made a serious run at overturning the results of a democratic election need to understand that their party is the abusive spouse in this scenario. It doesn't matter what the other party did first. What matters is that a Republican president brought an angry mob to Washington, told it there was a crime happening on Capitol Hill, and then urged it to do something about it.

The cheapest and easiest way for Republicans to make the necessary atonement is to cut Trump loose, completely. Vote to remove him from office and bar him from running again. Let the man who brought this down upon his country languish unlamented in electronic exile. This will make it clear to voters that they understand what a grave thing happened, and that they are determined to not just make amends,

What's that, you say, your base will punish you? It's not realistic to expect anyone to do so but also to ensure that nothing like it ever happens again. Something so politically costly?

If the Republicans cannot do this, then the wounds that they allegedly want to heal will only deepen and fester, especially within their own party. They might purchase a little temporary peace by catering to the mob-friendly base. But doing so will drive off the moderates who want no part of what happened last Wednesday — and further empower a mob that has already terrorized their party into submission, and would like to do the same to the rest of us.

A MAJORITY OF AMERICANS WANT TRUMP CONVICTED BUT REPUBLICANS CAN'T UNLATCH THEIR LIPS FROM HIS ASS:

FEBRUARY 8, 2021

A remark is in order here, on the last words of this title from VANITY FAIR. I feel a little uncomfortable, but rather, if I was in their shoes, I would take sanitary precautions with this guy since the Republicans can't unlatch their lips from his ass.

Why it matters that McCarthy went to Mar-a-Lago to kiss the ring Kevin, the Yes man, and also two-faced, was not only summoned to Mar-a-Lago to place a venom kiss on the dictator's ring, but also to make sure that he will be his slave in the future. A good start with a shoeshine, as illustrated further in the end of this book.

On Tuesday, Donald Trump's second impeachment trial kicks off in the Senate. Unlike his first impeachable offense, which took place largely behind the scenes, this time everything the ex-president did was right out in the open, from spending months insisting the election was stolen from him to whipping his supporters into a violent frenzy and sicking them on the Capitol. As the nine House impeachment managers wrote on Monday—in response to an attempt by Trump's lawyers to get the whole thing dismissed— "The evidence of President Trump's conduct is overwhelming.

PRESIDENT TRUMP VIOLATED HIS OATH OF OFFICE AND BETRAYED THE AMERICAN PEOPLE:

Trump tried to overthrow the U.S. government, leaving five people dead in the process—more Americans now say they want the 45th president convicted and barred from ever holding office again than did after he tried to extort Ukraine. This time 56% want him found guilty and banished from political life. Which is entirely reasonable given, again, that he led a failed coup against the federal government because he didn't like the results of the election.

With 67 senators needed to convict—or 17 Republicans, assuming no Democrat goes rogue—it is basically a certainty that Trump will get off, with the most shameless lawmakers on the right already previewing their excuses for letting him get away with everything. (Ted Cruz, who voted to block the certification of Joe Biden's win on January 6, thinks "impeaching and trying a president after he has left office is petty, vindictive, mean-spirited, and divisive." Tom Cotton claims "the Senate lacks constitutional authority to conduct impeachment proceedings against a former president." Lindsey Graham is trying to argue that this is all Nancy Pelosi 's fault. Daniel Goldman, the lead attorney for the House Intelligence Committee during the Ukraine impeachment told Chris Smith, "Having prosecuted the mafia, the mob boss doesn't say, 'Please go kill him for me. The mob boss says, 'Take care of him'. And no, Trump's words at the "Save America" rally are not protected by the First Amendment, as his apologists would like to claim. "The First Amendment is designed to protect individual speech from government intervention, not to protect government speech, or speech that leads to action.

Meanwhile Trump, apparently content in the knowledge that the vast majority of Republicans will do nothing to stop him, is reportedly already planning his "comeback tour," which involves campaigning against the (extremely) few House GOP lawmakers who supported his removal from office, as well as any Republicans even entertaining the idea of a symbolic vote to convict. "I'm sure he wants to get a roulette wheel out with all their faces on it," a source familiar with the matter told Business Insider.

MY OPINIONS AS A REMINDER:

February 3rd 2021

Could you believe, yes 199 cowards in the GOP voted today against the resolution to remove REP Marjorie Taylor Greene, oh yes! They are traitors, hypocrites, liars, and "Two-faced", that spineless group is the laughing stock. Shame on you!

You are a bunch of selfish and naïve people. You can run from accountability, but you can't hide. Now, by their cowardice, we can say that all these cowards are part of the QAnon group, the new Trumpists. But 11 representatives voted for democracy; those people have spines. To me they are my heroes.

The saliva you have in your mouth is mamba snake venom, and we don't need that kind of venom in the US so, traitors, we don't want to hear your lies. Do us a favor and get off the road, we don't need hypocrites like you, I am sick and tired of seeing your "two-faced" on Fox New, it's time to get rid of this Mob-Rep party, one day in near future you will be punish.

Finally, some good news, that just came out: a 2.7 billion $ lawsuit against Fox New and its conspirators: Lou Dobbs, Maria Bartiromo, Jeanine Pirro, Rudy Giuliani, and Sidney Powell.

Yesterday on CNN a few people were interviewed in Georgia regarding the lunatic liar, Rep Marjorie Taylor Green. I was stunned to hear the answer from these people, they still believe what that woman said, even crazy things like the 09-11 incident, even the Pentagon attack, even the Parkland shooting, the NASA didn't send mens to the moon didn't happen and all those crazy conspiracy theories. I repeat again, these people either are naïve or ignorant or stupid. Perhaps they should pay a visit to their doctor since it is possible that they are mentally ill. Or they live on another planet or on a Fantasy Island.

I knew that there were ignorant people in the USA, but not at this level. They are probably listening to FOX NEWS. In this organization, there are many ignorant people, and puppets, who, by their behavior and lies, are accomplices to the monster who poisoned the country for over 4 years. They have blood on their hands.

Meanwhile, Trump hinted last month about his plans should voters elect his opponent. "Could you imagine if I lost? I'm not going to feel so good. Maybe I'll have to leave the country—I don't know."

Moreover, the recent events that occurred with Donald Trump and his followers, I had to wait, to see the results of the charges and trials which are coming in the fall of 2023 and which are expected to conclude in the spring of 2024

Trump never put in place a coronavirus program.

CHAPTER THIRTY THREE

....

LET'S GO BACK TO A FEW MONTHS AGO!

On October 10, 2017, Rex Tillerson called Trump a moron, or a "fucking" moron. Trump refused to pass an IQ test with Mr. Tillerson. Why? Trump refused because he is a loser. A QC expert said that Trump would lose an IQ battle with Rex Tillerson. I would put money on Tillerson any day. But Trump still lashed out at the secretary of State, Rex Tillerson.

The Washington Post fact-checker team first started cataloguing the former president's four hundred and ninety-two (492) suspected claims in the first one hundred days of his presidency, averaging about twenty-one erroneous claims a day.

Trump was indicted over the 2020 election and block transfer to overturn power. The first impeachment trial of Donald Trump began in the US senate on January 16, 2020, and concluded with his acquittal on February 5, 2020.

Donald Trump was impeached for the second time on January 13, 2021, one week before his term expired.

In late December 2020, Mike Pence called vice-president Dan Quayle. Pence wanted advice because of Trump's efforts to cajole him. But Quayle believed that that could precipitate a constitutional crisis and Dan said, "Mike, you have no flexibility on this; none, zero, forget it! That's all you do, you just have no power, so just forget it." Quayle said, "It's nonsense! Today, the election was stolen!" Quayle assured Pence that things would go fine, to just 'follow the constitution'.

A FEW MONTHS LATER

As I write these words in January 2022, the GOP, aided by media such as Fox News, continues to spread lies, which a good portion of the population is hoarding into truth. Even after fifteen months following the defeat of Trump's Republicans, some still claim that they won this same election. It is grotesque!

On August 8, 2022, the Federal Bureau of Investigation executed a search warrant at Mar-a-Lago, Donald Trump's residence, and the FBI agents retrieved about a dozen boxes in the Mar-A-Lago raid.

But later, the FBI said that Trump's aide, Walt Nauta, moved documents from Mar-a-Lago one day before the FBI visit. This person was indicted later on June 9, 2023.

The former president, Donald Trump, was indicted in a Miami federal court on June 10, 2023, on thirty-seven criminal charges of withholding classified documents. The trial is forthcoming in a few months, as well as the other cases, such as the attack at the Capitol on January 6, 2021, and also the January 2, 2021 event concerning an hour-long conference call, asking the secretary of State of Georgia, Brad Raffensperger, to change the state's election result from the 2020 presidential election by modifying eleven thousand seven hundred and eighty (11 780) votes to his name.

Finally, we are not out of the woods yet, since democracy is in danger and as long as these heinous traitors are not accused and put behind bars, the future of this country is heading towards a second civil war.

Let's review Donald trump starting with the beginning of the end of his reign from the summer of 2023 to the spring of 2024.

On August 1, 2023, the Grand Jury meets as Trump braces for a possible third indictment. Special counsel, Jack Smith, indicted Trump for the events of January 6, 2021. Trump will appear before the DC court on Thursday, August 3, 2023.

On August 4, 2023, the lawyers signal that they will try to delay the trials. The indictments reveal themselves to be quicksand for Trump. The 14th amendment disqualifies Trump from office.

DEFINITION OF THE 14TH AMENDMENT

No person holding any office and having previously taken an oath to support the constitution of the United States, shall have engaged in insurrection or rebellion against the same, or given aid or comfort to enemies thereof.

Trump now faces a potential fourth indictment in Georgia and a January 6th federal charge by Fani Willis. Even today, in August 2023, Trump still says that the 2020 election was corrupted; but Trump is three-times accused, three-times impeached, and three-times indicted, and it's not over yet.

On August 4, 2023, Trump vents his fury at the third indictment. He launches a new attack on special counsel, Jack Smith. Trump is being charged by Smith in a federal case in Florida relating to the mishandling of documents. The top charges carry a penalty of up to twenty (20) years in prison.

At Trump's Florida estate, having been charged of lying to federal investigators, the case is going to trial on May 20, 2024.

On August 8, 2023, Rudy Giuliani, John Eastman, Sidney Powell, Jeffrey Clark, and Kenneth Chesebro schedule hearings on August 11, 2023.

The release of a recording on January 2, 2021, during a phone call between Trump and Georgia secretary of state, Brad Raffensberger, in which Trump asks him to find eleven thousand seven hundred and eighty (11 780) votes; during the investigations of the Special Grand Jury to hear testimonies from witnesses such as Rudy Giuliani, Sen. Lindsey Graham and, also, Brad Raffensperger and Brian Kemp.

Donald Trump was arrested on Tuesday, June 13, 2023, and is facing forty charges in a Miami federal court.

E. Jean Carroll has filed suit against Trump alleging that he defamed, sexually assaulted, and raped her in 1990.

On August 10, 2023, Judge Tanya Chutkan said it was a bedrock principle of the judicial process in this country that legal trials are not like elections, to be won through the use of the meeting hall.

On August 14, 2023, Trump is possibly days away from a fourth indictment. Former Georgia GOP chairs, David Sharer and Rudy Giuliani and sixteen activists who attempted to subvert the electoral college. Trump says that the Georgia witnesses "shouldn't" testify.

On Trump's Georgia indictment: 1) must surrender by August 25, 2023; 2) must negotiate a bond, if applicable and terms of release; 3) Fulton County sheriff's office and the secret service must work out the surrender details.

August 15, 2023, to August 31, 2023

Trump's fourth indictment and ninety-one counts of criminal charges. Judge Fani Willis said that eighteen others were indicted in the Georgia election. Trump chief-of-staff, Mark Meadows, also faces criminal charges.

Asa Hutchinson said that Trump should be disqualified from ever serving as president again. Those words are truer today than ever before. What is next in the Georgia case: 1) defendants must surrender by August 25, 2023; 2) all nineteen are to be tried together; 3) the district attorney wants the trials to start in the next six months. But the judge will decide. Also, the judge said that those charged in Georgia, would be under the racketeering law (RICO).

The 2020 election in Georgia was not stolen. For nearly three years now, anyone with evidence of fraud has failed to come forward under oath and prove anything in a court of law. "The election in Georgia was secure, accessible, and fair and will continue to be so as long as I am governor," said Brian Kemp.

Rudy Giuliani is charged with thirteen counts. In the meantime, Rudy makes a desperate appeal to Trump to pay his legal bill. Nothing new here, Trump never pays his bills.

Judge Chutkan receives threats from a Trump supporter in a voicemail, "If Trump doesn't get elected in 2024, we are coming to kill you!"

On the 17th of August, federal agents arrested a woman who had left racist voicemails threatening to kill the judge assigned to the Trump trials. This woman said, "You re in our sights; we want to kill you" to Judge Chutkan. The police investigated the threats against a Georgia Grand Juror.

Trump is expected to surrender at a Georgia jail next Thursday or Friday, August 24 or 25. Legal scholars say: The constitution bars Trump from office.

Trump's legal team agrees to a $200K bond in Fulton County. The constitution prohibits Trump from ever being president again. Enemies of that constitution are automatically disqualified from holding future office and must therefore be barred from elections to that office. Trump should be disqualified from the White House according to the 14th amendment, article 3. The 14th amendment to the American Constitution was ratified on July 9, 1868, after the American civil war.

All this "baloney" is, in my opinion, the only way to make sure that this dictator is not around the political arena anymore and will not have his name on a ballot; he should be confined to his residence in Mar-a-Lago, Florida.

Presently, Georgia is ground zero of democracy.

Trump trial calendar

1. October 2, 2023, New York gags civil trial
2. January 15, 2024, E. Jean Carroll defamation case
3. March 25, 2024, N.Y. State hush money
4. January 2, 2024, 2020 election subversion trial
5. March 4, 2024, Georgia 2020 election subversion trial
6. May 20-27, 2024, Classified documents criminal trial

A Trump employee changes their story and, together with Nauto-de-Olivera, gives false testimony; they attempted to delete security footage. On August 23, 2023, Rudy Giuliani surrenders at Fulton County jail. Bond is set at $150 000.

Trump is to be arrested in Atlanta on August 24, 2023. He is on his way to a Georgia jail surrendering to 13 criminal charges. The 45th president, inmate no. po1135809, becomes the first president with a mug shot. Trump is charged in the Georgia election probe with one count of racketeering, three counts of solicitation of violation of the oath, six counts of conspiracy, two counts of false statements and, one count of filing false documents.

At the jail, Trump said that he weighed 215 pounds, (Ty Cobb said on T.V.: "No way"). For Trump, it is normal to lie even regarding his weight which, some say, is closer to 265 pounds.

Ex-Trump lawyer, Sidney Powell, is charged with seven counts including violating the Georgie RICO Act, conspiracy to commit election fraud and conspiracy to defraud the state.

On August 31, 2023, New York attorney general's office: Trump has inflated his net worth over a span of years. Trump's net worth over ten years equals between 8.2 million and 2.2 billion.

Today, the proud boys were sentenced to 17 years in prison. Zachary Rehl was sentenced to 15 years. The proud boy's plea to the judge, "I know that I have to be punished and I understand, but please give me another chance. I beg you, I have to take my daughter to school, and I have to pick her up." But, to me, those were crocodile tears; he should have thought of that before doing something criminal at the Capitol on January 6, 2021. Also, Joseph Biggs being sentenced, crying and begging for leniency is also a demonstration of crocodile tears.

On September 1, 2023, and September 2, 2023, the proud boys Dominic

Pezzola, Etan Nordean and Enrique Tarrio were awaiting sentencing. The proud boy who smashed the Capitol window was sentenced to 10 years.

Trump and Meadows were charged with soliciting violation of an oath by a public officer.

Trump to secretary of State, Raff Raffensperger, "You know what they did and you're not reporting it. You know it was a crime, a criminal offense and, you know, you can't let that happen. It's a big risk to you." And he continued a few seconds later saying, "I just want to find 11 780 votes which is one more than we have because we won the state." And then, Raffensperger answered, "Well, Mr. President, the challenge that you face is that the data you have is wrong."

Pastor Stephen Lee is charged with five crimes including a criminal attempt to influence witnesses. Publicist Trevian Kutti is charged with three crimes including conspiracy to commit solicitation of false statements. Trump attorney, John Eastman, is charged with nine crimes including conspiracy to commit false statements.

Let us go back to December 13 and 14, 2020!

Donald Trump tweeted that day: What a fool the governor of Georgia is. It could have been so easy, but now, we have to do it the hard way. David Schafer, former Georgia GOP chair is charged with eight crimes including impersonating a public officer. He sent a message to fourteen unindicted co-conspirator individuals, "Listen, tell them to go straight to room 216 and to avoid drawing attention to what we are doing."

Kenneth Chesebro, pro-Trump attorney, is charged with seven crimes including conspiracy to impersonate a public officer. Chesebro sent an email to Michael A. Roman saying that Rudy Giuliani "wants to keep quiet until all the voting is done."

Scott Hall is charged with seven crimes including racketeering and conspiracy to commit election fraud. Also, Misty Hampton, Coffee County elections supervisor, is charged with seven crimes and, Cathy Latham, fake GOP elector, is charged with eleven crimes. All these people were caught on tape.

RICO-RACKETEER

What is RICO? "Racketeer Influenced and Corrupt Organizations Act". It allows for the prosecution of individuals or organizations involved in multiple related crimes over a certain period.

On September 5, 2023, Jack Smith accused Trump of "daily" statements that could taint the jury pool. Will Trump's co-defendants turn against him in some cases? Trump won't spend a penny on co-defendants.

September 6, 2023, on this day was the first televised hearing in Trump's Georgia subversion case, to determine when the Georgia trial will begin. The trial for Chesebro and Powell are to begin on October 23, 2023. The Colorado lawsuit seeks to keep Trump off the 2024 ballot. Ex-Trump aide, Navarro, is found guilty of contempt of congress. A trial will also be held for defying a subpoena in the January house probe.

Judge Fanny Hill received a threat, "We are coming for you, Fanny! We are going to 'fuck' you up! Don't go out at night, you black bitch! We are going to separate you from your car driver!" The judge rejected the bid to move the case to a federal court.

Judge Tanya Chutkan said, "The people that mobbed the Capitol were there because of their fealty, their loyalty, to one man and not to the constitution. It was blind loyalty to one person who, by the way, remains free to this day."

Trump said that Biden was too old to be president. 'He is incompetent'. Trump says that the idea of prison-time "doesn't affect me at all." Trump spoke out on potentially pardoning himself. Trump says that he would testify. He never directed employees to delete Mar-a-Lago security footage.

Special counsel seeks a limited gag order on Trump. He cites Trump's threatening post, "If you go after me, I am coming after you!"

On September 16, 2023, special counsel said, "Trump is 'cherry-picking' comments made by Judge Chutkan in his bid for her recusal. Trump says it was his 'decision' to try to overturn the 2020 election, and Trump says he is not worried about going to jail.

On September 18, 2023, Jeffrey Clark is charged with one count of violating Georgia's RICO Act, one count of criminal attempt to commit false statements and writings. Trump said, "I was listening to 'myself' when I said that the election was rigged, and I acknowledged multiple people telling me that the 2020 presidential election was not rigged." Trump admits he was told that the 2020 election lies were false. He says that he didn't listen to his attorney who told him he had lost.

On September 19, 2023, the judge hoped to decide by Thanksgiving whether the 14th amendment disqualified Trump from Colorado's 2024 ballot.

BIDEN IS RUNNING AGAIN IN 2024

Biden is on the ballot again in 2024 and, let there be no question, Donald Trump and his MAGA republicans are determined to destroy American democracy, and he said, "I will always defend and fight for our democracy. That is why I am running."

On September 21, 2023, Robert Murdoch stepped down as chair of Fox News Corporation with the mess he left behind. Oh yes! Leaving chaos in his wake.

On September 22, 2023, Cassidy Hutchinson said, "Trump is dangerous for this country. He represents the worst crime threat to our democracy. People are evading the truth."

On September 24, 2023, Trump, the demagogue, accused Gen. Milley of treason. He suggested that the top military leader, Gen Milley be executed.

On September 25, 2023, the ignorant Trump appears to blame Jeb Bush, instead of George W. Bush, for starting the Iraqi war.

A New York judge finds Donald Trump committed fraud for years and wrongly inflated his property values, living in a 'fantasy world' when it was good for business. On September 27, 2023, trial is set for October 2, 2023, after Trump is found liable for fraud. On September 28, 2023, a surprise in the Trump Georgia election subversion case, he won't try to move criminal charges to a federal court.

Trump's New York fraud trial is set to begin on Monday, October 2, 2023. Biden defends Gen. Milley after Trump threatened him. The outgoing US General stepped-up safety measure after Trump alleged treason, suggesting 'death' to Fani Willis, the Fulton County DA, Alvin Bragg, the Manhattan DA, and Judge Tanya Chutkan.

On September 29, 2023, the first Trump co-defendant pleaded guilty in the Georgia election case (the first one to flip). Scott Hall pleaded guilty to five counts in the 2020 election subversion case in Georgia. He was the first defendant in the case brought by the Fulton County district attorney's office to take a plea agreement with the prosecutors and was fined $5 000.

Gen. Milley said that the military didn't swear oaths to 'wannabe dictators' in an apparent swipe at Trump, and Milley said that Trump disrespected the military with an execution comment.

On September 30, 2023, Jack Smith referenced Trump's attack on Milley in a new filing about the urgency of a partial gag order request. He said he was firstly focused on Trump and his followers.

On October 1, 2023, Trump was set to appear, in person, at the civil fraud trial in New York on Monday, October 2, 2023. It was the first ever glimpse of Trump in a courtroom.

The Claims vs Trump

1. Persistent and repeated fraud;
2. Falsifying business records;
3. Conspiracy to falsify business records;
4. Issuing false financial statements;
5. Conspiracy to falsify financial statements;
6. Insurance fraud;
7. Conspiracy to commit insurance fraud.

The properties Trump may be forced to sell:

1. Trump tower;
2. Trump International;
3. Chester golf club;
4. The Trump building at 40 Wall Street.

On October 2, 2023, a civil trial posing a mortal threat to Trump's business starts. Trump insults a judge in New York. The attorney general said, "No one is above the law."

The trial against Trump' and his adult sons' business begins. Opening statements conclude in the Trump $250 M civil trial.

The prosecutor urged the judge to bar Trump from doing business in New York. The former chief-of-staff, John Kelly, confirmed disturbing Trump military comments and said, "A person that has nothing but contempt for our democratic institutions, our constitution, and the rule of law."

Trump lashed out at his fraud trial that threatens his business empire, "racist attorney", "horror show" and, "rogue judge".

Trump said that he attended this trial because he wanted to watch this 'witch hunt' himself.

On October 3, 2023, Trumps called the fraud trial 'rigged' but, he said he would testify. The judge issued a gag order on Trump after his attack on a clerk.

On October 4, 2023, for the first time in the United States, eight representatives voted to oust the speaker of the house, McCarthy.

Trump railed against a judge in New York. The attorney general said outside the courtroom, "I won't be 'bullied' by Trump. The Donal Trump show is over."

Trump falls off the Forbes 400 list of the richest Americans: his net worth tumbles $600 M as his social media site stalls.

On October 5 and 6, 2023, the New York fraud trial resumed without Trump in the courtroom. Week one of the Trump civil trial ended with former Trump organizer and co-defendant revealing details of the fraud.

Aired on ABC: Trump allegedly shared potentially sensitive information about the US nuclear subs with foreign interests with a Mar-a-Lago member. Trump's rhetoric is growing more violent in recent weeks.

On October 16, 2023, a federal judge issued a limited gag order against Trump. The judge in Trump's federal election subversion trial issued an order limiting what he could say about the case. According to the federal judge: Trump's presidential campaign does not allow him to do whatever he wants.

Court personnel, potential witnesses, special counsel, and his staff.

On October 17, 2023, Trump is set to give a deposition in the suit by a former FBI official who says firing was a political vendetta.

Trump never put in place a coronavirus program.

CHAPTER THIRTY FOUR

SIDNEY POWELL PLEADING

On October 19, 2023, in the morning, in Atlanta, Georgia, Sidney Powell pleaded guilty in an election case; the former lawyer reached a plea deal. Prosecutors recommended six years probation and, as part of the plea deal, she will be required to testify at future trials.

Details of Sidney Powell's plea deal: 1) Prosecutors recommended six (6) years' probation; 2) Trump will be required to testify at future trials; 3) Trump will write a letter of apology to the Georgia citizens. Added are the seven (7) counts including violating Georgia's RICO Act, conspiracy to commit election fraud and conspiracy to defraud the state. Oh yes! And it's only the beginning! Trump's lawyer, Sidney Powell, flipped in October 2023. We will see later for the other co-defendants.

One morning in October 2023, in a New York court, an employee was arrested for disrupting proceedings at a Trump civil fraud trial.

KENNETH CHESEBRO IS OFFERED A PLEA DEAL.

On October 20, 2023, at the Fulton County courthouse in Atlanta, Ex-Trump attorney, Kenneth Chesebro, was offered a plea deal in the Georgia election subversion case; now, both Powell and Chesebro agree to testify at future trials. Chesebro admits that he conspired to put forward fake electors in Georgia with Trump, Giuliani, and Eastman.

At 2:05 p.m. on the 20th, Jordan lost the secret ballot on whether he should drop the speaker race. This two-faced person, with his mustard-coloured tie, bit the dust, so to speak. He still says that the 2020 election was rigged; 'he is a traitor of the worst kind'.

In New York, on October 20,2023, at 2:45 p.m., Trump's trial for fraud took place. The judge suggested that a gag order violation could result in imprisonments.

TRUMP IS FINED $ 5 000.

On October 21, 2023, Trump was fined $ 5000 for violating a gag order in the New York fraud trial.

On October 23, 2023, Trump claimed his former attorney, who may testify against him, was never really his attorney at all. He told a Mar-a-Lago member about his calls with foreign leaders while he was president. Ex-Trump attorney, Jenna Ellis, is expected to plead guilty in the Georgia election case. Ellis said, "I failed to do my due diligence" pertaining to facts of the Georgia election. The charges are one count of violating Georgia's RICO Act and soliciting a public officer to violate their oath.

Michael Cohen testifies against Trump in the New York fraud trial.

On October 24, 2023, in the case against Jenna Ellis, the prosecutors recommended 5 years probation and payment of $5000 in restitution. Ellis will cooperate with the prosecutors.

Trump's former acolytes turn against him while under legal heat.

On October 25, 2023, in a Manhattan court, the judge in Trump's civil fraud trial found him 'not credible' and fined him $10 K for violating a gag order once again. The judge warned Trump: "Don't do it again or it'll be worse."

The Fulton County prosecutors talk about a potential plea deal with at least six (6) more defendants in Georgia's election subversion case. The judge, Arthur Engoron said, "I don't want anyone killed." The judge admonished Trump for disparaging a court clerk before fining him $10 000.

TRUMP'S FAMILY FRAUD TRIAL.

On October 27, 2023, a judge said, "Ivanka Trump must testify at her father's fraud trial." Michael Cohen spoke out for the first time in five (5) years. Cohen testified that, while working for Trump, concerning the assets, he (Trump) would look at the total assets and say, for example, "I'm actually not worth $4.5 billion, I'm really worth more like 6."

On October 30, 2023, trial began in Colorado on whether the 14th amendment's 'insurrectionist ban' disqualified Trump from office. A federal judge reinstated the gag order on Trump. The Colorado trial into whether Trump can be blocked from Colorado ballots resumed. Trump attacked potential witness, Bill Barr, just hours after the judge reinstated the gag order in the Department of Justice election case. Trump said, "I called Bill Barr dumb, weak, slow-moving, lethargic, gutless, and lazy. A rhino who couldn't do the job…"

TRUMP CHILDREN SET TO TESTIFY IN THEIR FATHER'S FRAUD TRIAL INCLUDING TRUMP.

On October 31, 2023, Trump moved to block witnesses from testifying at the civil fraud trial. The Trump children are set to testify this week in their father's fraud trial; the case threatens his real estate empire. Donald Trump jr. will testify on November 1, 2023; Eric Trump on November 2, 2023; Donald Trump on November 6, 2023; and Ivanka Trump on November 8, 2023.

November 1, 2023 – On this day, Donald Trump jr. is expected in a civil fraud trial in a New York courtroom. The Trump lawyers are looking to delay the Mar-a-Lago documents trial. According to an expert, Trump & Company saved $168 M in loan interest due to fraud. Ivanka Trump is appealing a judge's ruling ordering her to testify at the NYC civil fraud trial next week. In a NY court, Donald jr. said, on the accounting practices at Trump organizations, "I leave it to my accountants." Trump's inflammatory rhetoric cost him in the courtroom but fuels his campaign. Trump struggles with his own gaffe as he mocks Biden's age.

On November 2, 2023, the judge signaled that she may postpone the classified documents trial. Donald Trump said that Judge Engoron is 'a political hack who ruled against me before the trial even started. He is doing the dirty work for the democrats. Trump claims his sons are being 'persecuted' as they testify.

The judge admonished Trump lawyers over their comment criticizing a law clerk.

Donald Trump jr. is likely to say that he doesn't remember his being involved in preparing financial statements. Now, Trump jr. is in court to wrap up his testimony in a fraud trial.

Eric Trump is on the stand in court on November 2. He will testify in the New York civil fraud trial later at the attorney general's office. Eric Trump emailed, after his testimony, that he wasn't familiar with the Trump organization financial statements.

On November 3, 2023, the federal appeals court temporarily froze Trump's gag order in the election interference case. Jack Smith 'fired up' Trump to testify on Monday, November 6, 2023, in the fraud trial. The gag order against Trump in the January 6 case is put on hold. The former president and his daughter, Ivanka, are due to testify in the New Yok civil fraud trial next week. Ivanka will be ordered to court despite claims of 'undue hardship'.

Trump never <u>put in place a coronavirus program.</u>

CHAPTER THIRTY FIVE

TRUMP ARGUMENTS WITH JUDGES ON MULTIPLE OCCASIONS

On November 6, 2023, Donald Trump took the stand in the New York civil fraud trial in the absence of cameras. He attacked New York Attorney General, Letitia James, including court officials preceding the trial testimony.

Judge Arthur Engoron told Trump to answer the questions and not give speeches. Trump responded, "I'm sure the Judge will rule against me, he always does." The Judge answered, "You can attack me, but answer the questions." Trump repeatedly sparred with the Judge during his testimony. The Judge, to Trump's attorney during his testimony, "Can you control your client, this is not a rally." Trump said, "This is a very, very unfair trial, very. And I hope the people are watching."

Trump, after his clash with the Judge called the investigation 'disgraceful'. He pressed on his real estate evaluation, financial penalties of $250 million. When asked if he maintained accurate records since August 2014, he said, "I hope so." He also said that the testimony went well; the trial is a 'scam'. Trump admitted he would occasionally have 'suggestions' about financial documents at the center of the trial that threatened his empire.

The New York Attorney General, Letitia James, said after Trump's testimony, "I will not be 'bullied'. Trump then finished his testimony in the NY fraud trial.

According to some sources, Trump and his allies are plotting revenge on the justice department control in a second term of office.

On November 8, 2023, Ivanka is now on the stand at her father's civil fraud trial. The New York Attorney General, Letitia James, said Ivanka Trump was 'inextricably tied' to the Trump organization.

Ivanka Trump distanced herself from the inflated value of the penthouse apartment she leases from her father. She explained, during her testimony, why she discussed Trump organization business with her husband. She repeatedly testifies, "I don't recall."

The New York Attorney General said, after Ivanka Trump testified, "You cannot distance yourself from that fact, the documents do not lie."

On November 9, 2023, some sources say that the prosecutors may call Mar-a-Lago workers, including a plumber and a maid, to testify against Trump in the 'documents trial'. Also, a chauffeur and a woodworker may be called to testify. Trump attorneys say that Donald Trump jr. will be the first witness to be called upon on Monday, November 13, 2023, in the civil fraud trial.

On November 10, 2023, the judge rejected Trump's bid to delay the classified documents trial, for the time being. The judge kept the Trump classified documents trial scheduled for May 2024.

On November 12, 2023, Trump's team began its defense in the New York fraud trial. Trump again suggested that he would weaponize the DOJ against political enemies if re-elected.

On November 13, 2023, Donald Trump jr. was back on the stand in 250 civil fraud cases in a Manhattan courtroom. "My father is an artist with real estate," he said. Under oath, Donald Trump jr.: 1) denied any role in preparing his father's financial statements; 2) said he consulted with lawyers and accountants for the statements as a trustee, and; 3) said he certified the accuracy of the statements annually. Donald Trump called his political enemies' 'vermin' and 'radical left thugs'. Special counsel argued against live TV; It says Trump wants to turn the 2020 election subversion trial into a 'spectacle'.

On the same day, Marianne Trump Barry, Donald Trump's sister, died at the age of 86 years old.

On November 14, 2023, ex-Trump lawyers who pleaded guilty in the Georgia case, shed light on the election reversal efforts in a talk with the prosecutors. The Justice Department wants the Trump gag order upheld, and points to verbal attacks on the special counsel' family. Former Trump loyalists shed new light on the Georgia election case in leaked video statements.

Former Trump attorney, Jenna Ellis, said her 'Boss' was not going to leave the White House after losing the election. Former Trump campaign lawyer, Sidney Powell, admitted in a leaked video that she had never practiced election law before.

On November 15, 2023, Biden compared Trump's 'vermin' remark to Nazi rhetoric. Hunter Biden wants to subpoena Donald Trump and Bill Barr.

A Georgia judge in the election subversion trial will issue a protective order for evidence after the video leak. Georgia prosecutors asked the judge to jail a subversion defendant over 'effort to intimidate' witnesses. The Georgia judge plans to issue a protective order to lock down 'sensitive' evidence in the Trump election case.

On November 16, 2023, Fulton County prosecutors asked the judge to jail Trump co-defendants. The former president laid out more aggressive for a potential second White House term. "This is all bullshit! He will never be president again!

On November 17, 2023, an appeals court judge from the New York court, lifted an order in Trump's civil fraud trial.

Trump's legal team complains that the judge in the New York civil fraud trial is trying to censor him. Biden says, "It echoes language you heard in Nazi Germany in the 1930's; there are a lot of reasons to be against Donald Trump, but, damn, he shouldn't be president."

On November 20, 2023, Trump's lawyer says that the gag order in the federal election subversion case is 'categorically unconstitutional' as it restricts political speech. Trump's legal team fights the gag order in that particular case.

On November 21, 2023, a federal appeals court is inclined to restore the Trump gag order but loosens some of its restrictions. Several threats were received in the Trump civil fraud trial by the clerk.

On November 23, 2023, Trump slams 'racist' attorney general 'psycho' judge.

On December 13, 2023, Judge pauses Trump election interference case; the trial may be delayed. Visibly shaken, Georgia election worker recalls racist messages she received after Giuliani smears. Jury in the Giuliani; defamation damages trial will resume deliberations tomorrow.

On December 14, 2023, The Georgia election workers seeking $48 M. from Giuliani. But the Jury awards $148 M in Giuliani defamation damages trial. Giuliani got to close to the sun, and he got burn.

On December 16, 2023, Biden campaign says Trump "channeled his role models" and "parroted Adolf Hitler." And the White House fires back by Trump's "fascist" rhetoric. Trump says migrants are "poisoning the blood of our country" echoing white supremacist rhetoric, oh ya? what about your 2 wives Yvana & Melania who are immigrants; you are an idiot, He doesn't know what he is talking about: he continues to double-down on his anti-immigrant rhetoric.

On December 19,2023, Judge slams defense experts: "A lie is still a lie." Colorado supreme court removes Trump from 2024 primary ballot; finds "insurrectionist ban" applies to the presidency.

> No person shall. hold any office (who) having previously taken an oath.to support the constitution of United-States, shall have engaged in insurrection or rebellion, or given aid or comfort to the enemies thereof, "14th amendment to the U.S. constitution."

"No person shall. hold any office (who) having previously taken an oath.to support the constitution of United-States, shall have engaged in insurrection or rebellion, or given aid or comfort to the enemies thereof, "14th amendment to the U.S. constitution."

On December 20,2023, NYT poll: nearly a quarter of Trump supporters think Trump shouldn't be nominee if convicted. Today Detroit news: Trump recorded pressuring Michigan canvassers not to certify 2020 votes. Rona McDaniel on the phone with Trump: "do not sign it, we will get you attorneys" "we'll take care of that" and Trump on the call "We can't let these people take our country away from us." everybody knows Detroit is crooked as hell, and Trump said: "how can anybody sign something when you have more votes than people."

On December 22,2023, Trump said "I know nothing about Hitler." he defends anti-immigrant remarks. Appeals court to hear immunity arguments as march 4 trial nears.

On December 24,2023, Trump urges federal appeals court to grant him immunity against election subversion charges. Biden campaign heads into 2024 ready to make a case against Trump.

On December 26 and December 27, 2023, Trump's Christmas message to legal & political foes "rot in hell." Special counsel: Trump shouldn't be allowed to spread false info in court. The madman said, Biden's flunky, deranged Jack Smith, should go to hell. Imagine how the other country is thinking about us, are we a "banana republic". Recording reveal how Trump operatives flew fake elector ballots to DC in a last-minute bid to overturn 2020 election. Audio reveals frantic 11th hour efforts to keep Trump in office.

THE DOMINO EFFECTS!

The state Maine's top election official removes Trump from 2024 ballot. Secretary of state Shenna Bellows said barred Trump from ballot because of 14th amendment's insurrectionist ban. So, Maines joins Colorado in removing Trump from ballot. Trump from ballots in multiple states, the domino effects will see in the future. There more states to come, Michigan, Arizona, Minnesota, New Hampshire, California, and Oregon. This is good for democracy.

Illinois voters ask election board to take Trump off 2024 ballot.

Trump legal team continued the fight with the most ridiculous allegations, let remember that 59 out of 60 lawsuits were dismissed,

What kind of crazy system there're in this country, there're surely asylums, maybe they are filled to the maximum, and even, if the senate decides that, the case of this madman, could be presented to the supreme court, there is no point in having a good result, since there're two black sheep in the sheepfold, one in the past, was accused of raping, and the other one his wife received cash payment's from conservative, it sure sounds like Clar- and Gen are the most corrupt couple in Washington, also that women, praise MAGA supporters on January 6-2021, she actually attended the "stop the steal rally".

House democrat demand justice Thomas recuse himself from Colorado ballot ban case, supreme court sets February 8 oral arguments for Trump's Colorado ballot appeal.

January 4, 2024, Trump files barrage of appeals. Court will "swiftly" reject Trump immunity claim. Trump ask judge in jan.6 case to sanction special counsel.

House report: Trump org. made $5m from China when Trump was president yes, Trump, his business raked in at least $7.8 m from foreign governments during his time in WH.

Jan.5 and 6, supreme court to hear Trump Colorado ballot ban appeal, 34% of republicans falsely believes FBI organized and encouraged Jan.6, insurrection.

Three years later DOJ January 6th prosecution: 1265 arrested, 890 found guilty, 467 received jail time, and today FBI arrested 3 defendants Jan.6 Olivia Michele Pollock Jonathan Daniel Pollock and Joseph Daniel Hutchinson in Florida.

Jan 7, 2024 Congresswoman democrat from California said Trump is a "dangerous" and "sick" man. Trump is the worst disgusting and filthy person we ever had in the country, don't forget what Trump said in the past loud and clear, he "admires dictators". Trump claims Jan,6 criminals are "hostages". Stefanick parrots' false claims Jan.6, this crazy woman should be sent to jail, she's stupid, she probably has a tumor in her brain, please pay yourself a visit to your doctor, you need it, she's echo's Trump.

ABC News: Trump's fmr, deputy chief of staff talking to Jack Smith. Trump ask for Georgia election case to be dismissed. Trump expected to spend two days this week in court. Trump: treatment of Jan.6 rioters "very unfair" oh ya, one day he will say, release all prisoners from 2850 jails in the United-States. Find me someone as crazy as him, when are we going to sent this demagogue liar to jail, for ever.

Trump expected to attend court in DC and NY this week, Jan 8 and 9, Trump takes 2024 campaign to the courtroom. Judge appear skeptical of Trump's immunity claims.

Trump attorney: Former president would have immunity for assassinating rival unless impeached & convicted, "what kind of world are we living in?" Jack Smith.

Jan 10, 2024, Judge says Trump can't speak during closing arguments in NY civil fraud trial, and the Judge says former president has failed to accept preconditioned terms set by court.

Trump's NY civil fraud trial: What's at stake.

- NY civil fraud trial: NY AG seeking more than $370 M from Trump and co-defendants.
- Also looks to bar Trump from doing business in the state.
- And asking for a 5-year ban for Donald Trump Jr & Eric Trump.

Hon. Arthur Engoron: not having heard from you by the third intended deadline (noon today) I assume that Mr. Trump will not agree to the reasonable, lawful limits I have imposed as a precondition to living a closing statement above, therefore, he will not be speaking in court tomorrow, Judge Engoron: "you have your own agenda I understand that, Mr. Kise please control your client." Trump: "your honor look, I did nothing wrong, they should pay me for what we had to go through. Trump what they done to me reputationally and everything else."

Jan 11,2024, Dramatic final day of Trump civil fraud trial wraps; Judge admonishes Trump for rambling monologue, and NY AG says "justice will be done."

THE CARROLL SAGA AND MORE

On January 16, 2024, Trump arrived at the courthouse for the second time for the E. Jean Carroll defamation trial. She filed suit in 2009 over Trump's statements denying he had sexually assaulted her in the mid 90's in a department store. In the 2022 suit, Trump was found liable for sexually assaulting and defaming Carroll, in a New York federal court. Trump did not appear in person at any time during the Carroll defamation trial.

E. Jean Carroll said, "I am here because I was assaulted by Donald Trump, and he said it never happened. He lied and he shattered my reputation, and he has continued to lie; he lied last month, he lied on Sunday, he lied yesterday, and I am here to get my reputation back and to stop him from telling lies about me." Because of the Trump rhetoric, she took precautions, sleeping with a gun because she had received threats.

Carroll said, "I was known simply as a journalist, and now as a liar, a fraud, and a whack job". Trump reacted physically and verbally during Carroll's testimony; the Judge threatened to kick Trump out of court for audible comments.

On January 17, 2024, Roger Stone, one of Trump's good friends, was allegedly caught on tape talking about discussing the assassination of Democrats. "Go find Swalwell or Nadler and get this over with, it's time to do it. Then we'll see how brave the rest of them are. Either Swalwell or Nadler must die before the election, they need to get the message." By the way, for those who don't know Stone, he met Trump in the 1970's through his former lawyer, Roy Cohn.

Trump said, "Presidents must have immunity, even in events that cross the line."

On January 18, 2024, E. Jean Carroll's expert witness and former boss, Robbie Myers, took the stand and estimated the damages from $7.2M to $12.1M. The judge has not ruled yet.

Jessica Leeds and Natasha Stoynoff are two Trump accusers.

Garland agrees with special counsel's call for a "speedy" Trump trial.

On January 20, 2004, Haley attacked Trump's "mental fitness" after he confused her with Nancy Pelosi. Haley was not in office on January 6, and falsely claims that she was responsible for security, another lie from Trump, as usual. Geraldo Rivera, former Fox news host, said that Trump was unfit to be president. Trump says that U.S. presidents should be given "total immunity"; same as for a "dictator or a King". Mark Hesper, former secretary of defense, called Trump a "threat to democracy". The judge, Judy Sheindlin, on Trump, said that "chaos follows him."

On January 21 and January 22, 2004, Trump said, "I got indicted more than Al Capone." He hails far-right Hungarian Prime Minister as a "very strong man". Again, you see this dictator likes and praises only other dictators.

Now: Trump at a New York federal court for the civil defamation trial. The Trump civil defamation trial adjourns for four days due to a sick juror.

On January 24 and January 25, 2024, Judge Kaplan said that Trump was back in court as the civil defamation trial resumes. Closing arguments are set for tomorrow.

On January 26, 2024, an historic trial. Trump walks out of court in the middle of closing arguments. Judge Lewis Kaplan said, "There are to be no interruptions by anybody, no audible comments by anybody else." The judge also threatened Trump's attorney, "You are on the verge of spending some time in lock-up. Now, sit down."

According to Carroll's attorney, Roberta Kaplan, jurors should decide "what it will take to get Donald Trump to stop". She says he caused $12 M of reputation damage. And she also said "this case is also about punishing Donald Trump for what he has done and what he continues to do. Punishing him for the malicious nature of his attack, and his continuing attacks right up to and during this very trial."

The judge said to Trump's lawyer: "You will not quarrel with me." The jury is deliberating in the Trump defamation trial.

Finally, the jury says that Trump should pay $83.3 M in damages to E. Jean. Carroll. Emotional harm $7.3 M / Reputation repair $11 M / Punitive damages $65 M. Carroll's attorney said: "Standing up to a bully takes courage and bravery." The verdict proves that the law applies to everyone, "even former presidents". E. Jean Carroll said, "The decision is a huge defeat for every bully who has tried to keep a woman down."

Trump never put in place a coronavirus program.

CHAPTER THIRTY SIX

THE YEAR 2024, WILL BE A NIGHTMARISH ONE FOR TRUMP

- Accused = E. Jean Carroll. Defamation Trial...................... Guilty.
- Accused = Stormy Daniels. Hush Money Trial....... .... Guilty.
- Accused = Penalties and damages across New York trials........Guilty.
- Accused = The Capitol attack on January 6, 2021................. Guilty.
- Accused = Classified documents trial................................ Guilty.
- Accused = The phone call to Georgia Secretary of State............ Guilty.

Today, January 26, 2024, Former National Rifle Association CEO, Wayne Lapierre, testified in the corruption trial where he was accused of using funds as his "personal piggy bank." But, on January 4, 2024, Wayne Lapierre announced his resignation. Finally, a person whose hands are stained with blood disappears from circulation. This person and his acolytes have received, from manufacturers, more than 1 billion dollars in bribes for decades. There are 116 586-gun ammunition stores in the U.S. So those people also have their hands full of blood and they are happy to sell these toys, which kill millions of people each year. Bravo! More than 40 000 people killed in gun violence, in 2023.

Nicki Haley, in a South Carolina rally, again calls Trump "unhinged". On January 28, 2024, Haley slammed Trump and defended the $83.3 M verdict in the Carroll case: "One must absolutely trust the jury."

On January 29 and January 30, 2024, Trump's attorney, Alina Habba, makes and then backs off on "conflicting" claims against Carroll's attorney. Trump packs spent $50 million on legal expenses in 2023. Judge Arthur Engoron said, "It's up to me now, and I will do my best to have a final decision by January 31".

January 31, 2024, the judge could rule in Trump's New York civil fraud trial. In a South Carolina rally, Haley said, "Trump is "toxic" and lacks "moral clarity". Trump's business empire is at stake in the New York civil fraud trial.

Lindsey Graham, the yes-no man, testified in front of a Georgia grand jury: "If you told Trump that Martians stole the election, he would probably believe you." The answer is yes, he would, what a clown!

On February 1, 2024, sources said that the Trump organization's chief financial officer is in talks to plead guilty to perjury charges tied to a civil fraud probe. Representative Gaetz's ex-girlfriend was contacted in a house ethics probe.

Donald Trump's federal trial, which was to open on March 4 in Washington, has been delayed, notably due to the request for "immunity". Judge Tania Chutkan formally announced the postponement of the trial on Friday February 2, 2024.

The prosecutor responsible for investigating the case against Trump is from the state of Georgia, so Trump, has pleaded not guilty in this case.

The Fulton district attorney, Fani Willis, proposed that the trial of the ex-president and his 14 co-defendants, begin on August 5, 2024, three months before the presidential election.

On February 4, 2024, the Supreme Court is to hear arguments in the 14th amendment case on Thursday February 8, 2024. Trump urges the Supreme Court to keep him on the Colorado ballot.

On February 6, 2024, Trump said that he wants to debate Biden "immediately".

A US federal appeals court, on Tuesday, rejected Donald Trump's request for criminal immunity, reopening the way for his trial in Washington on charges of trying to illegally overturn the results of the 2020 election. He is entitled to "all the defense as any other criminal defendant". The Appeals court said that Trump's immunity argument "would collapse our system of separated powers by placing the president beyond reach of all branches". Trump does not have "unbounded authority to commit crimes that would neutralize implementation of election results".

The court gives Trump until Monday, February 12, 2024, to appeal ruling of the Supreme Court. The Court's allegation, if proven, is that it was an "unprecedented assault" on "the structure of our government". The Court said that Trump is not immune from prosecution in the election case.

On February 8, 2024, at the Supreme Court, Jason Murray, representing the Colorado voters, Jonathan Mitchell, the attorney representing Donald Trump, and Shannon Stevenson, Colorado solicitor general, plus 9 Justices from the Supreme Court, met. What could the Supreme Court decide? With this case, the country's high court is placed at the very uncomfortable intersection of law and politics, a collision point not particularly appreciated by the nine justices who make up this body. The U.S. Supreme Court could say the case is not mature enough to make a decision.

Currently, the ex-president's right to put his name on a ballot is contested in 35 states across the country, according to a review by the New York Times. Of these states, in which ineligibility appeals were filed against Donald Trump, only two were successful, in Colorado and Maine. Several states are nevertheless waiting for the Supreme Court to rule definitively.

The Colorado courts considered that Donald Trump's actions on January 6, 2021, fell within the 14th Amendment. "Remove Trump" and "Trump led a conspiracy" could be read on posters brandished Thursday by demonstrators in front of the Supreme Court.

Special counsel warns of the "risk" of outing more witnesses after several were "harassed and intimidated" on February 10, 2024.

Niki Haley said to Trump, "My husband Michael is deployed serving our country, something you know nothing about. Someone who continually disrespects the sacrifices of military families has no business being commander-in-chief. Your NATO comments "make me sick to my stomach."

In a rally, Trump said that mass deportations would begin "within moments" of taking office. He again called jailed January 6 rioters "hostages."

The traitor House republican conference chair, Elise Stefanik (R-H-Y.), said that she would not have allowed the 2020 election results to be certified on January 6, 2021, had she been in former Vice President Mike Pence's position. "I would not have done what Mike Pence did. I don't think that was the right approach".

It's clear that, this demagogue is preparing to become vice-president in the event that the dictator returns to the White House. But this loser hypocrite sucker, with a lack of knowledge, won't go far.

Donald Trump asked the United States Supreme Court on Monday

February 12, 2024, to suspend an appeal decision denying the former Republican president any criminal immunity.

Trump says that if NATO allies didn't spend enough on defence, he "encouraged" "Russia to do whatever the hell they want".

Biden said that Trump's NATO comments were "dumb, shameful, dangerous, unamerican".

Faced with Trump's threats, France, Germany, and Poland pleaded for a united Europe. On February 14, 2024, Trump was confronted by a busy legal week as a major case collided with the February 15, 2024, hush money to Stormy Daniels case. On February 16, 2024, it was the New York civil fraud case.

The judge said that the Trump hush money trial would likely last six weeks. Following this, Trump could owe hundreds of millions of dollars in penalties across the New York trials.

McCarthy said that Matt Gaetz "probably lies about who he sleeps with".

On February 15, 2024, a NY Judge ruled that Trump's first criminal trial will begin on March 25, in New York. Today, February 16, 2024, a ruling is expected in Donald Trump's civil fraud trial. At 3.00 pm, the judge issued a ruling against Trump and his sons in the civil fraud trial. The judge ordered Trump to pay nearly $355 million in the civil fraud trial. His sons, Don Jr and Eric, were ordered to pay $4 million each, and Trump CFO, Allen Weisselberg, $1 million. Trump's sons were also banned from doing business in New York state and cannot apply for loans from banks registered in New York for 3 years.

The judge, Arthur Engoron, ruled that Michael Cohen told the truth; the court found his testimony credible.

And it's not over yet, there are 4 trials to come.

Following the death of Alexey Navalny today, Niki Haley said, "Putin did this, the same Putin whom Donald Trump praises and defends. The same Trump who said: "In all fairness to Putin, you're saying he kills people. I haven't seen that". According to Haley, Trump is siding with a "thug who kills his political opponents". Trump's threats to NATO "emboldened" Putin. She said that the U.S. "will not survive" four more years of Trump chaos.

Ms. Haley, the next time you have a chance to respond to that dictator, know that his friend Putin has, so far, killed 14 people. What an ignorant guy he is.

And do not forget that Trump gave his approval to the crown Prince,

Mohammed Bin Salman, to kill Jamal Khashoggi in the Saudi Consulate in Istanbul on October 2, 2018. His body was dismembered with a bone saw.

So, let's imagine that this dictator returns to the White House and that this demagogue will have, as a partner, another dictator like Putin. Europe and America will no longer be the same, and that is the end of Democracy.

Haley said that Trump is "Weak in the knees" when it comes to Putin. Trump attacks Biden instead of Putin in his first public reaction to the Navalny death. What do you expect from a dictator to another dictator.

Donald Trump being called the worst president of the United States is another American paradox. He has been described as the worst president in the history of the country by a panel of experts from the American political science association. At the bottom of the list, Donald Trump is judged more harshly than James Buchanan, who plunged the United States in a civil war.

The totalitarian regime of Trump is to seek to obtain the complete support of the entire population and plays on the fear of repression. It will seek to provide the population with a feeling of power and collective strength. So, if this demagogue returns to the White House, be assured that we are heading toward a civil war. Wake-up America!

Firearms are not made to protect oneself.

Yet once again, two mass killings in the same week. Firearms are not made to protect oneself as the Americans like say or to be used against our fellow human beings, but rather they are made to kill. This stupid idea, that the National Rifle Association likes to tell you, and to deceive you with, is just smoke in your eyes. On the other hand, it is true that weapons can protect you from certain types of wild animals in the forest, and do not forget that this butchery, hypocrite that you are where you cry at each mass killing, is forgotten until the next one. And it only exists in the United States. You prefer to cherish your toys, rather than your dead.

On February 22, 2024, a judge rejected Trump's request to delay the $355 million civil fraud order. Trump now has 30 days to pay $454 million which includes the interest, as the judgment was finalized.

In Charleston, Donald Trump came under fire Saturday after his "racist" remarks to black voters. Trump sleeked to pit judges against each other to avoid trial.

Bannon falsely claimed that Trump is the "legitimate president" as he said on February 26, 2024. What are you waiting for, put this troublemaker in jail for life, normally that what's what we do with a traitor.

A Republican National Committee resolution would ban the party from paying Trump's legal bills.

Trump is searching like crazy to find the millions he needs for various trials.

New York State attorney, Letitia James, said that the interest per day for Trump, is $114,533.04. Trump is still searching for ways to pay the half-billion-dollar judgement. The appeals court judge said that Trump must come up with the full bond amount to cover the $454 million civil fraud trial judgment.

An Illinois judge declared that Donald Trump was ineligible on Wednesday, February 28,2024, because of his actions during the assault on the capitol and ordered the withdrawal of the ballots in his name during the republican primary in that state.

On March 02,2024, Donald Trump could be moving towards bankruptcy as he struggles to pay the $454 million, he owes from his New York fraud trial. A legal expert told Newsweek that New York judge, Anil Singh, rejected Trump's 100 million bond offer on Wednesday to cover less than a third of the fine for financial fraud within his real estate empire and ordered that the former president pay the full penalty or cash bond amount by the original deadline.

On March 04, 2024, the Supreme Court keeps Trump on the Colorado ballot, rejecting a 14th amendment push. Allen Weisselberg, ex-Trump CFO, pleaded guilty to lying under oath and faces 5 months in prison.

On March 05,2024, Trump asked the judge to cut the $83.3 million penalty in the E. Jean Carroll case or grant him a new trial.

Mitch McConnell endorses Trump despite years of clashes and tension.

I wrote in my book, a few months ago, that we remember what McConnell, this two-faced traitor, said about Trump during the attack of the capitol on January 6, 2021, and today he is ready to "kiss his ass". It's a disgrace against the democracy. We have eight months to save our republic and ensure that Donald Trump is never anywhere near the oval office again.

In a rally, a few weeks ago, what exactly did Donald Trump say? "We're going to drill, baby, we have more liquid gold under our feet, more energy, oil, and gas than any other country in the world! We have a lot of potential revenue", said this crazy demagogue. Bravo for the future, with an increase of hurricanes for the south of the United-States, and elsewhere.

At a town hall meeting organized by Fox News in July 2023, Trump said, "Think of President Xi, a brilliant guy, and when I say he's brilliant, everyone says, 'oh, that's terrible' he runs 1.4 billion people with an iron fist; smart, brilliant, everything perfect, there is nobody in Hollywood like this guy."

Former advisers sounded the alarm that Trump praises despots in private and on the campaign trail. Trump praises "fanatic" Hungarian autocrat Viktor Orban at Mar-A-Lago. Trump said, "If I am re-elected in 2024 I will "end" the war by not giving Ukraine a penny."

Trump employee # 5, Brian Butler, speaks publicly for the first time about the Mar-A-Lago classified documents case, and he said the public must know before they vote in November.

A Manhattan District Attorney does not oppose a move to delay the Trump hush money trial. The delay is one month, not two months as proposed by Trump's lawyers.

A judge ruled that Fani Willis could stay on the Trump election case. He said that the case may continue if prosecutor Nathan Wade is removed. On March 15, 2024, the Fulton County Prosecutor quit after judges' ruling.

Mike Pence, former vice president, will not support Donald Trump in the 2024 election.

A New York judge, on Friday March 14, 2024, postponed until mid-April the historic Donald Trump criminal case, scheduled for March 25. This is the case of concealed payments to an adult film actress. The postponement offers a new respite to the presidential candidate, some 31,000 pages of court documents have been produced in recent days,

The $130,000 payment to Miz Stephanie Clifford (her real name), was intended to keep her silent about a sexual relationship in 2006 when Trump was already married to Melania.

Trump said "If I don't get elected, it's going to be bloodbath". His lawyer said that Trump can't make the $464 million civil fraud case. It is a "practical improbability". No insurance can back the Trump bond as they approached 30 firms. Trump's attorney also said that they are seeking a stay of payment from the appellate division of the New York State Supreme Court to prevent the state from seizing their assets, a legal consequence Donald Trump faces if he does not pay, in accordance with the judgment.

The prosecutor, Alvin Bragg, will decide to authorize the testimony of former playboy model Karen McDougal, who claims to have been Donald Trump's mistress from 2006 to 2007. She sold her story for $150,000 to the National Enquire.

Believe it or not, Paul Manafort wants to enter into Trump's orbit.

This guy, already in the past, did some prison time for fraud, as mentioned earlier in this book, and remember, I repeat, "Tell me who your friends are, and I will tell you who you are."

On March 18, 2024, Stefanie Lambert, a pro-forma lawyer who tried to overturn the 2020 election, was arrested after a court hearing about her recent leak of internal emails belonging to Dominion voting systems.

On March 20, 2024, the New-York Attorney General said that the appeals court shouldn't consider Trump's claim that it's impossible to get a $464 million bond. Trump is in panic mode; he has until Monday to secure the $464 M bond in the civil fraud case.

The GOP nominee, Michele Morrow, another Trump friend who runs North Carolina public schools, called for violence against democrats including executing Obama and Biden; she's a killer. Why doesn't the FBI send such a traitor to jail.

Seen in the New York Times: Valet testified that Trump told Pence on January 6 that certifying the 2020 election would be a "career killer." The New York Attorney General takes initial steps to prepare to seize Trump's assets. But Trump says he has almost $500 M cash in a new truth social post.

On March 24, 2024, Trump races to meet tomorrow's deadline to secure the $464 M bond. The New York Attorney General could start seizing Trump assets if he can't meet the $464 M bond.

A judge said that the Trump hush money trial will begin on April 15 and slaps Trump with a new gag order, blasting his "threatening, inflammatory, denigrating" statements.

Larry David said that Trump is the "greatest con man". David rails against the sociopath, Donald Trump. "He's sick man and a little baby who just couldn't admit to losing."

On March 28, 2024, district attorney, Fani Willis is back, "the train is coming" for Donald Trump and she "may ask for an August trial".

On April 01, 2024, Trump ramps up inflammatory rhetoric as critical month begins; Jack Smith, Fani Willis, Alvin Bragg family, The judge Juan Merchan, Prosecutors, and Judges.

On April 02,2024, Trump renews attack on Judge who extended speech restrictions, Donald Trump once again described Judge Juan Merchan as "corrupt" on Tuesday, who will preside over his criminal trial starting April 15, in New York.

The expected witnesses, Michael Cohen, Stormy Daniel, Hope Hick, David Pecker, Karen McDougal, Kellyanne Conway, and more.

Donald Trump is facing 91 felony charges. And he claims America will "cease to exist" if he loses elections.

On April 04,2024, Judge rejects Trump's bid to get Georgia election subversion case dismissed on free speech grounds.

Trump never put in place a coronavirus program

On August 19, 2024 at the DNC convention in Chicago, Biden passed the torch to Kamala Harris in a moving speech, which he would never have wanted to give, on August 22 it was Tim Walz who was named as Kamala Harris' running mate. And finally Kamala Harris accepted the nomination for the presidency in a historic speech.

On September 13, 2024 Robert De Niro: Trump: Thinks he's a thug.

On September 15, 2024, second assassination attempt on Trump by Ryan Wesley at the West Palm Beach, Florida golf club.

North Carolina Governor Mark Robinson, said he was a Black Nazi, and expressed his support for bringing back black slavery. This person surely has a brain of gelatin.

Trump's accusers have said, he is a "predator, not a "Protector".

CHAPTER THIRTY SEVEN

THE BEGINNING OF THE END FOR TRUMP

Donald Trump dumped by several ex-members of his cabinet, and they aren't Mike pence, John Bolton, mark Esper, John Kelly, Ty Cobb, Antony Scaramucci, Alyssa Ellis, Cassidy Hutchinson, Stephanie Grisham, Alissa Farah Griffin.

The traitor John Eastman fights to get his law license back. The Donald Trump bond was rejected by the county's filling system NY Attorney General Lititia James.

"Donald Trump" Jury selection is scheduled to begin April 15,2024, and hundreds of Manhattan residents have received summons to appear in court, from them, twelve jurors and up to six alternates will be chosen.

On April 09,2024, today, again, Trump loses another attempt to delay Hush money trial. Ex former CFO Allen Weisselberg expected to be sentenced to 5 months on perjury charges. Trump plans vengeance if he wins white house in November. According to Reuters Ipsos poll data, 64% Voters take Trump's hush money charges seriously: A majority of Us voters consider the criminal charges in NY related to a hush money payment against former president Trump to be serious.

What we're watching: Trump the first US president indicted with criminal charges, face 34 felony counts of falsifying business records in the first degree in NY.

Day two jury selection, Trump smirked at pool when introduced as defendant, and bashes judge over gag order in the hush money case. Again, Judge to Trump lawyers "I will not have any jurors intimidated" in the court room.

On April 17,2024, Trump's stock stumbles again; down 70% since March, why "truth" investor I still hopeful, it's in Trump's hands. The next day his shares value drops from $ 5.28 B .to $1.9 B.

Prosecutors submit list of Trump's past legal troubles they may bring up in hush money case.

On April 18,2024, Trump's is back in court: "The Judge Juan Merchan said, now we have our jury" he is presiding over Donald Trump's trial, for falsifying documents in connection with election interference.

The man who hopes to make a triumphant return to the white house is on trial in a case of hidden payments to buy the silence of a former porn star, a few days before election 2016.

Donald Trump "he's the object of derision, it's his nightmare, he can't control the script, he can't control what's being said about him, and the outcome could go in a direction he really doesn't want".

Good news: Jos Biden receives support from the Kennedys; the entire legendary Kennedy family, no fewer than 15 members of the Kennedy clan, show their support to Jos Biden.

THE "HUSH MONEY TRIAL" & MORE

On April 19,2024, seven men, five women, and six alternate jurors selected; with the full jury for the Trump's criminal trial, which will start on next Monday April 22, in the NY court.

April 22, 2024, Trump back in court after lashing out at judge, gag order. Trump money trial, live coverage of former president Donald Trump in Manhattan, New-York. Tabloid ex David Pecker is first witness in historic Trump's trial. Prosecutor: this case is about a criminal conspiracy and cover-up.

The plot began in august 2015, during a meeting witch notably brought together at Trump tower. Donald Trump, his long-time friend, David Pecker, then CEO of the American Media inc. (AMI) press group, as well as his former lawyer, Michael Cohen.

A year after being indicted by the Manhattan district attorney, Donald Trump is undergoing a criminal trial without precedent in American political history. The very first brought against a former president.

April 23, 2024, Trump fines up to $1000.00 per violations-30 days in jail per violation. Trump "Sexual infidelity especially with a porn star on the heels of the access Hollywood tape would have been devastation his campaign".

Prosecutor: "It was election fraud, pure and simple" "criminal conspiracy".

David Pecker told Trump "I told him we're going to try to help the campaign, and to do that, I want to keep this as quiet as possible".

Donald Trump hatched a "plot to rig" the 2016 presidential election by buying the silence of a former porn star about sexual relationship.

Pecker testifies about decade long friendship with Trump and said I will publish positive stories about Mr. Trump, and will publish negative stories about his opponents and said I would be your eyes and ears.

Pecker bought doorman's story to prevent others from publishing it, "embarrassing" Trump's campaign.

April 24, 2024, Trump blasts Michael Cohen despite judge's gag order. Court officers discussing what to do if Trump is jailed for contempt of court.

Key Trump allies indicted in Arizona election subversion case: Mark Meadow, Rudy Giuliani, Jenna Ellis, John Easman, Mike Roman, Boris Epshteyn, Christina Bobb.

April 25, 2024, David Pecker "when I got on the phone, Mr. Trump said to me: I spoke to Michael Cohen, Karen is a nice girl". "I believe that when Mr. Trump said that she was a nice girl. I believe that he knew who she was".

Pecker: Trump ask how McDougal was doing during 2017 WH dinner; told president: she's doing well and "she's quiet". Pecker: Cohen told me Trump would be furious if I didn't purchase Stormy Daniels story.

April 26, 2024 Trump says he would testify "if it's necessary". Pecker admits he killed stories to influence the 2016 election. Michael Cohen's former banker testifies in Trump trial. Justice seems skeptical that Trump has absolute immunity, but may not greenlight quick trial in January 6 case.

Trump, say he wants to debate Biden "tell me where".

Melania keeps her distance, absent from the trial & trail.

Special counsel's lawyer: "Framers knew too well the dangers of a king who could do no wrong".

The US state of Arizona has charged 18 people in an attempt to overturn the results of the 2020 election, among those charged, Rudy Giuliani, Mark Medows, Jenna Ellis, and John Easman, Boris Epshteyn.

April 29, 2024, Testimony from Cohen's banker begins to lay out details of $ 130k payment to Stormy Daniels.

The supreme court on Monday the 29, April, reject former Trump adviser Peter Navarro's request that he be released from prison. Hope Hicks, Stormy Daniels, Michael Cohen expected to testify.

Second gag-order hearing set for this Thursday may,02,2024, How far

Trump would go: "if we don't win, you know, it depends" he tells Time Magazine "It always depends on the fairness of the election".

Judge Merchan has fined Trump $1000 for each violation for violating gag order, the judge warns Trump of "incarceratory punishment" if he continues to violate his gag order. Ex-attorney Keith Davidson for Stormy Daniels & Karen McDougall testifying.

Judge fines Trump $9 K for violating gag order nine time.

May 01, 02,2024, How far Trump would go, if he wins, a second term in November, pardons for all Jan.6 attackers, and more, what a disgrace.

Now: former lawyer Keith Davidson for Stormy Daniels, on the stand. is looking at the jury as he's speaking, and Trump's eyes remain closed while Davidson is speaking.

The prosecutor Steinglass ask "would you use the phrase hush money to describe the money that was paid to your client by Donald Trump". Davidson says Daniels was in tough spot at the time. And Davidson confirms that Karen McDougal never wanted her story to be public, and he confirms he did not speak with Cohen about the Mcdougal deal.

Again, the judge holds hearing on Trump's latest alleged gag order violation. And the judge to rule on four more alleged Trump gag order violation.

Davidson testimony about phone call with Michael Cohen: "I've saved that guy money so many times you don't even know, that fucking guy is not even paying me $130,000 back" The prosecutors are now playing the recording from September 2016 Trump's voice can be heard in it.

Donald Trump: contrary to the fake news media I don't fall asleep in the court I simply close my beautiful blue eyes.

May 03,2024, Hope Hicks called to testify, a long time Trump aide, Hicks on her role as press secretary. Hicks says she reached out to Cohen to run down a rumor she had heard about another tape. "That would be problematic for the campaign" she says.

Hicks testifies about Trump's reaction to "access Hollywood tape». Hope Hicks get emotional, cries on the stand in hush money trial.

May 06,2024, Trump return to NY court for hush money trial week 4. Judge fins Trump in contempt for violating gag order again.

Judge "court will have to consider a jail sanction" if Donald Trump continues to violate his gag order, the statement list the $130,000 wire transfer to the Keith Davidson trust made in October 2017.

Payments to Michael Cohen, Allen Weisselberg said, "we have to get some money to Michael" (Mcconney the controller.

Up-to-date, Prosecutors: Two more weeks needed to finish case.

Sources: If judge decides to give Trump short jail sentence for gag order violation, would be at courthouse with court officers, secret service working together.

May 07,2024, threatened with jail, Trump says he's willing to make "sacrifice".

Prosecutors expected to call Stormy Daniels to the stand today. Defence attorney Susan Neckeles "to Stormy Daniels is you are looking to extort money from president Trump". Neckeles ask. «false", Daniels says, raising her voice.

Judge Merchan says it's fine to elicit that Trump and Daniels had sex, "that fine, but we don't need to know the details" the judge says. Daniels recalls that Trump said, «we don't sleep in the same room», Trump closed his eyes and shook his head at the defence table and murmured to his attorney as she responded.

Daniels says she mentioned lake Tahoe and hotel room which was «obviously" about Trump, Stormy Daniels testifies about alleged affair with Trump. Stormy Daniels resumes testimony in Trump trial, and case ends for the day.

New sources: Former G.A, Lt.Gov. Duncan aid I am voting for Biden in November.

May 08,2024, the key testimony takeaways: Recontend alleged affairs, said hush money came after "access Hollywood" tape, said she does "hate Trump, said she did not "extort money" from Trump. Neckeles attorney said: Am I correct that you hate president Trump? Daniels: yes, and you want him to go to jail; right? I want him to be held accountable.

May 09,2024, NY appeals court set final briefs for may 20.

Testimony resumes in day 14 in Trump hush money trial. Ex-Trump oval office director, Westerhout: Trump paid attention to detail', preferred to read things before signing them.

Now. Défense: prosecutors don't plan to call Karen Mcdougal.

Judge denies Trump's request to modify gag order. judge again denies Trump team's request for a mistrial. Judge denies Trump's request to modify gag order; says "your client's track record speak for itself. Trump again claims hush money trial judge "corrupt". Judge denies defense motion for a mistrial;

says there were "many times" Trump attorney "could have object" to Stormy Daniels' testimony, "but didn't.

May 10,2024, Ex-Trump lawyer Michael Cohen expected to testify next Monday may 13, 2024.Trump is back in court, 014"Good morning, Mr. Trump," judge Merchan says. Testimony resumes in Trump hush money. trial. Awaiting testimony from next witness in Trump trial.

Judge suggests bringing former Trump Org.CFO Weisselberg to testify outside of jury's presence. Prosecution says "entirely possible" they will finish by end of next week. NYT/ problica report: Trump may owe $ 100,000 tax bill for questionable IRS tax break on Chicago tower.

Appeals court upholds Steve Bannon's contempt connection for defying January 6. Committee subpoena.

May13,2024, **Michael Cohen Testifies,**

Trump in a rally yesterday said stupid thing as usual, and I quote tokes "Hannibal Lecter" was a "wonderful man". Shame on you this guy is nut it's time to put him in jail.

Sources: Who is Michael Cohen? # 1 once called himself Trump's "thug, Pitbull &lawless lawyer". # 2 once vowed to take a bullet for Trump. # 3 wrote "& know where the skeletons are buried because I was the one who buried them.

At 9.38 am this morning, the prosecution has called Michael Cohen to the stand, prosecutor Susa Hoffinger will conduct the direct examination of Michael.

Michael Cohen says, Trump never pay him for the bill from entertainment resorts. And Trump said «he asked me it I wanted to get fired on the first day. Hoffinger asks whether Cohen would sometimes lie for Trump "yes, Ma'am" Cohen says.

About the love affairs "he told me to make sure that the story doesn't get out, you handle it. Cohen says that he went to Trump to tell him the agreement was completed.

The prosecution moves to Karen Mcdougal, Cohen says he went to Trump's office and said, "hey, boss, I got to talk to you." Cohen says he asked Trump if he knew who Haren Mcdougal was. "She really beautiful." Cohen says Trump said at the time, Cohen testifies" I said, ok but there's a story that's right now being shopped." Cohen: Trump told me "Make sure it doesn't get released".

Trump is still sitting back with his eyes closed.

Cohen says he wanted to talk to Trump regarding "the Karen Mcdougal matter." Dylan Howard former national Enquirer editor texted Cohen on June 20, "I am about to meet her, her name is Karen Mcdougal, a former play boy playmate." Cohen responds: "ok, we need to speak."

Now: Cohen testifies about working with David Pecker to kill Karen McDougal's story about alleged Trump affairs. Cohen says he was in Trump's office when had a call with David Pecker about the Karen Mcdougal matter. Cohen recalls Pecker said "he had this under control, and we'll take care of this." Pecker told them it would cost $150,000 to «control the story "Fantastic: great job" was Trump's reaction.

Hoffinger: To your knowledge was Mr. Trump aware that you were recording? "Cohen: "no Ma'am." Cohen: "what I was doing was at the direction and for the benefit of Mr. Trump.

At 12,14 pm Trump is sitting back in his chair with his eyes closed. At 12,29 pm the prosecution moves on to discuss Stormy Daniels, Cohen on the possible impact of Daniels' story: "catastrophic this is horrible for the campaign. "Trump's: Cohen "He told me work with David and get control over this."

Cohen says Trump told him, "Because if, I win, it will have no relevance because I'm president, and if I lose, I don't really care, Cohen: "he wasn't even thinking about Melania, this was all about the campaign."

AT 12,52 the court is breaking for lunch. judge Merchan said see you at 2,00 pm.

I called Mr. Trump, in order to advise him of the situation, the story was going to go to the daily mail. Weisselberg aked if AMI could pay Daniels. Eventually Weisselberg suggested that Cohen front the money to Daniels. Don't worry, you'll get the money back. Said Trump. Cohen said he checked in with Davidson to ensure the deal was in order so he could tell Trump "That the matter is under control."

Cohen had two phone calls with Trump around 8,30am on October 26 before Cohen went across the street to the bank to make the payment to Davidson. "I want to ensure what once again he approved what I was doing because I require approval from him on all of this, «Cohen says.

Cohen: Trump "expressed to me,' just do it on hush money payment. Cohen: «everything required Mr. Trump sign off, on top of what I wanted the money back." Cohen testifies he "immediately" notified Trump when payment was made,

At 3,21 the court is taking an afternoon break.

Cohen confirms he was disappointed he wasn't considered for WH chief of staff. "because of my close proximity to him for a decade, I did understand him" Cohen continues.

Trump, on paying Stormy Daniels "there're no reason to keep this thing out there so do it, he expressed to me, just do it, meet with Weisselberg and figure this whole thing out. Cohen" I was just personally insulted," Cohen: wouldn't have paid his money without Trump's approval. Cohen said he was in the room when Weisselberg wrote on the document calculating what Trump owed Cohen based on their conversations.

The attorney Hoffinger: reimbursements were not crossed up "correct." Cohen says. Cohen also explains the red finch $50,000 payment. At 4,26 "have a good night, see you tomorrow, judge Merchan says. Court is adjourned for the day in Donald Trump's criminal hush money trial in New York

May-14-2024. Michael Cohen resumes testimony in Trump trial at 9,39 judge Merchan: "Mcconney's email "just reminder to get me the invoices you spoke to Allen about. «Cohen: I was sitting with President Trump and he asked me if I was ok. He asked me it I need money." I Cohen: I said no, all good,' he said because I can get a check, I said no I am ok, he said alright. Just make sure you deal with Allen,"

Cohen emailed an invoice to Mcconney on Feb.14 including the $35,000 payments for Jan. And Feb. Hoffinger ask if the invoices Cohen sent were consistent with directions given by Allen Weisselberg "yes Maman." Cohen responds. Asked who sign each of the checks, Cohen confirms each time: "Donald Trump,"

Asked why he continued to lie, Cohen said. "Out of loyalty and in order to protect him. Cohen say "I will always protect Mr. Trump."

Eventually Cohen says he figured out "Michael Avenatti was going to be representing Daniels."

Cohen says he was raided by the FBI in April 2018. Cohen on the FBI: I look through the pep hole, I saw a ton of people out in the hallway, I saw the badge so I opened the door Cohen on the FBI raid: "they identified themselves as the FBI, asked me to step into the hallways. «Cohen testifies about the FBI raid of his hotel room, apartment and office. Cohen explains the FBI's search warrant gave them the right to take my two-cell phone, any electronic devices as well as records.

Cohen is asked to describe his feeling around the FBI raids «concerned, despondent, angry. "Cohen testifies Trump told him," Everything's going to be ok. stay tough, you're going to be ok." Cohen says it was the last time he and Trump spoke.

The court is taking a brief morning break.at 11,31 am. Hoffinger attorney "are you familiar with an attorney Robert Costello," Cohen I was introduced by a lawyer Jeffrey Citron a close friend to Rudy Giuliani, Cohen says he wasn't sure about Costello. Cohen: "I didn't trust him, meaning Bob Costello, and I was still remaining loyal to Mr. Trump.

Cohen confirms that he paid Daniels «on behalf of Mr. Trump». Cohen says he worked on the Mcdougal deal "at the direction of Donald J. Trump and "for the benefit of Donal J. Trump".

Cohen says his family told him "That it was about time to listen to them." Cohen, "I made e decision that I would not lie for president Trump any more". Jurors are watching Cohen as he explains he was sentenced 36months in prison and fines.

"I apologized to congress, I apologized to the country, I apologized to my family, Cohen says, nodding his head slightly.

At 12,58 pm court resume after a lunch break.

Todd Blanche; "is this trial important to you Mr. Cohen?" Cohen: "Personally yes." Blanche; "have you regularly commented on your podcasts that you want president Trump to be convicted in this case?" yes, probably," Cohen says.

Blanche: "You admire is financial success, his high profile, his tenacity?" "Cohen" "very much so yes." Cohen confirms he said in 2017 that he "missed President Trump."

May 16,2024,

Now: Biden & Trump to face off CNN debate June 27 at 9 pm ET.

"Let's get the witness please" Merchan says.

Judge Merchan tells the jury that it maybe necessary to have the Court convene next Wednesday. Merchan added that if any juror can't work on Wednesday, that's fine and the Court won't sit.

Blanche asks if Cohen said he was "going" to hold President Trump accountable" in one of the texts.

Blanche asks if the detective told Cohen that the DA's office "told the NY Times about the indictment before they told you?" "No sir." Cohen says. Cohen, confirm he viewed himself as David and Trump as Goliath.

Blanche says "You continues to call President Trump various names on your podcast, correct!" Blanche asks "correct?" Cohen says.

"Went you stopped the (Trump tower Moscow) project was a lie, correct?" "Blanche asks, "correct," Cohen says.

Blanche: you knew you were lying, correct? "Cohen" "yes". "And you lied again when you met with the special counsel, correct? Blanche asks Cohen, "correct," he says.

"Nobody induced you or threatened you to plead guilty, correct, Blanche asks, Cohen:" I was provided 48 hours within which to accept the plea or the (SDNY) was going to file an 80-page indictment that included my wife. "Cohen; "and elected to protect my family,"

"You say you want the truth to come out that the prosecutors in the southern district of NY were corrupt:" Blanche asked, "correct," Cohen says. Blanche, I challenging Cohen on his past statements that he never asked for nor would ever accept a pardon from Trump. He also said a pardon was "being dangled," "at the time it was accurate," Cohen says.

Cohen says he "always ran everything by the boss immediately, I believe I also spoke to Mr. Trump and told him everything regarding the Stormy Daniels matter,"

Trump appears to have his eyes closed as the testimony gets underway after lunch. Cohen says it was his routine to always advise Trump. Because if Trump didn't like it Cohen says, "one, it would cause him to blow up at me and two, it would probably be the end of my job."

Blanche now asks Cohen about his relationship with NY reporter Maggie Haberman, Cohen says he feels he's had a strong relationship with her

Blanche: turn to AMI's payment to the former Trump tower doorman to suppress his false claim that Trump had an alleged love child with with a maid. Blanche: "Money was paid to keep the story from getting out but the story was false" correct? Cohen "I believe so yes".

Blanche: "want to talk for a few minutes about the $130,000 payment you made to Stormy Daniels," "Cohen yes Sir," Blanche begins by asking about ABC news 'interest in the Daniels story. Blanche askes who Davidson was speaking to ABC news about the story. "I'm actually blanking on this name," Cohen say, before remembering it was John Santucci.

Cohen says Santucci, "used to come to the office quite a bit" so he was surprised when he heard ABC though Santucci was fighting for Daniels 'story. "Yes. I recall making a statement like that," Cohen says, "that they were extorting Mr. trump,"

Referring to the Daniels settlement, Blanche asks, "make no mistake, this was a completely legal binding contract, correct? "Yes sir," Cohen says,

Judge Merchan is ending court for the day, be back Monday may -20- 2024.Cross-examination of Michael Cohen to continue Monday,

Jury hears recording of Michael Cohen's podcast: "I truly fucking hope that this man ends up in prison."

May-20,2024, The president of Red-Finch: Cohen says, the full payment of $50,000, but they accepted the money they received. "To cover up this $130,000 payment, "you lied to Weisselberg about how much you needed for Red-Finch?" Blanche asks "correct" Cohen says

"So, you stole from the Trump organization?" Blanche says, noting Cohen was reimbursed $100,000.

Blanche walks through the payments Cohen received again asking "How much were you paid" directly by Trump in 2017: "nine checks," Cohen says, $35,000 a piece.

At 11.57 Blanche ends his cross-examination oh Cohen,

Hoffinger ask what Red-Finch did for Trump, Trump was polling low in the Forbes poll, "and it upset him," Cohen says, "and he had me come to his office and provide a sheet of paper that showed it," Cohen says. Trump wanted to be number 1 in the poll but after Red Finch's work ended up 9 Cohen says "despite cheating," Trump felt he didn't get his moneys worth for the worth, Cohen says Trump did not pay Red-Finch because CNBC ended up not moving forward with this poll.

Judge Merchan instructs the jury to keep an open mind, "I'll see you at 2.15 he says. Prosecutors are back in the courtroom, The judge Merchan: "we agreed this morning we're basically going to have week down, we're sending this jury home for a week to do nothing", there's no prejudice. At 2.35 p m.

Former Trump attorney John Eastman to be arraigned in "fake electors" scheme charged with 9 counts in Georgia, Including violating Georgia's Rici act. Conspiracy to commit false documents. Conspiracy to commit impersonating a public Officer.

NYT: Alito's home displayed "stop the steal" flag after Jan.6 2021, this supreme court judge Samuel Alito had the upside-down flag at his home, this inverted U.S flag known as symbol of stop the steal movement.

THE CLOSING ARGUMENTS & MORE

May,28,2024 Closing arguments in Donald Trump's trial. The jury is back in the courtroom. Prosecutor Joshua Steinglass is at the podium to deliver his closing argument, He says the defense wants to name this case about Cohen, "it isn't, that's a deflection." Steinglass: "this case is not about Michael Cohen.

Steinglass: It's about Mr. Trump and whether he should be held accountable for making false business entries in his own business records." Steinglass notes that Blanche told the jury there was no discussion of catch and kill during the 2015 meeting. "that's not true." He says.

Steinglass says the catch and kill says the catch and kill scheme to suppress the sajudin story was election interference, "this was overt election fraud." Steinglass says, telling the story it was an act in furtherance of the conspiracy to interfere with the election.

May,29,2024, The courtroom has been informed that once the judge begins the jury charge, no one can enter or leave the room. Merchan to jury: "It is not my responsibility to judge the evidence here. It is yours." Merchan to jury: You are the judges of the facts, and you are responsible for deciding whether the defendant is guilty or not guilty.

Merchan tells the jurors that their decision should be guided "solely on a full and fair evaluation of the evidence," The judge is now giving instructions about how the jury should deliberate. Merchan says the jury will work until 4.30 pm today.

The jurors are now leaving the courtroom to deliberate.

Jury asks to be read testimony from David Pecker & Michael Cohen, Jury note: "we the jury request to rehear the judge instructions.

At 4.05 pm the judge says deliberations will start again at 9.30 am tomorrow and dismisses the jury for the day.

May,30,2024, The judge reads the limiting instruction on Michael Cohen and his guilty plea. Judge says he'll be happy to clarify "if jury has more questions."

THE JURY INSTRUCTION

Here are the jury instructions #1 set aside personal differences. # 2 Be unanimous on verdict # 3 Can't hold not testifying against Trump.

At 4.38 pm the jury has request 30 minutes to fill out the correct forms after reaching a verdict. At 5.00 pm the judge has called for the jury.

At 5.05 the 12 jurors and the jury alternates are now in the courtroom, verdict reached judge Merchan is turned to the jurors, "we received a note from you signed by your jury foreperson at 4.20" he says. 34 counts guilty.

Judge Merchan: "jurors, I want to thank you very much for your service in this case." The sentencing date is set for July 11 at 11.00 am et.

To come for Trump June 27 CNN presidential debate, and July 11 Trump hush money sentencing.

Alvin Bragg the Manhattan district Attorney, said the jury made a decision based on the facts, the only voice that counts is that of the jury.

Special note: Robert De Niro slams Trump outside courtroom amid trial calling the republican candidate a "clown" when Trump ran in 2016, he was like a joke, a bouffon running for president this clown will become a ferocious dictator.

Trump's false or misleading claims total 30,573 over 4 years during his presidential term, that a good liar.

It's not over, Trump will have to undergo 3 more trials in 2025 and this is true if he is not chosen for a second time as president. On the other hand, if it unfortunately turns out that he returns to the White House, it will be chaos for another 4 years and goodbye to democracy which will be crushed by this dictator. Let's remember what he said a few months ago, that he will be dictator for one day, really, who will believe him, his ignorant and hypocritical supporters surely.

Here are the three trials:

#01 Phone call, president Trump pressured Georgia secretary of state Brad Raffensperger, to overturn the 2020 election results, Trump said, "I just want to fin 11,780 votes.

#02 On Jan. 6 2021, the United States capitol building in Washington, Dc, was attack by a mob of supporters of ten-US president Donald Trump.

#03 According to several American media, the 45th president will have to answer to seven charges related to his management of classified documents after his departure from the White House, to Mar-A-Lago residence Florida.

NEWS UPDATE:

Saturday July 13- 2024 Trump assassination attempt by Thomas Mattew Crooks in a rally, Butler Pennsylvania.

23 July-2024 The Vice-President Kamala Harris become the Democratic presidential nominee, and later Mr Tim Walt as Colister

SUMMARY

This character has behaved like a pariah towards his brother and his mother who never really controlled him, even since his early childhood. He was sent to military college and then to university and, not having good grades or SAT's, he asked for help from a friend named **Shapiro** as well as his sister, who corrected his grades and SAT's. This was the beginning of his cheating life.

Later, in business, in the 60's, with the help of his mentor, **Roy Cohn**, he learned how to defraud the government and the city of New York, by not paying his taxes.

Between the years 1970 to 2000, he made panoply of fraudulent bankruptcies in many different ways. Also, he did not pay his employees who were mostly undocumented immigrants.

He threatened his contractors in multiple legal ways in order to avoid paying them.

It is not surprising how this overly narcissistic, racist, lying character got along well with three dictators, including that of Saudi Arabia, Russia, and North Korea.

His biggest cheat was when he became, in 2016, President of the United States of America. And this, with the help of his fixer and childhood friend, **Felix Sater**, who had connections with relatives of **Vladimir Putin.** There was also a friend of **Michael Cohen's,** named **Gauger,** who knew how to cheat the electoral system by rigging the polls.

Another scam was to avoid going to Vietnam. He asked his father's doctor to obtain a document by pretending that he had a problem with an ankle. Trump's grandfather was 'kicked out of Germany in 1905 for avoiding military service 'It would seem that Donald has the same DNA as his Grandfather Friedrich.

This persona, with his 4500 lies and his shenanigans of all kinds, from

2016 to 2021, created an unimaginable chaos at the White House. He fomented, among other things, a lack of seriousness about the coronavirus pandemic. He lied to the American people throughout 2020 by making fun of the deaths for which he is 89% responsible, by repeating in his rallies that it was a hoax and an invention of the Democrats.

He never put a coronavirus program in place, mainly because he preferred to play golf, while Americans were dying by the hundreds of thousands.

The worst happened on January 6, 2021. **The "president"** with his big lies and his lying GOP accomplices of cowards attempted a coup against their own government. Finally, we are not out of the woods yet, since democracy is in danger and as long as these heinous traitors are not accused and put behind bars, the future of this country is heading towards a second civil war.

As I write these words, in January 2022, the GOP, aided by media such as **Fox News**, who continues to spread lies, which a good portion of the population is hoarding into truth. Even after 15 months of the defeat of **Trump's** Republicans, some still claim that they won this same election. **It is grotesque!**

Finally, once again the star Trump with the steal documents, The Mar-a-Lago raid occurred on August 8, 2022 when the Federal Bureau of Investigation (FBI) executed a search warrant at the Mar-a-Lago complex in Palm Beach, Florida, the residence of Donald Trump, former President of the United States.

According to the press and the political pundits, **Trump was the worst president ever.**

The infamous July 2019 call to President Volodymyr Zelensky: "I would like you to do us a favor though."

On Jan. 2-2021, he called Georgia Secretary of State Brad Raffensperger and tried to use the power of the presidency to pressure the secretary to "find 11,780 votes".

When Donald Trump, on January 13-2021, became the first president ever to be impeached twice, he did so as a leader increasingly isolated, sullen and vengeful.

He is the first U.S. president in history to be impeached twice; he lost the popular vote twice; he lost both the House and Senate for his party; and more than 383,000 Americans died from covid-19 on his watch.

Trump has famously survived two impeachments, two divorces, six bankruptcies, twenty-six accusations of sexual misconduct, and an estimated four thousand lawsuits.

He urged his supporters to "fight" and "fight like hell" He urged them, "Be there, will be wild!" And when they gathered, he exhorted them to march on the Capitol and said, "If you don't fight like hell you're not going to have a country anymore."

In the same way, Trump is inextricable from the mob he has spawned. He lives for their applause. Without it, he is lost, but he doesn't know why he seeks their plaudits.

More recently, several contractors filed $5 million in liens against Trump's new hotel in Washington, alleging he did not pay them for services rendered.

Nothing would have horrified the framers of the Constitution more than a president inciting an attack against his own Congress.

On Thursday, July 9, 2018 President Donald Trump's next pick for the United States Supreme Court, Brett Kavanagh, heads into hearings, the allegations about his behavior in the past will be top of mind for many.

As of Wednesday, three women -- Julie Swetnick, Christine Blasey Ford and Deborah Ramirez -- have come forward to accuse the nominee of either sexual misconduct or sexual assault.

Since Trump is a traitor, therefore all those who are with him, with his rhetoric, are also, traitors against democracy.

They don't have brains, its gelatin, Who, most of the Trump followers.

Tell me who your friends are and I will tell you who you are.

To discuss available precautions for preventing an unstable president from initiating military hostilities or accessing the launch codes and ordering a nuclear strike.

Trump also appears to have used $258,000 in foundation money, most of it given by other donors and not himself, to settle legal disputes, including donations to charity in lieu of paying fines.

Trump used donor money to his campaign to buy a book, sending the cash back to himself.

Trump empowered loyalists who were willing to tell him what he wanted to hear.

Usually we harvest what we sow, that's what my grandfather used to say, so what you have to do now is cry some kind of crocodile tears for having created chaos and violence for over 50 months! That is why this country now looks like a banana republic; but Mr. Biden will get our democracy back. I HOPE.

Hitler, who was fully aware of this interdependence, expressed it once in a speech addressed to the SA [the Nazis' paramilitary gang]: 'All that you are, you are through me; all that I am, I am through you alone.'

What do you mean cheated? He is a master in cheating! Do you think he really knows how many thousands of people he has been cheating during his whole life! This is ridiculous! He cheated his family, cheated his staff, cheated his customers, and cheated his contractors! Cheated the government of the United States, cheated the New York City, cheated his foundation, cheated all his mistresses, cheated all his wives, cheated his landlords, cheated the election results, cheated the election officials, and others, but, worst of all, he cheated the CNBC nomination on-line poll, for the 2016 election results, that why he's an impostor. Without this scheme, mounted from scratch by his fixer, this monster would never have been President of the United States of America.

Please Vote to remove him from office and bar him from running again.

Donald Trump says so many absurd things, what can I say to answer his gags, the question should rather be asked of his enablers and the GOP, because all these people live on a fantasy island.

Trump's future looks rotten. The Americans want Trump convicted but republicans can't unlatch their lips from his ass.

The year 2024, will be a nightmarish for Trump.

To date Trump has been accused and guilty in 3 cases, the first for rape Ms. Jean Carroll and civil fraud for the New York case. Also, the Hush money case.

In an INTERVIEW with Henri Leconte, he described the American president as "a thug, a full-fledged racist, a son of a bitch, a relentless narcissist, and a weirdo."

ACKNOWLEDGMENTS

I am a foreign resident in Canada, I am retired, I have devoted 9 years of research to the construction of this first book.

I dedicate this book to my entire large family of 4 sisters, 4 brothers, also my3 children, 6 grandchildren, and 5 great grandchildren.

Special thanks to a friend Nathalie for her psychological help during all this time spent, distant in thought, since I was locked up for several months, with my computer.

A special thanks to Yves, for his expertise in the field of electronic writing.

It was a great pleasure to dissect the various files that I had accumulated over time for the assembly of this book,

Thanks also to Mr. Machael, for having corrected the multiple errors in my manuscript; without him, I am convinced that my document would have ended up in the publishing house shredder.

A special thanks to my graphic designer.

Also, a special thanks to my confidant and organizer, Nasib.

A big thank you to Simon & Schuster for agreeing to launch this book.

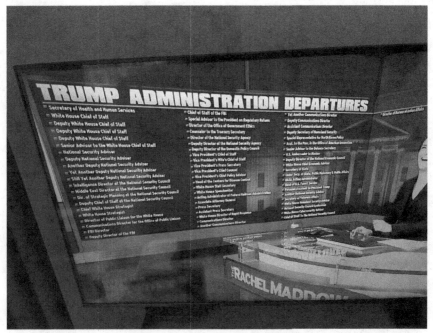

Trump in his first year in office he laid off 64 of his staff.

The End

ABOUT THE AUTHOR

I was born in 1938 in a small village on the Atlantic coast called Gaspé, From the age of 8 my father and grandfather showed me to do small jobs on the farm, Much later at 18 I left for the city of Montreal, and worked as an assistant manager in a Hilton Hotel after another 15 years I became president of 3 companies and in 2015 I decided that it was time to retire, after having worked hours and hours minimum 80 per week. It was from this period that I did some research on Donald Trump, I spend time over 9 years to complete the writing of this lbook. Now aged 86 I hope that the marketing of my work will satisfy me.

Printed in the United States
by Baker & Taylor Publisher Services

Printed in the United States
by Baker & Taylor Publisher Services